The IDG Books® Creating Cool™ Series Advantage

We at IDG Books Worldwide created *Creating Cool Photoshop 4 Web Graphics* to meet your growing need for quick access to the most complete and accurate computer information available. Our books work the way you do: They focus on accomplishing specific tasks — not on learning random functions. Our books are not long-winded manuals or dry reference tomes. In each book, expert authors tell you exactly what you can do with new technology and software and how to evaluate its usefulness for your needs. Easy to follow information, comprehensive coverage, and convenient access in language and design — it's all here.

The authors of IDG books are uniquely qualified to give you expert advice as well as to provide insightful tips and techniques not found anywhere else. Our authors maintain close contact with end users through feedback from articles, training sessions, e-mail exchanges, user group participation, and consulting work. Because our authors know the realities of daily computer use and are directly linked to the reader, our books have a strategic advantage.

Our experienced authors know how to approach a topic in the most efficient manner, and we know that you, the reader, will benefit from a "one-on-one" relationship with the author. Our research shows that readers make computer book purchases because they want expert advice. Because readers want to benefit from the author's experience, the author's voice is always present in an IDG book.

In addition, the author is free to include or recommend useful software in an IDG book. The software that accompanies each book is not intended to be a casual filler but is linked to the content, theme, or procedures of the book. We know that you will benefit from the included software.

You will find what you need in this book whether you read it from cover to cover, section by section, or simply one topic at a time. As a computer user, you deserve a comprehensive resource of answers. We at IDG Books Worldwide are proud to deliver that resource with *Creating Cool Photoshop 4 Web Graphics.*

Brenda McLaughlin
Senior Vice President and Group Publisher

Internet: YouTellUs@idgbooks.com

CREATING COOL™ PHOTOSHOP® 4 WEB GRAPHICS

CREATING COOL™
PHOTOSHOP® 4
WEB GRAPHICS

David D. Busch

IDG Books Worldwide, Inc.
An International Data Group Company

Foster City, CA ◆ Chicago, IL ◆ Indianapolis, IN ◆ Southlake, TX

Creating Cool™ Photoshop® 4 Web Graphics

Published by
IDG Books Worldwide, Inc.
An International Data Group Company
919 E. Hillsdale Blvd.
Suite 400
Foster City, CA 94404

http://www.idgbooks.com (IDG Books World Wide Web site)

Library of Congress Catalog Card No.: 96-79588

ISBN: 0-7645-3033-X

Printed in the United States of America

10 9 8 7 6 5 4 3 2 1

1B/QX/QS/ZX/FC

Distributed in the United States by IDG Books Worldwide, Inc.

Distributed by Macmillan Canada for Canada; by Contemporanea de Ediciones for Venezuela; by Distribuidora Cuspide for Argentina; by CITEC for Brazil; by Ediciones ZETA S.C.R. Ltda. for Peru; by Editorial Limusa SA for Mexico; by Transworld Publishers Limited in the United Kingdom and Europe; by Academic Bookshop for Egypt; by Levant Distributors S.A.R.L. for Lebanon; by Al Jassim for Saudi Arabia; by Simron Pty. Ltd. for South Africa; by Pustak Mahal for India; by The Computer Bookshop for India; by Toppan Company Ltd. for Japan; by Addison Wesley Publishing Company for Korea; by Longman Singapore Publishers Ltd. for Singapore, Malaysia, Thailand, and Indonesia; by Unalis Corporation for Taiwan; by WS Computer Publishing Company, Inc. for the Philippines; by WoodsLane Pty. Ltd. for Australia; by WoodsLane Enterprises Ltd. for New Zealand. Authorized Sales Agent: Anthony Rudkin Associates for the Middle East and North Africa.

For general information on IDG Books Worldwide's books in the U.S., please call our Consumer Customer Service department at 800-762-2974. For reseller information, including discounts and premium sales, please call our Reseller Customer Service department at 800-434-3422.

For information on where to purchase IDG Books Worldwide's books outside the U.S., please contact our International Sales department at 415-655-3172 or fax 415-655-3295.

For information on foreign language translations, please contact our Foreign & Subsidiary Rights department at 415-655-3021 or fax 415-655-3281.

For sales inquiries and special prices for bulk quantities, please contact our Sales department at 415-655-3200 or write to the address above.

For information on using IDG Books Worldwide's books in the classroom or for ordering examination copies, please contact our Educational Sales department at 800-434-2086 or fax 817-251-8174.

For press review copies, author interviews, or other publicity information, please contact our Public Relations department at 415-655-3000 or fax 415-655-3299.

For authorization to photocopy items for corporate, personal, or educational use, please contact Copyright Clearance Center, 222 Rosewood Drive, Danvers, MA 01923, or fax 508-750-4470.

is a trademark under exclusive license
to IDG Books Worldwide, Inc.,
from International Data Group, Inc.

ABOUT IDG BOOKS WORLDWIDE

Welcome to the world of IDG Books Worldwide.

IDG Books Worldwide, Inc., is a subsidiary of International Data Group, the world's largest publisher of computer-related information and the leading global provider of information services on information technology. IDG was founded more than 25 years ago and now employs more than 8,500 people worldwide. IDG publishes more than 275 computer publications in over 75 countries (see listing below). More than 60 million people read one or more IDG publications each month.

Launched in 1990, IDG Books Worldwide is today the #1 publisher of best-selling computer books in the United States. We are proud to have received eight awards from the Computer Press Association in recognition of editorial excellence and three from *Computer Currents*' First Annual Readers' Choice Awards. Our best-selling *...For Dummies*® series has more than 30 million copies in print with translations in 30 languages. IDG Books Worldwide, through a joint venture with IDG's Hi-Tech Beijing, became the first U.S. publisher to publish a computer book in the People's Republic of China. In record time, IDG Books Worldwide has become the first choice for millions of readers around the world who want to learn how to better manage their businesses.

Our mission is simple: Every one of our books is designed to bring extra value and skill-building instructions to the reader. Our books are written by experts who understand and care about our readers. The knowledge base of our editorial staff comes from years of experience in publishing, education, and journalism — experience we use to produce books for the '90s. In short, we care about books, so we attract the best people. We devote special attention to details such as audience, interior design, use of icons, and illustrations. And because we use an efficient process of authoring, editing, and desktop publishing our books electronically, we can spend more time ensuring superior content and spend less time on the technicalities of making books.

You can count on our commitment to deliver high-quality books at competitive prices on topics you want to read about. At IDG Books Worldwide, we continue in the IDG tradition of delivering quality for more than 25 years. You'll find no better book on a subject than one from IDG Books Worldwide.

John Kilcullen
President and CEO
IDG Books Worldwide, Inc.

Eighth Annual
Computer Press
Awards ≥1992

Ninth Annual
Computer Press
Awards ≥1993

Tenth Annual
Computer Press
Awards ≥1994

Eleventh Annual
Computer Press
Awards ≥1995

IDG Books Worldwide, Inc., is a subsidiary of International Data Group, the world's largest publisher of computer-related information and the leading global provider of information services on information technology. International Data Group publishes over 275 computer publications in over 75 countries. Sixty million people read one or more International Data Group publications each month. International Data Group's publications include: **ARGENTINA:** Buyer's Guide, Computerworld Argentina, PC World Argentina; **AUSTRALIA:** Australian Macworld, Australian PC World, Australian Reseller News, Computerworld, IT Casebook, Network World, Publish, Webmaster; **AUSTRIA:** Computerwelt Osterreich, Networks Austria, PC Tip Austria; **BANGLADESH:** PC World Bangladesh; **BELARUS:** PC World Belarus; **BELGIUM:** Data News; **BRAZIL:** Annuário de Informática, Computerworld, Connections, Macworld, PC Player, PC World, Publish, Reseller News, Supergamepower; **BULGARIA:** Computerworld Bulgaria, Network World Bulgaria, PC & MacWorld Bulgaria; **CANADA:** CIO Canada, Client/Server World, ComputerWorld Canada, InfoWorld Canada, NetworkWorld Canada, WebWorld; **CHILE:** Computerworld Chile, PC World Chile; **COLOMBIA:** Computerworld Colombia, PC World Colombia; **COSTA RICA:** PC World Centro America; **THE CZECH AND SLOVAK REPUBLICS:** Computerworld Czechoslovakia, Macworld Czech Republic, PC World Czechoslovakia; **DENMARK:** Communications World Danmark, Computerworld Danmark, Computerworld Danmark, Macworld Danmark, PC World Danmark, Techworld Denmark; **DOMINICAN REPUBLIC:** PC World Republica Dominicana; **ECUADOR:** PC World Ecuador; **EGYPT:** Computerworld Middle East, PC World Middle East; **EL SALVADOR:** PC World Centro America; **FINLAND:** MikroPC, Tietoverkko, Tietoviikko; **FRANCE:** Distributique, Hebdo, Info PC, Le Monde Informatique, Macworld, Reseaux & Telecoms, WebMaster France; **GERMANY:** Computer Partner, Computerwoche, Computerwoche Extra, Computerwoche FOCUS, Global Online, Macwelt, PC Welt; **GREECE:** Amiga Computing, GamePro Greece, Multimedia World; **GUATEMALA:** PC World Centro America; **HONDURAS:** PC World Centro America; **HONG KONG:** Computerworld Hong Kong, PC World Hong Kong, Publish in Asia; **HUNGARY:** ABCD CD-ROM, Computerworld Szamitastechnika, Internetto online Magazine, PC World Hungary, PC-X Magazin Hungary; **ICELAND:** Tolvuheimur PC World Island; **INDIA:** Information Communications World, Information Systems Computerworld, PC World India, Publish in Asia; **INDONESIA:** InfoKomputer PC World, Komputek Computerworld, Publish in Asia; **IRELAND:** ComputerScope, PC Live!; **ISRAEL:** Macworld Israel, People & Computers/Computerworld; **ITALY:** Computerworld Italia, Macworld Italia, Networking Italia, PC World Italia; **JAPAN:** DTP World, Macworld Japan, Nikkei Personal Computing, OS/2 World Japan, SunWorld Japan, Windows NT World, Windows World Japan; **KENYA:** PC World East African; **KOREA:** Hi-Tech Information, Macworld Korea, PC World Korea; **MACEDONIA:** PC World Macedonia; **MALAYSIA:** Computerworld Malaysia, PC World Malaysia, Publish in Asia; **MALTA:** PC World Malta; **MEXICO:** Computerworld Mexico, PC World Mexico; **MYANMAR:** PC World Myanmar; **NETHERLANDS:** Computer! Totaal, LAN Internetworking Magazine, LAN World Buyers Guide, Macworld Netherlands, Net, WebWereld; **NEW ZEALAND:** Absolute Beginners Guide and Plain & Simple Series, Computer Buyer, Computer Industry Directory, Computerworld New Zealand, MTB, Network World, PC World New Zealand; **NICARAGUA:** PC World Centro America; **NORWAY:** Computerworld Norge, CW Rapport, Datamagasinet, Financial Rapport, Kursguide Norge, Macworld Norge, Multimediaworld Norge, PC World Ekspress Norge, PC World Nettverk, PC World Norge, PC World ProduktGuide Norge; **PAKISTAN:** Computerworld Pakistan; **PANAMA:** PC World Panama; **PEOPLE'S REPUBLIC OF CHINA:** China Computer Users, China Computerworld, China InfoWorld, China Telecom World Weekly, Computer & Communication, Electronic Design China, Electronics Today, Electronics Weekly, Game Software, PC World China, Popular Computer Week, Software Weekly, Software World, Telecom World; **PERU:** Computerworld Peru, PC World Profesional Peru, PC World SoHo Peru; **PHILIPPINES:** Click!, Computerworld Philippines, PC World Philippines, Publish in Asia; **POLAND:** Computerworld Poland, Computerworld Special Report Poland, Cyber, Macworld Poland, Networld Poland, PC World Komputer; **PORTUGAL:** Cerebro/PC World, Computerworld/Correio Informatico, Dealer World Portugal, Mac*In/PC*In Portugal, Multimedia World; **PUERTO RICO:** PC World Puerto Rico; **ROMANIA:** Computerworld Romania, PC World Romania, Telecom Romania; **RUSSIA:** Computerworld Russia, Mir PK, Publish, Set; **SINGAPORE:** Computerworld Singapore, PC World Singapore, Publish in Asia; **SLOVENIA:** Monitor; **SOUTH AFRICA:** Computing SA, Network World SA, Software World SA; **SPAIN:** Communicaciones World España, Computerworld España, Dealer World España, Macworld España, PC World España; **SRI LANKA:** Infolink PC World; **SWEDEN:** CAP&Design, Computer Sweden, Corporate Computing Sweden, Internetworld Sweden, it.branschen, MaxiData Sweden, MikroDatorn, Nätverk & Kommunikation, PC World Sweden, PCaktiv, Windows World Sweden; **SWITZERLAND:** Computerworld Schweiz, Macworld Schweiz, PCtip; **TAIWAN:** Computerworld Taiwan, Macworld Taiwan, NEW ViSiON/Publish, PC World Taiwan, Windows World Taiwan; **THAILAND:** Publish in Asia, Thai Computerworld; **TURKEY:** Computerworld Turkiye, Macworld Turkiye, Network World Turkiye, PC World Turkiye; **UKRAINE:** Computerworld Kiev, Multimedia World Ukraine, PC World Ukraine; **UNITED KINGDOM:** Acorn User UK, Amiga Action UK, Amiga Computing UK, Apple Talk UK, Computing, Macworld, Parents and Computers UK, PC Advisor, PC Home, PSX Pro, The WEB; **UNITED STATES:** Cable in the Classroom, CIO Magazine, Computerworld, DOS World, Federal Computer Week, GamePro Magazine, InfoWorld, I-Way, Macworld, Network World, PC Games, PC World, Publish, Video Event, THE WEB Magazine, and WebMaster; online webzines: JavaWorld, NetscapeWorld, and SunWorld Online; **URUGUAY:** InfoWorld Uruguay; **VENEZUELA:** Computerworld Venezuela, PC World Venezuela; and **VIETNAM:** PC World Vietnam. 10/1/96

For Cathy

Preface

Morphing! Fractal textures! Undetectable composites! Extruded, spherized, edge-enhanced images! 3D rendering! You don't need to be a special effects technician to perform graphics magic on your Web pages. All you need is Adobe Photoshop 4.0 and some time to let your ideas bubble through the creativity-sparking suggestions in this book.

Creating Cool Photoshop 4 Web Graphics focuses on eye-catching ways to transform ordinary images into triumphant prize-winners for Web publication. It presents Photoshop users with ways to create irresistible Web pages. You'll learn how to do new, exciting, sexy stuff: graphics that jump out of Web pages and seduce visitors as they explore every nook and cranny of a site.

This book is a double treat for budding Webmeisters and graphics gurus. It bristles with new ways to use Photoshop — whether you're a Photoshop neophyte or grizzled veteran — and offers a painless introduction to creating Web pages themselves. With some special emphasis on Photoshop's new Internet-friendly features, you'll find *Creating Cool Photoshop 4 Web Graphics* a perfect introduction to the most powerful graphics tool.

If you don't believe a picture's worth a thousand words, ask visitors to your site for feedback on your Web graphics. Depending on how well they're crafted, images on the Net can be an attraction or a distraction, and the difference often is in how well you apply the graphics tools you have at your disposal.

Used wisely, graphics can add an alluring touch that captures the attention of visitors to your site and tempts them to linger and read your painstakingly orchestrated text and check out all of your links. Good Web graphics can be just a few buttons to help visitors jump to selected anchors and page links, or they can be page-filling photographs.

Badly designed graphics, on the other hand, can kill a Web site. Internet cruisers disdain ugly Web images *and* they're not going to waste a lot of time waiting for them to download. To attract and keep visitors, your graphics have to be clean, lean, and meaningful.

Fortunately for those of us who love Adobe's premiere image editor, Photoshop is a natural tool for Web graphics development. Because Photoshop is the leading image editor on both Macintosh and PC platforms, millions of potential Web page developers either already know how to use the program, or are looking for a good excuse to learn. Moreover, Photoshop has many built-in tools that lend themselves to effective Web graphics. Images are easily resized, resampled, and reduced to reusable 256-color palettes for GIFs, or squeezed down using one of Photoshop's JPEG compression options. Photoshop 4.0 includes transparent GIF facilities built-in, and, now that Adobe Gallery Effects is a standard part of the Photoshop package, it offers an overwhelming variety of filters that can dress up and spice up Internet graphics.

What You'll Need to Use This Book

Serious Photoshop users (and Photoshop dilettantes are masochists) already have just about everything they need to work with this book. If you're new to the Internet, you may have to add a few new tools and facilities to your repertoire. But, in brief, the basics you'll want to have at hand include all of the items listed below.

Mac-oriented stuff

Your basic complement will include Macintosh essentials such as the following:

Photoshop 3.05 or 4.0

Just about every technique in this book works with either version of Photoshop, although in some cases, users of the older edition will need add-ons or plug-ins that are now built into Version 4.0. In other cases, users won't be able to perform a function as easily without one of the new features Photoshop now offers. Even so, owners of any recent version of the program will be able to work with the examples in this book.

A fast Macintosh with decent RAM

Anyone who tries to use Photoshop on a slow Mac and an indecently small amount of RAM won't be having very much fun. Fortunately, because of the relatively slow speeds at which images are downloaded from the Internet, Web page graphics tend to be much less RAM-hungry than those you'll work with outside of the Internet environment. Having said that, the *working* size of a graphic can be substantial. Any time you deal with layers or have several images open at once, you'll want to have about five to six times as much RAM available as the largest image(s) you'll be manipulating. The 16MB plugged into most new Macs these days is a bare minimum, while 32MB is better. My main Photoshop computers have 128, 64, and 40MB of RAM respectively. With DIMMs costing $7 a megabyte or less from mail-order firms, even a few hundred dollars worth of memory can double or triple the performance of your Mac when you are working with demanding images.

A CD-ROM drive

Apple led the industry in offering basic models that include a CD-ROM drive, and your Mac should include one. You didn't really want to install Photoshop 4.0 from a zillion floppy disks did you? External 4X drives cost only two or three times as much as this book, so I can reasonably expect you to have one to access the files we'll be working with.

Internet-oriented stuff

Of the following items, only a browser is mandatory for working with cool Web pages. You can create perfectly good Web pages on your Mac and view them with your browser without once logging onto the Internet. It's even possible to set up an internal Web site using only a network connection between other Macintoshes, forming what is called an intranet. However, I'm assuming most of you are creating Web pages for distribution over the World Wide Web, and for that you'll need the following items:

A browser

Some Web creation tools, like Adobe PageMill, allow you to view your creations without a browser, but you'll need at least one actual copy of Netscape Navigator and/or Microsoft Internet Explorer to view pages under real-world conditions. There are quite a few other browsers available for the Mac, and you may want to use one of them to see how others may be viewing your pages. However, before this book is out of date, most users will be using either Navigator or Internet Explorer.

An Internet account

You'll want an account with an Internet Service Provider (ISP) so that you can at least view Web pages that others have set up, as a source for ideas, information, and downloads. Many ISPs also give you some free Web space to set up pages of your own.

Web space

You'll want some space on a Web server (such as the space provided by your ISP, as mentioned above) to make the Web pages you create available to the public. Even if you're making pages for others, it's a good idea to have some Web space of your own to use as a testing ground for your own pages. At worst, you can see how long it may take to download those scintillating graphics of yours under real-life conditions.

A modem

A modem makes connecting to the Internet much easier (an understatement!), unless you can link over your company's network to a direct Internet connection. Nothing slower than 28.8Kbps (and 33.3Kbps is better if you can actually connect to your ISP at that speed) should be considered.

A text editor or Web page creation package

You'll need a tool to type in or edit the HTML (Hypertext Markup Language) pages you create. Since the HTML instructions are simple text, you can use SimpleText, your favorite word processing program (with files saved in Text Only format), or a full-fledged Web authoring package.

About the Book

I've tried to make *Creating Cool Photoshop 4 Web Graphics* a mix of just the right amount of background information with follow-along examples — and then enhance as your expertise grows. Each chapter is filled with examples that can be used to master the techniques described, then used as a springboard to creating new variations. Within minutes of opening this book, even casual browsers will spot useful tips such as the following:

➡ Seamless backgrounds are easy to create. Crop the image to an appropriate square (say, 100 × 100 pixels), then offset down and to the right by half the height/width. In Photoshop, use Filter ➪ Other ➪ Offset. Choose wrap-around so that the frame is filled. Then disguise the "joints" running through the middle with a clone tool. Save the file as a GIF file that can be tiled seamlessly by browsers (Chapter 1, "Ten-Minute Guide to Graphics that Grab").

➡ To generate a 3D button in a few moments, add a light-to-dark gradient using your choice of two colors, from the upper left corner to lower right corner of your button. Then select the center portion of the button (leaving an outer edge) and apply the same gradient in the reverse direction (Chapter 6, "Creating 3D Imagery in Photoshop").

➠ Want an irregularly-shaped transparent GIF? Select a strong color that is scarce in your image and use an airbrush tool to mask out the surrounding area. Then choose that hue as your transparent tone when exporting the GIF (Chapter 7, "Creating Transparent GIFs").

➠ Add a drop shadow to any text or object by experimenting with a Gaussian blur on a copy of the object. Fill the fuzzy background copy with the shadow tone you want, skew it if you like, and paste behind the original object. If you work on a transparent layer or strong color that can be dropped out, your drop-shadowed object can rest right on the background of your page (Chapter 11, "Great Text Effects in Photoshop").

➠ When resizing a GIF file, convert to 24-bit RGB first, then convert back to 256 colors after adjusting the size to reduce "jaggies" (Chapter 12, "Color Correction").

Other chapters show you how to use add-ons such as Kai's Power Tools or Alien Skin's Black Box to transform images into something new; create 3D type with shadows, cut-outs, and perspective; build stunning Web images by combining two or more photos seamlessly; produce correct color even if you don't know color correction or gamma correction from brightness-contrast controls, and think a histogram is a cold remedy; create impressive images from scratch, since even the best photo destined for Web use may need some sort of object created with painting and drawing tools.

You'll also find plenty of information about crafting Web pages with HTML here. I concentrate on the basics, plus all of the special HTML instructions that pertain to graphics. After you've spiced up your pages with images, if you want to get fancy with forms, frames, or other Web magic tricks, I recommend *Macworld Creating Cool HTML 3.2 Web Pages* by Dave Taylor, also available from IDG Books Worldwide.

For the moderately Photoshop-literate reader who wants to come up to speed with version 4.0, *Creating Cool Photoshop 4 Web Graphics* will be a dream guide. Instead of basic instructions on how to load Photoshop, save files, or use individual tools, this book jumps right in — from the very first chapter — and demonstrates how to apply the latest Photoshop features creatively to dozens of example Web pages. I arm you with a selection of powerful tools, including the following:

➠ A living, breathing Internet Web site (http://www.dbusch.com/CoolWeb/) that contains sample pages, new graphics you can download, plus links to other important Web sites that boast nifty Photoshop add-ons and other graphics tools.

➠ A CD-ROM bundled with this book that includes HTML templates, royalty-free photographs, buttons, rules, arrows, and other graphics that can be dropped into pages as is, or modified using the techniques discussed in the book.

➡ Full-color versions of every figure in the book right on the CD-ROM, plus the original files used to produce the effects discussed, and many intermediate files (saved in individual layers in Photoshop native-format files). You can load these into your own copy of Photoshop and follow along, or just see how to easily perform the most-confusing — and most-desired — functions, using the step-by-step examples.

About You

I wrote *Creating Cool Photoshop 4 Web Graphics* for intermediate Photoshop users who want to spread their wings and learn more, and who need to learn how to incorporate graphics into Web pages. The impatient, the harried, and those who must use image editing programs to enhance their HTML documents, but aren't quite ready to make a career out of learning this complex program, will love this book. These are the people who never read the manuals — unless they have to — but instead call Technical Support lines and ask "Just tell me how to do this one thing...." *Creating Cool Photoshop 4 Web Graphics* serves up exactly the sort of information you are looking for.

It also will serve as a tutorial for experienced HTML authors who may lack graphics expertise, and an idea generator for Web or Photoshop veterans who want to spice up their work.

About Me

Kelly Bundy, one of television's great unintentional, if fictitious, philosophers, once paraphrased a famous truism by saying, "Those who can, do. Those who cannot, don't."

When it comes to graphics and Web pages, I *can*, I *do*, and I want to share my discoveries and my mistakes with you. I'm a former commercial photographer who, since the early 1970s, has written hundreds of articles on photographic topics for magazines such as *Petersen's PhotoGraphic*, *Professional Photographer*, and *The Rangefinder*. In 1977, I was seduced by the dark side of technology, and managed to morph into a dogged demystifier of computer technology. Because of my photography background, computer graphics have always been a specialty of mine, which was something of a challenge until I got my first graphics-friendly Macintosh in March 1984.

I've also been a denizen of the online world since 1981, back when the Internet was ARPANET, and you had to be connected to the military, civilian government, an educational institution, or prepared to fake it, to gain access.

The World Wide Web was only a gleam in the eye of a few science fiction writers and some bona fide computer folks who eventually made it happen.

So, the marriage of graphics and online life that we know as the Web was a perfect match for me, and for the last several years I've divided my time between writing books about image editing programs, such as *Macworld Photoshop 4 Instant Expert* with David Field (1997, IDG Books Worldwide), and more Internet-oriented tomes, including *60 Minute Guide to Internet Explorer 3* with J.W. Olsen (1996, IDG Books Worldwide). In sum, I've racked up a lot of time creating and using Web graphics, and now you have the opportunity to not only laugh with me over some mistakes I have made that you won't have to repeat, but also share with me some genuinely useful findings.

How This Book Is Organized

I packed everything into 16 concise chapters and four appendixes, organized by the Internet- and graphics-oriented topics most directly applicable to Photoshop and related tools.

Chapter 1. Ten-Minute Guide to Graphics that Grab
Spend ten minutes creating a background and a simple transparent GIF file, and you'll see that creating cool Web pages with Photoshop is easy, fun, and ripe with creative possibilities.

Chapter 2. Using Photoshop Graphics Effectively
This chapter explains how graphics can be used effectively — or misused — in Web pages, and describes some of the ways Photoshop can be wielded to optimize graphic images.

Chapter 3. Graphics Formats
Internet graphics aren't just GIF anymore. This chapter clearly explains how inline graphics work, the difference between GIF and JPEG file formats and when you might want to use each.

Chapter 4. Adding Graphics to HTML Pages
You have a graphic. How do you get it displayed on your page? This chapter explains the simple HTML tags needed to add graphics to Web pages.

Chapter 5. Working with Existing Photos and Images
This chapter offers some cool techniques for transforming graphics into suitable images for Web pages, including compositing, retouching, clever selection techniques, and other effects.

Chapter 6. Creating 3D Imagery in Photoshop

This chapter describes creating buttons, rules, arrows, and other graphics that seem to jump out of the page at you, using Photoshop's gradient, spheroid, and other tools.

Chapter 7. Creating Transparent GIFs

Step-by-step hints for creating effective transparent GIFs are included in this chapter, in addition to tricks for fading an image into the background, creating irregularly-shaped transparent images, and more.

Chapter 8. Building Interactive Image Maps

Photoshop has all of the tools you need to build your own clickable image maps, so visitors to your Web page can jump to other sections or other sites just by clicking part of an image.

Chapter 9. Photoshop's Native Filters

These filters can be your key to softening and modifying images for best display on a Web page; creating special effects that give your page a unique personality; or improving defective images. This chapter shows which Photoshop filters are most effective, and provides a clutch of clever projects to help you put them to use.

Chapter 10. Cool Effects with Add-on Filters

In this chapter I discuss third-party filter add-ons you can use to augment Photoshop's built-in abilities, including Kai's Power Tools, KPT Convolver, Squizz, and others.

Chapter 11. Great Text Effects in Photoshop

Specialized tools like Pixar Typestry are great — but you can achieve sensational text effects right within Photoshop. This chapter explains how.

Chapter 12. Color Correction

Web page designers who have high-color displays may not realize that many visitors to their sites could be using 256-color graphics. This chapter discusses this issue as well as explains exactly how colors can shift when several graphics using different palettes are shown on the same page.

Chapter 13. Acquiring Additional Images

Using scanners, digital cameras, video capture devices, and other hardware add-ons to grab images that make good Photoshop fodder is discussed in this chapter. Here I also explain how these devices work, and how they can best be applied to acquire Web graphics.

Chapter 14. Finding Images

Your Web pages can bristle with sensational artwork even if you don't own a scanner or digital camera. This chapter discusses the wealth of royalty-free clip art, including photographs, fractal backgrounds, line art, logos, and tons of other stuff available for downloading right off of the Net.

Chapter 15. Beyond Photoshop
This chapter highlights some cool shareware and commercial products that extend Photoshop's capabilities, such as KPT Bryce.

Chapter 16. Beyond HTML
What can you expect in the future in terms of extensions to Netscape and HTML that will affect how you create and use graphics in your Web pages? This chapter explores the emerging standards, and offers hints on how you may use them.

Appendix A: Glossary

Appendix B: About the CD-ROM

How to Reach the Author

Want to contact me? You can send e-mail to dbusch@dbusch.com, or visit my main home page on the Web at http://www.dbusch.com/, where you'll find separate pages dedicated to the topics of some of my other recent books, in addition to this one.

Our exploration of Photoshop 4.0 and Web graphics promises to be an enjoyable one. Let's get started.

Acknowledgments

While my name is on the cover, many other creative people worked long and hard to contribute to push me along to creating cooler and better Web effects with Photoshop. I would like to thank my untiring editors, Barb Guerra and Katie Dvorak, for their help in keeping this book both focused and literate. Thanks, too, to Eric Thomas for his insightful suggestions and tips, and to Ben Schroeter and the IDG Books Worldwide's production staff for doing such a good job as we tried to get this book on the shelves in concert with the latest version of Photoshop. I would also like to thank Michael Roney for his confidence that a book like this was needed, and that I was the best one to bring it to life.

(The Publisher would like to give special thanks to Patrick J. McGovern, who made this book possible.)

Contents at a Glance

Table of Contents

Ten-Minute Guide to Graphics that Grab

If you expected the first chapter of this book to dwell on ancient history or background — along the lines of "What Is a Web Page?," "What's HTML?," or "Everything You Wanted to Know about the Internet" — think again. If you don't already know that stuff, I'll slip in a bit of explanation as we wend our way through later chapters. But I know you didn't buy this book to gain a deeper understanding of the World Wide Web. You want to create cool Web pages with Photoshop and are reading this paragraph wondering exactly when we'll get underway.

In This Chapter

How to Create a Seamless Background

Using the Rubber Stamp Tool

Adding a Texture to Your Background

Saving in a Web-friendly File Format

Adding HTML Instructions

And now, gentlepersons, start your engines. Even if you've never created a Web page in your life, I promise you'll be looking at one in ten minutes. Not all of the chapters in this book will take the tutorial format, but just to get us started I'm going to provide some step-by-step instruction.

A Cool Graphics Page

This first exercise will leverage much of what you may already know about using Photoshop, in addition to a few things that you may not already know about Web pages. However, even if some or all of this information is totally new to you, you'll be able to follow along with the step-by-step instructions, and will find that everything makes a lot of sense by the time we're done.

You'll have the chance to catch up and learn how everything works in the chapters that follow. For now, just come along and have some fun.

Note to Windows Users: In Photoshop, the Macintosh Command key is the same as the Control key under Windows, and the Option key on the Mac offers the same function as the Alt key under Windows. To avoid clumsy dual instructions such as "Press Command/Ctrl+Shift" or "Press Command+Shift (Ctrl+Shift if you're using Windows)" I'm going to stick with Mac terminology throughout this book, even though roughly half of the illustrations you'll see were created with a Pentium-166 running Windows 95. When you see instructions to use the Command or Option keys, use Control or Alt instead.

Creating a basic background

Our first step is to create a background image for our Web page. You may have seen pages that use one of the default colors of your browser as a background. They're highly boring, aren't they? Most pages these days have a distinct underlay that give each page a certain theme. Follow these steps to create a basic background, and theme, of your own:

1. **Load Photoshop.** This is the first and only time we'll ask you to do this. All later exercises will assume that you already have Photoshop up and running when we begin.

2. **Create a new blank document, File ➪ New (or Command-N).** Title the document `backgrnd.jpg`, set the height and width of the document to 150 pixels, set the resolution to 72 dpi, and choose the RGB color mode, as shown in Figure 1-1.

Although your Macintosh or Windows 95 system can easily store files with names such as My Web Page Background, we'll use the lowest-common-denominator, DOS-style file naming conventions for the projects in this book. The Web pages you create can easily turn up on Macs, PCs, OS/2, or UNIX-based machines, and the DOS-style file naming convention works fine on all four. As you work with this book, try to keep the following rules in mind when naming files:

➡ Use an eight-character root name, since earlier versions of DOS can't handle long file names, and even Windows 95 has a tendency to create clumsy abbreviations for longer names in certain modes.

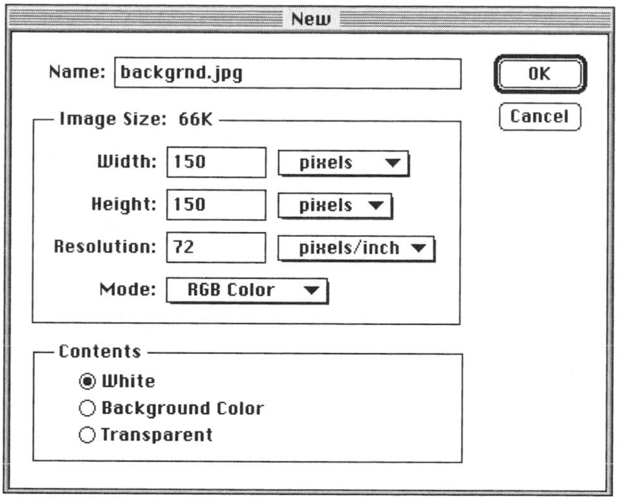

Figure 1-1: *Your new file, backgrnd.jpg, should include these settings.*

➥ Follow the root file name with a three-character extension that corresponds to the file type, as with `backgrnd.jpg`. All Macintosh files have file type and creator codes embedded into their resource forks that tell the MacOS not only what kind of file format it is, but also the name of the application that created it (or the application that should be used to open that file by default). The closest Windows machines and most browsers can come to that is a clumsy system of associations that are based on the extension, so we'll conform to that system for the sake of compatibility.

➥ Use all lowercase letters. Macs have always differentiated between upper- and lowercase letters, but some other operating systems see Background.jpg, Background.JPG, and background.jpg as identical under some circumstances, and different under others. We'll use lowercase for consistency and to avoid problems.

3. **Use Photoshop's Swatches palette to select a shade of sky blue as the current foreground color, and leave white as your background color.** (If the background has been left in some other hue from a previous session with Photoshop, change the background to white by pressing Option-click in any white space in the document window.)

4. **From the Filters ⇨ Render menu, choose Clouds to fill the frame with blue sky and puffy, white clouds.** Zoom in (Command-spacebar-click) to look at the image in detail. If you don't like the effect you get, press Command-F to reapply the filter until you get the cloud effect you prefer.

5. Use the Brightness/Contrast (Image ⇨ Adjust ⇨ Brightness/
   Contrast) controls to add a little snap to your background, and
   make the clouds stand out.

   While you now have a decent, cloud-filled background, it can't
   be used as the background for a Web page. That's because at
   150 × 150 pixels, it's not large enough to fill all of a page's window
   in a browser (which could be 400 or more pixels wide or deep).
   The browser can use a smaller background file to fill the area by
   tiling (placing duplicate copies side by side and top to bottom) but
   that won't work, either. If you were to tile the image as it is now,
   the edges wouldn't match, as you can see in Figure 1-2. Luckily,
   Photoshop has a quick way of creating images that tile together
   seamlessly.

   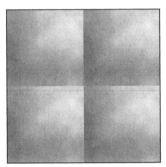

   Figure 1-2: Images don't normally tile together
   smoothly without some special techniques.

6. Use the Filter ⇨ Other ⇨ Offset command to shift the image
   around in the frame, moving it 75 pixels down and 75 pixels to
   the right (half the height and width of the original image). Click
   the Wrap Around button, as shown in Figure 1-3.

   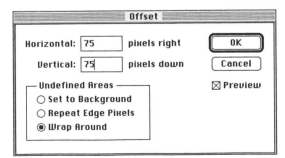

   Figure 1-3: Set the pixels and choose Wrap Around
   to produce smoother tiling.

You'll end up with an image like that shown in Figure 1-4. Photoshop rearranged the image so that the original outside edges are now in the middle, and the original center is evenly distributed along the new edges of the window. When tiled, the outer edges will match up perfectly to form a seamless boundary. Unfortunately, the *original* edge seams, now in the middle, show up like a sore digit. We can fix that, too.

Figure 1-4: Now the edges can be tiled smoothly, but the center still looks wrong.

7. **Select the Rubber Stamp/Clone tool.** Make sure that Clone Aligned is selected in the Options palette. Choose a fairly large brush size from the Brushes palette. The 35-pixel brush (the number 35 appears below its icon) is about right.

8. **Option-click somewhere in any of the four quadrants, then clone a bit of that area over one of the center seams.** Repeat until you've gently obliterated all traces of the seams, producing a uniformly cloudy frame. Avoid cloning right up to the edges, however. We want them to remain unchanged because they already tile seamlessly with each other. Your finished seamless background should look something like Figure 1-5, a seamless, cloudy sky.

Figure 1-5: This background image will tile smoothly in a browser window.

You now have a cloudy background that can be tiled smoothly on a Web page. Use this technique to create such backgrounds from any image you choose.

Saving in several file formats

All Web browsers recognize JPEG (Joint Photographic Experts Group) and GIF (Graphics Interchange Format) file formats and display them as they are downloaded, either inline with the text, or as a background. A browser may be able to display other graphics formats, but the type of files a browser can support varies from browser to browser. Additional programs, called add-ons, plug-ins, or helpers, may also be required to view different file formats. To be sure your pages are compatible with the broadest range of software, you'll want to stick with JPEG and GIF files for now. (We'll discuss the advantages and disadvantages of each type in Chapter 3.) The following steps explain how to save our background in both file formats:

1. **First, save the background as a JPEG file, using File ⇨ Save As.** Don't forget to select the JPEG file format from the pull-down list. When the JPEG Options dialog box (shown in Figure 1-6) pops up, choose Medium for Image Quality.

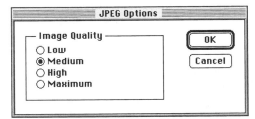

Figure 1-6: Image quality can be selected in the JPEG Options dialog box.

2. **Now use File ⇨ Export and select GIF89a Export.** A dialog box like the one shown in Figure 1-7 will appear. Make sure the Adaptive palette is selected, the Interlaced box is checked, and that 64 is checked off next to Colors.

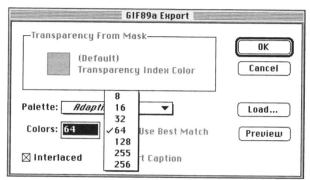

Figure 1-7: The GIF89a Export dialog box options include transparency and interlacing.

3. **Now click OK and fill in a file name —** `backgrnd.gif` **— to save the file to your hard disk.**

What you've done in the last two steps is saved a copy of the file using only 64 different hues, rather than the 16.7 million that can be represented by a JPEG file. You'll find that the original JPEG version is about 33K in size (actually a little too large for a "friendly" background image — it would take users 8 to 10 seconds or more to download over the Internet). While the GIF version looks almost as good, at 17K, it is half the size. We'll explore file sizes in more detail in Chapter 3.

Adding texture

I had you save the clouds background because you may prefer to use that background as is. However, we can do even more to add character to our first Web page's underlay by applying a bit of 3D texture. Just follow these steps:

1. **Go back to** `backgrnd.jpg`, **and re-save it under the name** `backgtex.jpg`.

2. **Use Filter ⇨ Texture ⇨ Texturizer to access Photoshop's Texturizer filter.**

NOTE Users of earlier versions of Photoshop will need Adobe Gallery Effects, Classic Art 2, to perform this step; these filters are now included as a part of Photoshop 4.0.

3. **The dialog box as shown in Figure 1-8 appears.** From the pull-down list, set Texture to Sandstone, Scaling to 50 percent, Relief to 5, and make sure the Light Dir setting is Top Right. Click OK, then Apply in the original dialog box.

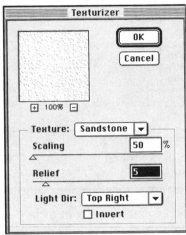

Figure 1-8: Set the type of texture, scaling, degree of relief, and position of the light source from this dialog box.

The cloudy background will now have a 3D texture. Believe it or not, it will still tile just fine; the texture maintains the seamless quality you already added. You can use this background as is, or modify it further in the next couple of steps. Try out both effects, if you like, and choose the one you prefer later on. Just make sure you save backgtex.jpg first so you can come back to it if you like.

4. **Use the Image ➪ Adjust ➪ Brightness/Contrast controls to reduce the contrast of the image a bit.** The texture and background fade and become less obtrusive, but the colors are now less vivid. You may like this effect when you don't want the background to be too strong. Save the resulting image as backgdim.jpg.

5. **Reload both** backgtex.jpg **and** backgrnd.jpg. Make the latter image active by clicking on its window, then use Select ➪ All to choose all of the image. Press Command-C to copy the untextured background.

6. **Now click** backgtex.jpg**'s window and use Edit Í Paste Layer to paste the untextured version onto a new layer beneath the textured image.** Click the Layers palette, make sure the new pasted layer is highlighted (it will be shown in a darker gray), and play with the Opacity controls until the untextured version mutes the rougher layer to your satisfaction.

7. **From the Layers palette's fly-out menu, select Flatten Image to merge the two layers.** You now have a smoother texture and retain the vivid colors of the original.

8. **Save this version as** backgsm.jpg.

Creating a quick button

Buttons are graphic elements that visitors to your Web page can click to jump to another page or a section of the same page. Buttons should be complementary to the other visual elements of your page and certainly should not clash. We'll use part of our background image to create a button for this initial Web page. Just follow these steps:

1. **Load** backgsm.jpg **into Photoshop.**

2. **Make sure Rulers are turned on.** (Press Command-R to toggle them on if they are not already showing on your screen.)

3. **Now, hold down the Shift key and drag with the rectangular marquee tool to produce a square selection.** Use the Ruler to help you produce a selection that is about one-half inch on each side. Drag down and to the right, watching the position of the marker on the horizontal ruler. You'll end up with a selection like that shown in Figure 1-9.

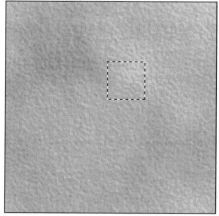

Figure 1-9: Select a perfect square from the background to begin creating a button.

4. **Now, use Select ⇨ Modify ⇨ Border, and type in a value of 4 pixels in the dialog box that pops up.** Click OK. Your selection now should look like Figure 1-10.

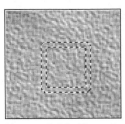

Figure 1-10: The selection has been transformed into a rounded border.

5. **Use Selection ⇨ Save Selection to save the border selection you've created.** Even if a procedure doesn't require retrieving a selection, I save a multistep selection anyway in case I make a mistake or deselect an area by mistake, and don't notice until I've done something else.

6. **Use the Swatches palette and the Eyedropper tool to choose a darker blue as the foreground color, and a lighter blue as the background color.** Click in the palette to choose the foreground color, and Option-click to select the background color.

7. **Choose the Gradient tool, then move the cursor to the lower right corner of the border-selection, and drag to the upper left.** A dark-to-light blue gradient will be applied, giving the border a 3D effect.

8. **With the border still selected, choose the rectangular marquee tool.** Position it inside the border and hold down the Shift key so that you can add the center part of the button to the current selection.

9. **Now use Select ⇨ Modify ⇨ Contract, and type in a value of 3 pixels.** Photoshop shrinks the selection slightly to eliminate the fuzzy edges of the button.

10. **Now, press Command-C to copy the button and choose Edit ⇨ Paste Layer to paste only the button in a new, transparent layer.** Your work should look something like Figure 1-11 if you make the original background invisible by clicking its icon in the Layers palette.

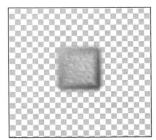

Figure 1-11: The button has been pasted onto a new, transparent layer.

11. **Use Image ⇨ Adjust ⇨ Brightness/Contrast and make the button a bit darker than the background image we copied it from.** That will make it show up better on our page.

12. **Deselect the button by pressing Command-D (which has the same effect as Select ⇨ None).**

13. **Now, return Photoshop's foreground and background colors to its default black/white value by clicking the default colors icon in the Color Control box (the small pair of black and white overlapping squares in the lower left of the Color Control box, just beneath the Tool palette).**

14. **Choose a font (I used Arial), activate the Type tool, and place the cursor to the right of the button and click.** Then type in the message:

   Click Here!

15. **Now, double-click the Line tool.** From the Line Options palette, select a line width of 2 pixels and check Arrowheads: End box. Draw a line that points at the button. Your image should now look like Figure 1-12.

Figure 1-12: Text and an arrow have been placed next to the button.

16. **With only the button's layer visible in the Layers palette, make a selection just outside the button, text message, and arrow (but well into the transparent area) with the rectangular marquee, and choose Edit ⇨ Crop to eliminate most of the extraneous area surrounding the button itself.**

17. **Now use File ⇨ Export, and select GIF89a Export.** You'll see the dialog box as shown in Figure 1-13. Note that the Transparency From Mask section of the box will be visible. That means the filter is about to create an image in which the transparent portions of the original (the layer's background) will appear transparent when the GIF file is displayed on the Web page. Only the button itself will show up.

Figure 1-13: In the GIF89a Export dialog box, transparency is already selected as the default.

18.   **Leave the other options as they are and click OK.** Name the file `button1.gif`, and save it to your hard disk.

You've just created your first transparent GIF file. You'll use this feature a lot while creating cool Web pages.

Putting It All Together

You now have a background and a simple button for your Web page. We're going to spend the rest of our time in this chapter creating the Web page itself. You're about to get your feet wet in HTML — and find out just how easy it is.

You HTML veterans will notice I've simplified the way the tags are set up for clarity. We'll learn faster and more efficient ways to code a page later on. (Beginners: Forget I said "code." I didn't mean it. Don't worry if you don't quite understand what all these program-like statements mean right now. We'll learn more about HTML in upcoming chapters.)

If you already have a favorite HTML editor, you can use that. Those who are just beginning to work with Web pages may not have an HTML editor at all, but that's OK. For the simple page we're creating, any text editor will do fine. For now, just follow these easy steps:

1.   **Load an editor that can save simple text files.** Actually SimpleText on the Macintosh or WordPad or NotePad under Windows will do, but you can also use Microsoft Word, WordPerfect, or another application. Just remember to save in Text Only when you've finished.

2.   **Type the following on a line by itself at the top of the page:**

```
<HTML>
```

This is a line that tells the browser reading this page that it can expect to see a set of HTML instructions. It's something like noticing that a page begins "Chapter 1." You'd expect the text that follows to begin the story.

The <HTML> text is called a *tag*. Most HTML tags are used in pairs that enclose instructions. The directions to the browser begin with an *opening tag* (such as <HTML>) and end with a *closing tag* (such as </HTML>) at the end. Most HTML instructions use the <tag>, </tag> format, as you'll see in the example in the next step.

3.   **Now, move down a line and type the following:**

```
<TITLE>My First Page</TITLE>
```

The title you enter between the tags will be displayed by the browser in the title bar of the page's window. You can leave the area between the opening and closing title tags empty if you like, but most HTML authors put a meaningful title here.

4.   **Now, move down another line and type this line:**

```
<BODY>
```

This tag tells the browser that the instructions on what to display for that particular page and what formats to use to show those elements follow immediately. The </BODY> tag at the very end marks the conclusion of these instructions. The simplest HTML page might look like this:

```
<HTML>
<TITLE>Very Simple Page</TITLE>
<BODY>
Some text!
</BODY>
</HTML>
```

Our page will actually have a bit more content than this, so we'll add a few more lines.

5.   **Move down another line and type:**

```
<BODY BACKGROUND="backgtex.jpg">
```

This tells the browser to download the file called `backgtex.jpg` and display it as the page's background, tiling if necessary. No closing tag is needed for BACKGROUND, since the word BACKGROUND is actually a parameter of the BODY tag itself. I've listed it on a separate line so I could explain the parent tag first, then describe how parameters are used separately. No harm is done by having two or more <BODY> tags, but experienced authors will include all the parameters that apply to a particular tag on the same line. This is your first page, though, so I cut you some slack.

6.   **Type on another line:**

```
<H1 ALIGN=CENTER>First Web Page</H1>
```

This is an example of including several parameters on a single line. I'll break up the individual pieces so you can see what's going on:

```
<H1 ALIGN=CENTER>
```

The `<H1>` tells the browser to display the text that follows this tag in the Heading 1 typeface and size. All browsers support six different heading sizes, from H1 through H6, with H1 being the largest and H6 the smallest. You, the page author, have no control over the exact size used for each heading — only the relative hierarchy among them. There's a good reason for that. Some folks will view your Web pages on a 640 × 480 pixel screen, while others may use a 1024 × 768 display. The browser needs to choose its own type size, or one specified by the user, to help everything fit in the available area. The actual font and point size can vary, depending on the browser and the settings established by the person using the browser, but the `<H1>` tag will always specify the largest type shown on the page. The ALIGN=CENTER instructs the browser to center the text in the middle of the line.

```
First Web Page
```

This is simply the text that follows the `<H1>` tag. It can be a few words, or several lines. Until a new formatting tag appears, all the text that follows will be displayed in the font and size specified by the `<H1>` tag. You'll discover that this is true for every text formatting tag.

```
</H1>
```

This is the closing tag that turns off display of text in Heading 1 style. All subsequent text will be shown in the default, Normal, type size and style until another formatting tag is encountered.

7.   On the next line, type:

```
<HR WIDTH="100%">
```

The <HR> tag tells the browser to display a horizontal rule. The WIDTH=100% parameter causes the rule to extend the full width of the window. Remember that browser windows can vary in size, so a percentage is used rather than a specific number to keep the rule proportionate on all visitors' screens. The <HR> tag does not need a matching closing tag.

8.   On the next line, type:

```
<H3 ALIGN=CENTER>This is it folks! My very first
Web page!</H3>
```

By now, you should have a good feeling for what is going on. This is a line of text displayed in Heading 3 size (per the <H3> tag), aligned in the center of the page. Simple, eh?

9.   **Now, type all of this on a single line:**

```
<P ALIGN=CENTER><A HREF="http://www.dbusch.com/
CoolWeb/"><IMG SRC="button1.jpg" border=0 </A></P>
```

Sorry. That's not as simple, is it? Well, once we've broken it down, what's going on will be a little easier to understand. Here's a part-by-part breakdown:

```
<P ALIGN=CENTER>
```

The <P> tag tells the browser to start a new paragraph. In this case, we've aligned the paragraph in the center of the page. You'll find a matching </P> tag at the end.

```
<A HREF="http://www.dbusch.com/CoolWeb/">
```

The <A HREF> tag is an anchor reference, which points to a link that the browser will jump to if you click the area specified by the tag. That's everything shown on the screen between the <A HREF> tag and the </A> closing tag. The "place" that will be jumped to is listed inside the quotes, after the equals sign. In this case, it's a URL (*uniform resource locator;* in other words, a World Wide Web address), but the link can also be another page in your Web site, or even another place on the same page. The link itself is not displayed on the page; you must add text or an image to provide the visitor something to click. We'll learn more about links in Chapter 4.

```
<IMG SRC="button1.jpg" border=0 </A></P>
```

The <IMG SRC> tag tells the browser to download an image and display it. If the viewer of the page clicks the image, the browser will jump to the link. The border=0 parameter tells the browser not to draw a colored border around the image. You can specify a border around an image, and the browser will change the color of the border — just like it will with text links — to show whether or not a visitor has clicked that link yet. Many Web authors elect to dispense with the distracting borders, and we wouldn't want one here in any case. It would tip off the boundaries of our transparent GIF. The </A> and </P> closing tags end the link reference and paragraph, respectively.

```
<CENTER><P><A HREF="http://www.dbusch.com/CoolWeb/">
[Click here to visit a very cool place!]</A></P>
</CENTER>
```

This is nothing more than a text equivalent of the line above. A reference to the same URL is provided, with some text, [Click here to visit a very cool place!], shown instead of the image.

10. **Type the following closing tags on separate lines:**

```
</BODY>
</HTML>
```

These finish up the page and tell the browser that it's been given all of its instructions.

11. **Save your first page as** mypage.htm. Remember to use Text Only format if you're not using SimpleText.

12. **Load your favorite browser and view the page.** With Netscape or Microsoft Internet Explorer, you'd use File ⇨ Open File in Browser (or Command-O). You should see something like what's shown in Figure 1-14.

Figure 1-14: Your finished page looks like this.

In about ten minutes, or perhaps a little longer if you took the time to read everything carefully, you've created your first Web page with some fairly good-looking graphics.

Moving On

Many of the techniques covered here — transparent GIFs, backgrounds, and so on — were just touched upon to help you get your feet wet. We'll investigate all of them in more detail in chapters to come. Up ahead are additional tutorial exercises such as these, but I'll also spend time simply explaining techniques you can apply on your own to create cool Web pages with Photoshop.

In the next chapter, I'll look at Web graphics in more detail, and pick up some tips on how to use them effectively.

Using Photoshop Graphics Effectively

Graphics intended for Web pages have special requirements. You can't simply take any old image you've cobbled together in Photoshop and drop it onto a page. At best, haphazard efforts make your otherwise cool page look ugly. At worst, you may make downloading your page difficult, impractical, or unappetizing for the very visitors you want to captivate. This chapter explains some of the ground rules for using Photoshop graphics effectively on a Web page.

In This Chapter

How Web Pages and Graphics Work

What Can Photoshop Do?

Image Requirements for Web Pages

Some Rules of Thumb for Web Graphics

How We Got Here

The idea of setting up pages rich with images and other graphics seems so natural to us today that it's easy to forget that as recently as two or three years ago, the World Wide Web mainly consisted of just linked text documents. Nor do we often stop to think that the Web itself didn't exist before 1991.

The only places you'll find the beginnings of the Web emphasized are in the introductory sections of books like this one. Every author feels obligated to describe how the Internet itself evolved from the U.S. Department of Defense's Advanced Research Projects Agency (ARPANET), which was originally intended as a way of linking military and scientific computers together, even after a nuclear attack. You'll also find ubiquitous discussions of how the

Web was dreamed up by a team headed by Tim Berners-Lee, a European physicist, and its miraculous transformation from a text database into a graphics playground for every computer user who has access to a bit of online server storage.

I'm not going to spend a lot of time on background of that sort. In fact, I've already dispensed with most of it. What you *really* need to know is how graphics fit in with Web pages, and what you need to do to display them properly. The good news is that Web graphics must meet some constraints, which end up simplifying how you handle them. The bad news is that those same constraints place some challenges in your path that require some creativity to overcome.

How Web Pages and Their Graphics Work

As you saw in the first chapter, Web pages consist of simple ASCII (American Standard Code for Information Interchange) files with text instructions that a browser is designed to understand, accompanied by actual content, which includes paragraphs of text.

When you point a browser at a specific URL address while connected to the Internet, the browser software sends out a set of commands to the Web server that you've identified in the URL, requesting that page or whatever default page is located there. As the browser receives the page, it follows the instructions encoded into the page in the form of tags.

Some of the instructions tell the browser how to format or lay out the text content on the page. You've already typed in tags that request various headline sizes, text placement, and so on. There aren't an overwhelming number of layout options on a Web page — just a few relative type sizes, some alignment choices (flush left, right, or centered), italics, bold-facing, a selection of special characters, and so on. That's because Web pages are designed to allow the browser to retain control over display of items in its window, making it possible for a particular page to be viewed in a broad range of window sizes, on a wide range of computers.

Other instructions tell the browser to set up a hypertext link, which is a place on the Web page you can click to jump to another place on the same page, a new page at the same site, or a completely different URL located on the other side of the globe, perhaps.

Still other instructions ask the browser to insert an image inline with the text on the page. The term *inline* is used because, for a long time there was no way to precisely position a graphic on a page — after all, the page was formatted by the browser to fit a particular window. Instead, the browser displays text and images in the order in which they are mentioned on the page. At best, the Web author can specify that text before or after an image be positioned to one side or the other of the graphic — wrapping around. Only frames and other recent extensions to HTML, implemented in browsers such as Microsoft Internet Explorer 3.0 and Netscape Navigator 3.0 and later, let you do much about placing your graphics on a page.

Inline graphics are dropped in the middle of a page using instructions like the <IMG SRC> tag you used in the last chapter. The browser downloads and displays text, finds an <IMG SRC> tag that points to a graphic, downloads and displays the graphic, then continues down the HTML page with the remaining text and pictures. Sometimes <IMG SRC> describes an image that resides on the same Web server as the HTML page itself, but that's not mandatory. You could create a Web page with six different graphics, each residing on a different computer in a different country. That page would take longer to display, but it could be done.

In a nutshell, here's what Web pages contain:

- ASCII text for display as content
- Other ASCII text tags that define how content is to be displayed
- Pointers that tell the browser to jump to other places
- Instructions to download and display images inline with the text
- Special instructions including embedded JavaScript instructions, Java applets, and pointers to other types of files, such as sound or video

How Web Connections Work

In addition to understanding how text and graphics files work on a Web page, you also need to know how Web connections work. If you are already familiar with computer programming or how other online exchanges of information work, the World Wide Web is not like either one of them in many ways.

For example, when you log onto CompuServe or America Online, your modem makes a direct connection with either of those services (or connects you through the Internet, which is another option for both). Once online, you are physically linked to the information provider's computer for the entire session. If, as has happened before, more users try to log on than can be served by the service's available hardware, some users are summarily dropped, and the online service reports that it is currently "busy." A new user cannot log on until another user exits.

With a few exceptions, your connection to a Web server lasts only as long as it takes to transmit a particular set of information over the Internet to your computer. Then, the connection is severed and the Web server is free to accept another user in your place. This is called a *non-persistent connection*. For that reason, even small computers with what you might view as narrow links to the Internet can service tens of thousands — even millions — of hits per day. It's no problem for 1,000 people to view a Web site at roughly the same time, since each of them connects to the server for just long enough to download the particular page and its graphics or other files.

If you spend half an hour browsing through 15 pages at a particular Web site, you may actually be linked to the site's server for only a few minutes; you may be linked through a different connection for each page you visit that may be routed through a completely different set of intermediary computers. It's a little like having a phone conversation in which a new call must be placed each time you speak or the person you're talking to speaks.

Microsoft Internet Explorer introduced a facility for maintaining live, persistent connections to a remote server, ostensibly to improve the browser's response. However, in most cases, Web connections operate as I've described, with the added provision that several simultaneous links to a Web server can be underway at one time from the same browser. You can, for example, download all of the graphics on a page at once through separate connections initiated by your browser.

One offshoot of this affects how you "program" your Web pages. In an ordinary computer program, the author has a great degree of control over where the user moves next. If a certain page is on display, there may be buttons that take the user to a menu of other pages, or to a help screen, or to exit the program. The application can be written to take care of (nearly) all of the possible branches from a given point.

However, once visitors have loaded your Web page, there is no guarantee that they will move to the pages you have set up through carefully designed links. They may hit the Back button, visit a few more sites, and perhaps return half an hour later — or never. This characteristic has a tremendous effect on those who use Web pages for transactions. A form may be filled out and never submitted, for example.

As a Photoshop graphics guru, you need to be aware of this for a simple reason. Because each page is (potentially) a one-time experience for visitors to your site, you will want to make sure that the graphics encourage — not discourage — users to view an entire page and explore the other pages your site links to. Web graphics not only help make a good first impression, they can determine whether that look is the only impression or not.

What Photoshop Can (and Can't) Do for You

Before we move on to talk about the special requirements of Web images, we should spend a little time looking at exactly what Photoshop can do for you. Photoshop is remarkably versatile when it comes to building Web graphics. Its chief functions can be summarized by the following four categories:

➡ **File conversion.** Graphics acquired from scanners, digital cameras, or pulled off a Photo CD or clip art disk still have to be converted to one of the formats supported by the Web. If you've already had some experience in Web page design, you know that it's essential to have some way of saving files in conventional, interlaced, and transparent GIF formats, as well as in JPEG and progressive JPEG formats (at selected compression/quality ratios). If the Portable Network Graphics (PNG) format becomes popular, Photoshop 4.0 can handle that, as well. If you haven't had much exposure to these mysterious file formats, we'll explore them in more detail in Chapter 3.

➡ **Image enhancement.** Even great images can benefit from cropping, flipping, or rotating. And, if a GIF format is your target, convert 24-bit, 16.7 million-color images to an optimized palette of 256 or fewer hues. If you plan to put several graphics on one page, the ability to use the same set of colors for all of them — so visitors using 256-color displays don't experience dramatic color shifts — is a plus. Photoshop handles all of these tasks with aplomb, as you'll discover in Chapter 12.

➡ **Image modification.** Images may require retouching, the addition of cool textures or special effects, and other modifications. Here, again, Photoshop shines, and we'll look at more of its possibilities in Chapter 5.

➡ **Image creation.** If you're building buttons, designing your own horizontal rules, creating a few arrows, or concocting a logo, you'll want the most flexible set of pixel-bending tools available for working with an empty canvas. Fancy options for creating type and 3D images that jump off the page are cool, too. You already created an image from scratch in the very first chapter of this book.

Photoshop can't do it all for you, however. I've set aside Chapter 15 to describe some of the other tools you'll want to consider adding to your kit. These include enhancements of Photoshop's existing features (such as Kai's Power Tools), as well as applications that handle the following functions:

➡ **Image management.** Web sites can grow faster than a mosh pit at a Lollapalooza show, so a way of collecting current and potential images to put into an album for offline browsing and selection is essential. You'll want to know about ways to catalog images and track them with thumbnails and text databases.

➡ **Miscellaneous capabilities.** While many Web tools are hand-me-downs from other graphics-oriented activities, special offers often contain libraries of Net-oriented images, programs that help create image maps, and applications that are geared toward generating visuals specifically for HTML use. Small gems like these can be real time-savers.

Image Requirements for Web Pages

Most of the requirements for graphics used on the Web involve compromises you must make between your desire to provide as much information and detail as possible, and your need to have folks actually stick around long enough to view your page. The following section examines some of those compromises, and how Photoshop can help you optimize your images.

File size counts

Photoshop does a wonderful job with big, beautiful images. A 640 x 480 graphic with 16.7 million colors can look stunning on the screen of your computer, especially after you've used Photoshop to tweak it a bit closer to perfection. Unfortunately, without compression, that image is nearly 1MB in size. Even under ideal conditions, it would take a user five to six minutes — and more likely much longer — to download an image of that size. So, you can forget about filling up someone's screen with a single dazzling image, or even with a batch of smaller ones.

Visitors to your page just don't have the time nor the patience to wait around for long periods while your images download. You must first, and foremost, make Web graphics as small as humanly possible, while retaining all the information you want to convey. In many cases, you'll find that size is the overriding factor, and you'll have to give up some information to ensure that your Web pages can be downloaded in a reasonable period of time.

So, forget about using 1MB images. Don't expect to use any 500K or even 100K images, either. Most of the graphics on your page should be well under 100K in size, and the most visitor-friendly sites stick to images that are 25K or smaller.

We're talking file size here, which is almost all that really counts, not the physical size that an image displays on your page. For reasons that will be explained in more detail in Chapter 3, a 25K file can occupy a relatively tiny nook on your page, or spread out over a larger expanse of real estate. Figure 2-1 shows the relative space a pair of images — both 50K in size — take up on the screen.

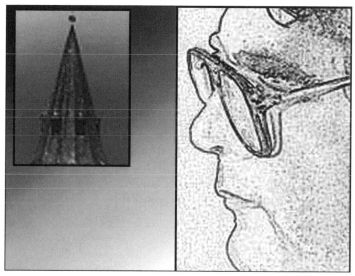

Figure 2-1: Both the castle tower in the upper left corner and the face at right are contained in files of identical size.

The reasons for this disparity will become apparent soon. For now, you just need to know that how you work with files and the format in which you save them can have a dramatic effect on how long it will take a user to download that file.

Real estate counts

The physical size of your image on the screen is also important when you create your cool Web pages, since the amount of real estate a graphic takes up affects how the browser displays other elements.

Remember that the available display area for your Web page may vary widely. Some visitors may have 640 x 480 displays, while others may be using an 832 x 624, 800 x 600, or 1024 x 678 window. On a 20- or 21-inch monitor, even larger displays are possible, and you must take into account portrait-type monitors like those from Pivot, which can set up a screen that is taller than it is wide. Even with a given display resolution, the user may have resized the browser window to something smaller.

You can see that the largest image you could possibly display without scrolling for all users on a Web page is less than 640 x 480, since the browser application's menus, window borders, scroll and size boxes, and so on, take up some space. In my own wildest fantasies, I entertain the idea of presenting images no bigger than about 400 x 300 pixels and rarely come anywhere close to that size in practice.

You can examine the size of an image you are working with in Photoshop by using the Image ⇨ Image Size dialog box. If you've changed the Preferences ⇨ Units defaults to pixels, the size will automatically be displayed in the Current Size box, shown in Figure 2-2, as pixels. Otherwise, you'll need to change the New Size measurement unit to pixels to see the exact dimensions of your image. If you use the Info palette, a faster way to find the dimensions of the image is just to select the entire image with Command-A. The height and width in pixels is displayed at the bottom of the palette. We'll talk more about sizing images for Web pages in Chapter 4.

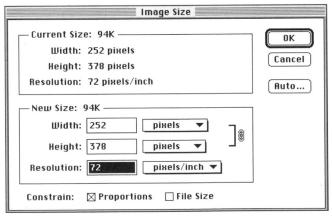

Figure 2-2: In the Image Size dialog box you can view the dimensions of your image.

Color depth counts

If you've worked with Photoshop much, you may have delved into the idea of color depth more than once in the past. Photoshop works best with 24-bit color images that have up to 16.7 million colors ("millions of colors," in Mac-speak). As you probably know, 24-bit images use one 8-bit byte to represent up to 256 different shades of each of the red-green-blue primary colors, or 24 bits in all (3 x 8). However, you may also encounter grayscale images, which have a maximum of 256 individual tones, and are considered 8-bit images. Further, a full-color image can be reduced to an 8-bit, 256-color format. (Photoshop calls this Indexed Color in the Mode menu.)

During this color reduction process, many groups of similar colors are grouped together and are represented by a single hue. Or, the intermediate colors can be simulated by dithering several of the available tones, allowing the eye to blend these different colored spots together into something that resembles the original color. Color reduction is possible because no 24-bit images actually contain a full 16.7 million colors. A 640 x 480 pixel image, after all, contains only 307,000 different pixels. Even if every one of them were a unique color, the file would have only 307,000 colors — not millions.

For this reason, some types of 24-bit color images can be represented fairly accurately in 8-bit, 256-color format, while others cannot. Images that have smooth gradations of tone from one shade to another suffer the worst under this treatment, since 256 colors can't provide an even gradient.

As you might expect, an image that uses 24 bits to represent each pixel is potentially three times as large as one that requires only 8 bits. So, in many cases, a 256-color image is smaller and faster to download than one that contains millions of colors. However, the rule is not as hard and fast as you might think, thanks to things like image compression, which I'll talk about more in Chapter 3. In addition, some images require a lot less than 256 colors — perhaps only 16 or 32, and the GIF file format can take advantage of this to produce even tinier files. We'll explore this idea more in the next chapter.

Ways Photoshop Can Help

Photoshop has some facilities built in that you can use to optimize the file size of your graphics. These include the following:

➡ **Cropping.** Make a rectangular selection that includes only the most essential portions of your image, choose Image ➪ Crop, and Photoshop trims the graphic to optimum size. As I mentioned earlier, activate the Info palette, turn on display of mouse coordinates in the fly-out Options menu, and a constant display of the height and width of your selection, in pixels, can be shown, as in Figure 2-3. This is an easy way to crop an image to the exact size you want. The Crop tool can also be used to specify a precise new size.

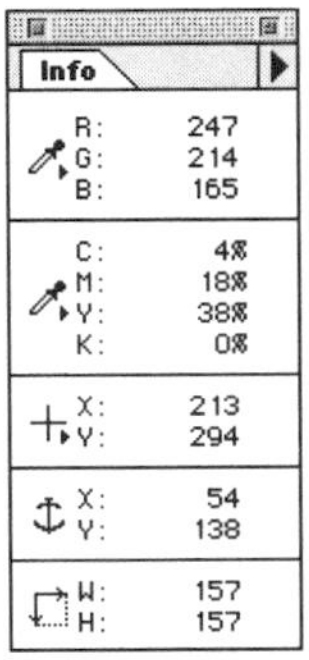

Figure 2-3: You can view the exact dimensions of a selection in the Info palette.

➡ **Size Reduction.** Photoshop does a pretty good job of squeezing an image down from one size to another, even if the reduction is not strictly proportionate. By changing the Image ➪ Image Size dialog box's New Size measurements to percent, you can type in values to decrease an image to 50 or 25 percent — or some odd value — of its current size. If you're looking for a specific height or width, you can change the measurements back to pixels and type in a new width or height (but just one of these, if you want to keep the same proportions or aspect ratio). Photoshop will then scale the picture, using interpolation algorithms to delete pixels, or create new ones that approximate the pixels that should fit within the specified dimensions.

➡ **Color Reduction.** Photoshop also has some flexible tools for changing the number of colors in an image, from 16.7 million to 256, and back again. We'll practice this procedure more in Chapter 12. The process is trickier than you might think. That's because reducing an image down to 256 colors involves creating a customized palette of the best 256 colors that can represent that image. A different image probably has 256 different colors. If a user's screen display is set for thousands or millions of colors, his or her monitor can probably accommodate both sets of 256 hues. But, if someone views your Web page on a display set for 256 colors, the two different palettes on one page can cause some bizarre color shifts.

Rules of Thumb

The following are some general rules of thumb you can use to check how your Web graphics stack up:

➥ Set up your pages to accommodate the lowest common denominator: a 640 x 480 display with a browser window that is smaller than that and has as few as 256 different colors available to show your graphics.

➥ Try to keep each Web graphic well below 50K in size, especially if you plan to include a lot of them on a page. You'll find that 25K is even better, and elements such as rules and buttons can often be trimmed to 7K or less. You'll learn techniques for optimizing file size in later chapters.

➥ Add up the sizes of all the images you want to display on a page, and keep the total smaller than 200K. A page with that much graphic content still takes a minute or so to download with a fast connection, but if you sprinkle in enough interesting text and spread the graphics around, visitors will have something to read while your page downloads.

➥ Confine the heavy-duty graphic images to certain pages, and provide your visitors with a warning — don't surprise them. If you have a graphics-intensive site (say, a display of your photographs or artwork), you might want to include only enough graphics on your main page to entice visitors into your gallery. Those who do not want to wait for long image downloads can avoid those pages.

➥ Small, thumbnail images, like those shown in Figure 2-4, can be placed on a page and used as a preview of a larger graphic image. You can place the full-size image on another page, or have it displayed when the visitor clicks the thumbnail image. That way, a visual clue is provided that helps the visitor decide whether to proceed with the full download.

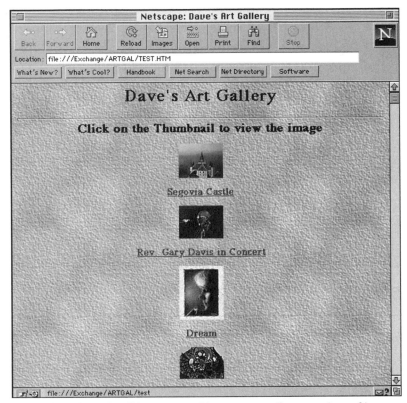

Figure 2-4: Thumbnail images provide a way to offer a preview of larger graphics.

Moving On

In this chapter you've learned how the size and number of colors affect how visitor-friendly your Web site is, and some of the basic rules of thumb you should use to adhere to the common-sense rules of effective Web graphics.

In Chapter 3, I'll explore some of the concepts introduced here in a little more detail. You'll learn how Photoshop works with JPEG and GIF files, and options for other kinds of files, including the new PNG format.

Graphics Formats

If your experience with images on the World Wide Web has mostly been from the outside looking in, you may be puzzled about which of the dozens of file formats Photoshop supports can be used for the graphics you embed in your HTML pages.

Fear not. The picture is not as cloudy as you might think. Two formats dominate among current Web browsers: GIF and JPEG. You should also be familiar with PICT, considered to be the Mac's native image format; PSD, which is Photoshop's own format (necessary to save files when using the special Layer features); and TIFF, a common format between Mac and PC platforms, and therefore one that you'll see often. For example, I used TIFF to save all the screen shots in this book on the CD-ROM, so both PC and Mac readers can easily work with them.

In This Chapter

In this chapter, we'll look at how all of these and other graphics formats work, discuss some of the advantages of each, and explain how Photoshop and your Web browser use the various formats.

The Birth of Computer Graphics

When you get right down to it, most of the work you do with a computer involves text, such as working with word-processing documents, spreadsheets, databases, accounting, and checkbook software. That's all boring stuff, in the long run. Most of the enjoyment you receive from your computer comes from the graphical side — the windows and icons of the operating system's interface; the colorful images that pop up when you run

Photoshop or your favorite business, educational, or game CD-ROM; the graphics that populate World Wide Web pages.

But let's be honest. Personal computers didn't become a basic home and office tool until graphical computers like the Macintosh and Windows PCs became common. The Internet didn't catch on until images became prevalent on Web pages. To judge the importance of images, consider this: You never really believe a picture is worth a thousand words until you try to describe an image file in a file name, or imagine a world without graphical computers.

While computers and the Internet didn't always have such a rich graphical environment, computer graphics themselves are nothing new. High-end systems like $250,000 computer-assisted drafting (CAD) workstations were common in the 1970s. I used a $10,000 Xerox 860 dedicated word processor with impressive graphics as far back as 1980. These systems pre-date both the Macintosh and IBM PC by a few years.

Users of the first sub-$5,000 personal computers, however, had no such access to graphics. Early pre-Macintosh systems could display only a fixed set of predefined characters that resided permanently in a read-only memory (ROM) chip. Those characters were limited to the alphabet, numbers, a few symbols, and a small group of chunky graphics blocks that could be assembled to create crude images. If you've ever seen one of those form-fed printouts of a male or female pinup reproduced solely by clever arrangement of alphanumeric characters, you'll realize just how limited early graphics were.

The first Macs made graphics a standard feature of computing by virtue of its rather unusual — at the time — standardization on a 100 percent-graphic display. Instead of fetching the letter *A* from a ROM chip every time the letter was displayed on the screen, the Mac operating system actually drew the letter, pixel by pixel, just as it created every other element displayed on-screen. A fast 32-bit processor, some clever screen drawing routines (called QuickDraw) that were built into the Mac's ROM, and a limitation to black-and-white — not color or grayscale — graphics made this dramatic leap possible. Windows PCs caught up when 486 and Pentium-class processors and fast graphics accelerator cards were created to work in tandem with the improved graphics capabilities of Windows 3.x and Windows 95.

As graphics became standard components of every computer's software through sophisticated programs like Photoshop, it was natural that images would come to the Internet, too. Early Web browsers offered a standardized way of formatting text for display on a wide variety of platforms. It was only a matter of time before formatting commands were added to permit images to be displayed inline with text. (That is, a Web page could be formatted with some text, followed by picture or two, some more text, more pictures, and so forth, in a scrolling page that could be viewed with any compatible browser.)

We'll learn more about how images are included in Web pages in Chapter 4.

The Way Graphics Work

To understand graphics file formats, you need to understand the two basic kinds of graphics used on the World Wide Web: *raster* and *vector* images. Raster images dominate today, but you can expect to see more of the vector variety eventually. The following section explains both graphics types.

Raster images

Photoshop's forte is bitmapped, or so-called raster-oriented, images, which can be visualized pixel by pixel, line by line, much as a raster image is drawn on a television screen (or monitor). Any kind of pixel image is often called a *bitmap*, because it can be described by specifying the value of each pixel in a map created by the rows and columns of the image. Figure 3-1 shows a close-up of the pixels in a typical image.

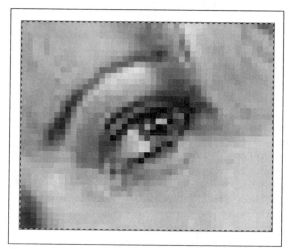

Figure 3-1: When you zoom in, you can see the pixels clearly.

Strictly speaking, at least among graphics professionals and in Photoshop's nomenclature, a bitmap is only a black-and-white image with each pixel represented by either black or white. That's why you see the Bit Map choice in Photoshop's Image ⇨ Mode menu. Chances are, when professional image workers are talking about a bitmap, they mean a black-and-white pixel image. Among the less fussy crowd, a bitmap can refer to any raster image. Because the raster term is clumsy, I'll often call any kind of pixel image a bitmap in this book. When I mean a black-and-white, non-grayscale, or color bitmap, I'll say so specifically.

The chief difference is the amount of information provided about each pixel in the image. In a black-and-white image, a 1 or a 0 is used to represent whether the pixel is black (1) or white (0). For this reason, bitmaps are also called 1-bit images.

Bits can also be described using long, binary numbers. If you use four bits to describe each pixel, you have 16 different combinations from 0000 (white) to 1111 (black) and the gray values in between. Eight bits allow numbers from 00000000 to 11111111, or 256 combinations of grays or colors. Even though as a Photoshop user you'll usually be working with more than 256 colors, it is important to be familiar with 8-bit color. Many visitors to your Web site may have only 256-color displays, and you may want to optimize your images for viewing on those displays. In practice, you may have as few as 216 colors to work with since browsers may use a common set of 216 hues (called a *palette*) and attempt to fit all of the images it encounters into that collection of colors.

More often, however, you'll begin your work in Photoshop using 15- or 16-bit color or better. That's "thousands of colors" in Macintosh parlance and is actually either 32,767 or 65,535 colors, depending on whether the mode is 15- or 16-bit.

If you have a newer computer your Photoshop efforts are probably geared toward 24-bit ("millions of colors") mode and a total of 16.8 million hues. Of course, you'll never actually use that many colors in a single image. On an 832 x 624 screen there are only 519,168 individual pixels. Even if each and every one of them were a different color (which is unlikely), you'd need only 519,168 colors. Figure 3-2 shows an image represented in 1-bit (bilevel), 4-bit (16 colors), and 8-bit (256 colors) formats.

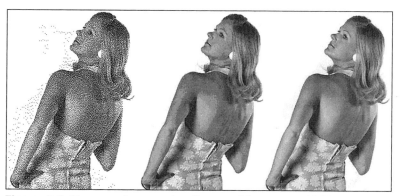

Figure 3-2: *The same image using 2 tones, 16 tones, and 256 tones.*

High color is important in providing you with a large enough choice of colors so that Photoshop can represent an image as accurately as possible. Imagine a forest scene in which most of the detail is represented by deep greens, browns, and yellows. In "thousands of colors" or 16-bit color mode, with the available tones equally distributed among all of the available colors, there may very well not be enough greens, browns, and yellows available to recreate the image. That's where millions of colors come in handy.

Actually, billions of colors can also be useful. Some types of artwork, such as color transparencies, may have such a broad range of colors, from the very bright to the very dark areas, that there are not enough tones in even 16-bit mode. That's why you'll see desktop color scanners billed as 30-bit, 32-bit, or even 36-bit devices. They are capable of capturing billions of colors, which are reduced down to an optimized palette of "only" 16.8 million colors before the file is saved on your hard disk.

Don't confuse 30- to 36-bit color — which is always converted to 24-bit format in the desktop scanner — with the 32-bit color files Photoshop is able to create. Those files are still 24-bit color files, with the extra eight bits used to store a grayscale alpha channel that you can use for masking. Photoshop's proprietary PSD format can also save layers and multiple alpha channels, in addition to paths. However, these files are still 24-bit color.

Raster images can store an amazing amount of information about an object. The chief disadvantage of these images is that they don't scale very well. When you enlarge a bitmap too much, the pixels quickly become apparent. When you reduce a bitmap image in size, it can lose sharpness through an interpolation process that may not be able to resize the image properly. (See the following sidebar, "What's Interpolation?")

Raster images also comprise an extremely large file, since a fixed number of bits (or bytes) is required to specify the contents of each and every pixel, even if the pixel is empty. Compression routines used by various file formats can reduce this overhead somewhat by representing long strings of repeated pixels with shorter codes. Still, image files can easily reach several megabytes or more in size. They tax your hard disk space, your computer's available memory, and Photoshop's ability to manage these swarms of bits efficiently. We'll learn more about raster/bitmap images as we work with them in this book.

What's Interpolation?

As we work with Web graphics, it's helpful to understand how Photoshop works with changing images through a process called *interpolation*. You'll often want to reduce an image to produce a thumbnail for your Web page or to create an image that is smaller and easier to view. At the very least, knowing about interpolation will help you appreciate why manipulating images in these ways can degrade the quality.

You already know that the images Photoshop works with are based on individual picture elements or pixels. Whenever you enlarge an image or selection, Photoshop must create the added pixels to produce the bigger image. Reduce an image or selection, and the program must decide which pixels to discard. Rotate, skew, or otherwise distort the same image, and some calculation must be done to figure out what new arrangement of pixels is needed to reorient the selection in its new configuration. This calculation is done through a process called interpolation.

Interpolation uses mathematical algorithms to create or delete pixels as required based on the values of the pixels in the original image. The process is relatively simple if you're just enlarging or reducing an image, particularly if even-number magnifications or reductions are involved, say, from 600 x 600 pixels to 1200 x 1200 or 300 x 300 pixels. Photoshop does not, as you might guess, duplicate every pixel to enlarge an image or discard every other pixel to reduce an image.

Instead, a more sophisticated method is used. To double the size of an image, the eight pixels that border each pixel are examined to get an accurate image of the four pixels needed to replace it. To halve the size, clumps of four pixels are averaged to determine the value of the one that will replace them. This works great when you're changing the size in multiples or fractions of 2, but not so great when any other factor is used. That's why Photoshop can increase the size of an image by 200 or 400 percent, or reduce it by 50 or 25 percent with optimum results, yet not do a very good job if you want to enlarge by 173 percent or reduce to 31 percent of the original size.

In these cases, Photoshop will have particular difficulty reproducing objects with diagonal lines, which are difficult enough to represent using square pixels without throwing unevenly added (or subtracted) picture elements into the mix. For the same reasons, rotating images (especially in increments other than 90 degrees) and slanting or skewing selections can produce rough-looking, jagged results.

The most important thing you should remember about interpolation is that it's always just an approximation of the pixels that should be in an image, so you should minimize the number of times Photoshop has to put your image through this wringer.

Vector images

Vector images are created through outlines, primarily with mathematical descriptions of the curves and straight lines that comprise an image. Photoshop's Pen tool and Paths palette allow you to work with such outlines, as you can see in Figure 3-3. Photoshop can also import outline art and convert (rasterize) it into a bitmapped image.

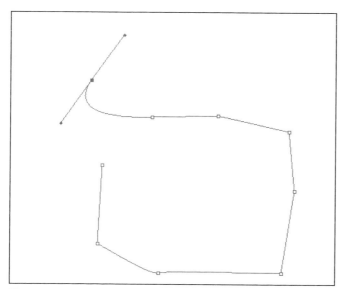

Figure 3-3: Photoshop's Pen tool creates smooth, scalable outlines.

The advantage of outline-oriented art is that the mathematical descriptions can create a given object at any particular size, so the object can be scaled up or down precisely without becoming rough or jagged. When you place an outline-oriented EPS (Encapsulated PostScript) file into Photoshop, you can resize the image without losing resolution until you're ready for Photoshop to rasterize it. After that, it becomes subject to the pixelation of any bitmapped image in Photoshop.

Because of that limitation, it's best to import vector art into Photoshop only as a last step, when you won't need to resize it any more. If you use Adobe Illustrator, this can be particularly easy, since Illustrator images can be dragged directly from an Illustrator window to a Photoshop document without converting the outline image into a bitmapped PICT file — a step that is usually necessary when you drag and drop from other drawing applications. Adobe is trying to make Illustrator and Photoshop work together as smoothly as possible, as well as with other Adobe applications (like PageMaker).

Vector files are typically much, much smaller than bitmapped files, since they contain only the information needed to reproduce the outlines and any fills or patterns contained in them.

Graphics Formats and Browsers

When you're creating cool Web graphics in Photoshop, you can work with any graphics format you like. However, when it comes time to save the image for use on a Web page, your choices break down into two formats: GIF and JPEG (and a couple variations of each). The following section describes each of the major graphics file types and offers tips on how you can best work with them in Photoshop.

GIF format

GIF stands for *Graphics Interchange Format,* a 256-color image format that was originally developed for use on the CompuServe Information Network. It was created so that subscribers to CompuServe would have a common graphics format in which to exchange images, regardless of whether they were using Macintoshes, PCs, Amigas, or some other platform. GIF quickly became a universal graphics format on the Web, and support for it has been built into all graphics-ready browsers.

A bit of controversy surrounded GIF a few years ago when Unisys, which owns the patent rights to some of the algorithms used to compress GIF files, started to indicate that it would expect royalties from vendors of applications that included GIF support. (Note that only the software vendors, not users of GIF, were threatened with sanctions.) However, because GIF capabilities are built into so many applications developed by very small vendors, including shareware authors, for awhile it appeared that there would be a mass exodus away from GIF to some other graphics file format. Some of the major vendors got in line, however, and signed arrangements with Unisys, and there have been no problems since. GIF appears to be viable online for awhile yet.

There are some advantages and disadvantages to GIF files with which you'll want to be familiar.

GIF supports only 256 colors or fewer. This is simultaneously an advantage and a disadvantage. On the plus side, working with 256 or fewer colors means that resulting images can potentially be viewed on any display screen offering 256 or more colors. Once you've reduced an image to 256 colors or less, the image should look just about as it will appear on the screen of any visitor to your Web site.

However, there are few guarantees in life. There are two complications to this rosy picture. First, in creating any image with 256 or fewer colors, Photoshop creates a palette of the required number of hues. The GIF89a Export filter (found in the File ⇨ Acquire menu and shown in Figure 3-4) even allows you to help build a palette that best portrays your image. If you're not careful, the palette may be different for every image you save in the GIF format. That can have some bad effects on how your images are viewed.

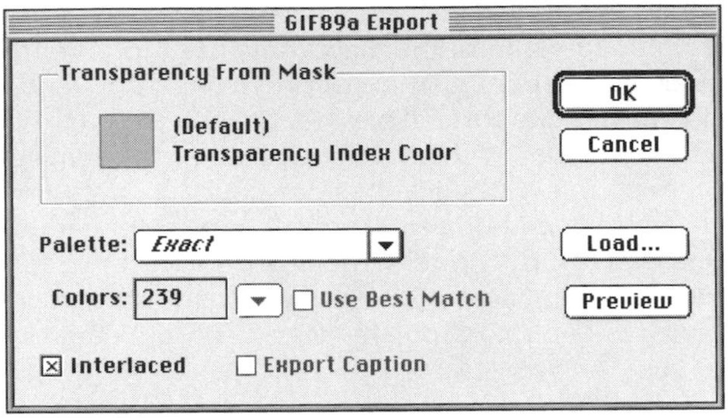

Figure 3-4: Photoshop's GIF89a Export filter can be used to create optimized 256 (or fewer) color palettes.

What happens is that the visitor's browser or operating system adjusts itself to display your GIF image using the closest it can come to your ideal palette. This may work reasonably well, but browsers actually have a standardized palette of 216 hues that can work even better than the one you create. (Photoshop contains an option for using such a palette, which we'll look at later in this chapter.)

Problems emerge, however, when you place more than one GIF file on a page that each uses a different palette and that are visible at the same time. A 256-color display can't show both palettes at once, and may shift back and forth between them in a bizarre way, or introduce speckled artifacts onto the image, as shown in Figure 3-5.

So, a 256-color file format like GIF isn't a panacea. We'll show you ways to minimize the problems later in this chapter.

Keep in mind that GIF doesn't require you to use a specific number of colors, as long as you use fewer than 256. If your image contains or looks good with only 87 colors, or 31, or 11, you can reduce the image to that number of hues. The benefits? Your reduced color image will be easier to display on the screen, and the file size will drop dramatically, especially when GIF's compression routines are applied.

For example, I took a rather massive 1.5MB TIFF file, reduced it to 256 colors, and saved it as a GIF file. It took just 83K of disk space — about one-twentieth its original size — when saved in that format. Using Photoshop's Mode ➪ Indexed Color ➪ Web option, the same file used 216 colors — and looked virtually identical on a Web page — yet took up only 66K of disk space. When a visitor is downloading your page at 14.4Kbps, that smaller size can shave up to 10 to 20 seconds or more from the time spent downloading the image.

Figure 3-5: Speckled artifacts show up when your palettes don't match.

If my test image had been suited to display using 128 colors, 64 colors, or some other number of hues (logos, line art, images with a preponderance of one color group, and other similar items with only a few colors), I can produce even more dramatic size and download-time savings.

There's more to know about GIF. Because it is limited to 256 colors, some types of images, particularly photographs with many different colors, just can't be represented accurately in that mode. Figure 3-6 shows an image in its original tones, and how it appears after it is reduced to 256 colors. Images with subtle gradations of color from one hue to another don't adapt well to GIF, since Photoshop must clump groups of similar colors together and represent them with a single hue. This produces a banding effect rather than a smooth transition, which is noticeable in images with much color gradation.

Figure 3-6: *Smooth gradations change into bands of color when reduced to 256 hues.*

Traditionally, GIF format has been only acceptable, at best, for many kinds of photographs. Its real strength is in images with fewer colors, especially those with strong lines and for which sharpness is an important element. That's because GIF's file compression scheme is lossless — no image information (other than the extra colors you discard) is lost during the conversion to GIF. If an image was sharp before GIF compression, it will be just as sharp when decompressed and displayed on the screen.

Text and lines show up especially well in GIF format. If you want to add some fancy text to a Web page, a GIF file is often your best choice. There's a special reason for that, in addition to GIF's inherent lossless compression: GIFs can be made transparent.

Well, perhaps that's a misnomer. Transparent GIFs aren't really translucent. Instead, you can select one color that will be ignored by the browser as if it weren't there. The background color will show through instead. If you create text on a background and then make that background transparent, the browser will merge the text smoothly with its own background. The text will appear to be embedded right into the background page itself, instead of within a rectangular image (which is the case with non-transparent Web images). Figure 3-7 shows a transparent GIF image on a Web page. We'll create some transparent GIFs in later chapters.

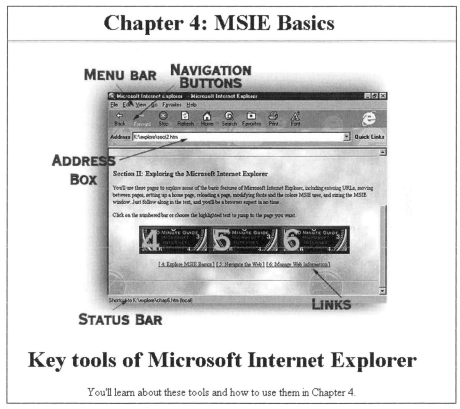

Figure 3-7: The transparent image is visible in the background.

There is one other advantage to GIF files: They can be interleaved. That is, alternating lines of the image can be downloaded from your page first, giving the browser a coarse preview of the final image, which then gradually becomes sharper and more detailed as the rest of the GIF data is received. Interleaved GIF images can grab visitors' eyes long enough to lure them further into your Web page.

Of course, interleaved images are a virtual necessity, because GIF files are still often relatively large and take awhile to download.

As a final advantage, GIFs can be animated. It's possible to incorporate several images within a GIF file, although Photoshop doesn't have the built-in ability to create such files. Most browsers will display each of these images in turn, producing alternating images, or if you've made only animation-like changes to small portions of the image, create an animated effect. Animated GIFs are a good way to add movement to your Web page without using Java or complex programming.

To summarize, GIF files have the following advantages:

➥ GIF files support only 256 or fewer colors for excellent display on all Web browsers regardless of the color capabilities of the visitor's monitor.

➥ GIF has smaller file sizes than TIFF because it uses fewer colors and efficient compression.

➥ A lossless compression scheme retains the sharpness of the original.

➥ Transparent images can float on a background.

➥ Interleaved GIFs can be revealed progressively as the files download.

➥ Animated GIFs can add action to your Web page.

And the following disadvantages:

➥ Some GIF palettes may not display well, even on 256-color monitors.

➥ Many photographic images don't look good in 256 colors.

➥ GIF file sizes are often larger than JPEG files, which are discussed in the section that follows.

JPEG format

JPEG is a flexible format that supports up to 16.8 million colors, making it suitable for photographic images and browsers that run on 24-bit color displays. JPEG also has a dial-a-quality mode that allows you to choose between high-quality, virtually lossless compression (and larger file sizes) or lower-quality, lossy compression that discards image information, but produces remarkably small image files. We were able to squeeze our 1.5MB TIFF image down to 27K using JPEG's highest compression ratio, for example.

JPEG, developed from the *Joint Photographic Experts Group* from which it got its name, supports very high compression rates that speed up downloads of JPEG images dramatically. Some image quality may be lost, but the amount of compression and degradation are selectable, enabling the Web builder to decide how much sharpness to compromise in the name of speed and viewer-friendliness. On the downside, not all browsers support inline display of any kind of JPEG images (yet), let alone the new

Progressive JPEG format that offers slick, interleaved images like GIF, and the even newer Transparent JPEG.

Because we've already discussed most of these points when we talked about GIF, it won't take long to explain JPEG's advantages and disadvantages. Consider the following advantages:

➡ JPEG handles 16.8 million colors without breaking stride, so full-color images reproduce well.

➡ JPEG offers smaller file sizes than GIF, and Photoshop provides a sliding control, shown in Figure 3-8, that allows choosing between smallest file size/lowest image quality and largest file size/highest image quality.

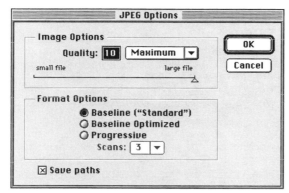

Figure 3-8: Photoshop's JPEG compression/quality slider control looks like this.

➡ The smaller file sizes of JPEG download very quickly, making it easy for a Web page to bristle with good-looking images without long download times.

JPEG's disadvantages include the following:

➡ The lossy compression scheme robs many images of needed sharpness, so JPEG may be a poor choice for finely-detailed artwork. Its high color rendition may be wasted on such images.

➡ Users with 256-color displays may not be able to view JPEG images as easily, or as you intend them to be seen.

➡ Not all browsers support Progressive and Transparent JPEG, so if you want to use those two features and remain as compatible with as many potential visitors as possible, you may want to stick with the GIF equivalents.

Figure 3-9 shows a JPEG image at low, medium, and high quality.

Figure 3-9: *This image has been saved at low, medium, and high quality in JPEG format.*

What's Compression?

When a computer is working with an image, it stores a binary number representing each part of the bitmap in a separate memory location. If those values are stored on your hard disk as is, a bitmap can be very large, even for small JPEG or GIF files displayed on a Web page. Fortunately, compression schemes come to our rescue.

All compression methods operate by replacing individual streams of bits with shorter streams that convey the same information. One way to do that is to examine a file, discover which values occur most frequently, and then represent those values by shorter codes. If an image contains a lot of dark blues and greens, those values would be represented by shorter codes. Less frequently-used colors might be represented by full-length or longer codes, but the savings accrued from the popular colors provides an overall reduction of 10 to 20 percent in a typical file size.

Another type of compression, usually called LZW after its developers, Lempel, Ziv, and Welch, replaces frequently used strings of numbers with fixed-length codes and uses pointers to tell the decompression software where long strings or runs of numbers are repeated within the file. Instead of storing these runs over and over, they are retained only once, and the pointer shows where the image information can be retrieved.

JPEG is yet another, more sophisticated compression scheme for continuous tone images that is efficient, and still retains the most valuable image information. JPEG uses three different algorithms — one called discrete cosine transformation (DCT), a quantization routine, and a numeric compression method like the ones described above.

JPEG first divides an image into larger cells — say 8 x 8 pixels — and performs a discrete cosine transformation on the information. This mathematical mumbo-jumbo simply analyzes the pixels in the 64-pixel cell and looks for similarities. Redundant pixels — those that have the same value as those around them — are discarded.

Next, quantization occurs, which causes some of the pixels that are nearly white to be represented as all-white. The grayscale and color information is then compressed by recording the differences in tone from one pixel to the next, and the resulting string of numbers is encoded using a combination of schemes. An 8 x 8 block with 24 bits of information per pixel (192 bytes) can often be squeezed down to 10 to 13 or fewer bytes. JPEG allows specifying various compression ratios, in which case larger amounts of information are discarded to produce higher compression ratios.

Other formats

Browsers can display other file formats using helper applications that you associate with file extensions. That is, you can tell your browser to automatically load Photoshop to display any file it encounters with the .PCX, .TIF, or other compatible extension. This is a slow way to operate, and you won't find many .PCX or .TIF files on Web pages for that reason. You certainly shouldn't include any on yours. PICT files are the native format of the Macintosh. When you copy an image to the Clipboard, it is converted to PICT. But Web pages can't display PICT files any more than they can .PCX or .TIF formats.

The *Portable Network Graphics* (PNG) format, another type of raster image, is well-supported by Photoshop (you'll find a PNG option in the File ⇨ Save pull-down format list), but is not widely used yet. PNG is a lossless, cross-platform, highly compressed RGB file format that can incorporate mask channels, as well as gamma and chromacity values. Potentially, browsers that support PNG would be able to display such files with much greater accuracy, regardless of the type of computer being used. PNG also supports progressive display.

Some other file types, such as the vector files produced by Macromedia Freehand, can be easily and automatically displayed by browsers through the use of plug-in programs such as Macromedia QuickSilver. Multimedia movie and sound files can also be played back in streaming format (that is, while they are actually downloading) using appropriate plug-in modules. However, such files can't be generated by Photoshop.

Finally, text- and design-oriented documents can be embedded into a Web page in Adobe Acrobat's Portable Document Format (PDF), downloaded, and displayed by most Web browsers using the Acrobat plug-in. Again, you can't create such files with Photoshop, but Acrobat is included on the Photoshop CD-ROM if you want to experiment with it.

Moving On

Now that you know something about individual graphics formats and how to select the best format for Web images, we'll move on to look at just how graphics can be included in Web pages in Chapter 4. In Chapter 5, you'll find step-by-step instructions for creating interlaced GIFs, JPEG files, and other images for your Web site.

Adding Graphics to HTML Pages

Most of this book concentrates on techniques for creating cool graphic images to place on a Web page. In this chapter you'll find a discussion of HTML (Hypertext Markup Language) and almost everything else you need to know to about placing Photoshop graphics on a Web page.

Some HTML features are beyond the scope of this book, and you certainly don't need to learn all of the ins and outs of this markup language to create effective, eye-catching Web pages. A WYSIWYG (What You See Is What You Get) Web authoring program like Adobe PageMill makes crafting Web pages drag-and-drop easy.

Unless you need advanced features, you don't even need to know the HTML basics described in this chapter. However, a solid grounding in the underpinnings of HTML will help if you plan to create a page from scratch without an authoring program, or need to edit a page's source listing to provide a minor tweak. The information you need is here. Should you want to explore HTML further, I recommend Dave Taylor's *Creating Cool HTML 3.2 Web Pages* (IDG Books Worldwide, 1997).

What's HTML?

The term *Hypertext Markup Language* sounds like one of those highly-technical jargon terms bandied about by those fellows who have beards, wear suspenders, and think UNIX is the only true operating system worth talking about. In practice, HTML isn't nearly as complicated as the programming tools we ordinarily think of as computer languages.

Basically, HTML is nothing more than a way of labeling text and pictures for display by a Web browser. One HTML tag may mark a line as a heading, while another may specify a paragraph of body text. HTML graphics instructions may also tell the browser how many pixels wide and tall an image is and ask the software to center the image, or place it at the right or left margin.

HTML tags also provide locations the browser can use to find the graphics or pages to display, even if the graphics or pages don't reside on the same computer as the current HTML page.

At its basic level, that's all HTML is — instructions for displaying text and graphics, and links to other pages and images. We'll look at some typical HTML listings shortly, so you can see exactly what I mean.

Linear versus hyper

First, it's important to understand the difference between *linear media* and *hypermedia*. This book is linear: the information I've collected here is best used if you start at the beginning and work your way to the end. You can skim quickly or skip sections if you already know the material, or come back later to refer to a particular section you want to concentrate on. In general, linear media is perused from the beginning to the end.

A "choose your own adventure" book for kids is a simple kind of hypermedia. Young readers can make decisions and jump around the text to create a story of their own choosing. Interactive computer games that let you carve your own path through a play scenario also can have hyper-oriented components. If you're researching a topic in an encyclopedia and follow multiple "see also" references, you're also working in a non-linear, hyper-like way.

True hypermedia bristles with "see also" links. A well-constructed Web page will lead you from one page to another in a logical, linear fashion, but will also include jumps to other interesting pages. You can follow along as the author intended, or skip from one page and image to another in whatever order the available links and your interests dictate. Figure 4-1 shows a Web page with text, graphics, and links to other pages and images.

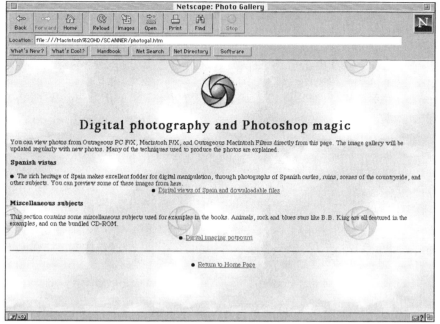

Figure 4-1: A typical Web page with text, graphics, and links.

What's in an HTML page?

A typical HTML page consists of text, images, and instructions on how to display them, which are all downloaded from the page's computer host. The host is usually called a Web server — although your browser can also read an HTML page and its files that may simply reside on your hard disk, somewhere on your network, or on the CD-ROM like the one packaged with this book.

As the HTML page — a simple ASCII text file like those you can create in SimpleText or any word processor — is retrieved, the browser sorts out which information is text to be displayed, which is instructions, and which are pointers to images that should also be downloaded and shown on the page.

Many of the HTML tags are similar to the styles used by word processing programs such as Microsoft Word, or page layout programs such as PageMaker. These styles determine how various levels of headings, body text, bulleted paragraphs, and so on, are displayed.

HTML allows the Web browser to control many of the parameters for displaying content. For example, you generally don't specify right and left margins for text. The browser automatically adjusts the line breaks so the text is shown correctly between the margins of the browser window. That makes it possible to display text in a variety of browsers, without worrying whether the user has a 1024 × 768- or 640 × 480-pixel screen. If all of the text can't be displayed on a given screen, the user can move down the page using the browser's scroll bars.

All HTML pages consist of three main components, plus an optional external fourth component. These include the following:

➡ **Text content.** These are the words that will be displayed on the page between and around your Photoshop images. Your page can include text paragraphs, captions for the images, and other plain text. Given no additional instructions, a browser such as Netscape Navigator or Microsoft Internet Explorer will simply display this text in a default body text font, within the margins of the browser window.

➡ **Markup instructions.** These are special codes, placed between angle brackets — for example, <TITLE> — that provide the browser with instructions on how to display a particular piece of text or image (flush right, flush left, or centered), or where to look for additional content to display. A simple set of instructions might look like this:

```
<HTML>
<BODY>
<H1>Cool Photoshop...</H1>
<P>You've reached the home page of Cool Photoshop
Web page effects. </P>
</BODY>
</HTML>
```

In these HTML instructions, <H1> indicates that the browser should start using the Heading 1 style. This is matched with a closing instruction using a forward slash, such as </H1>. The closing instruction tells the browser to stop using the Heading 1 style. Everything within angle brackets is a markup instruction; everything between the instruction tags is text that will be displayed on the page.

The style names and their properties are defined by the rules of HTML itself, rather than by the person creating the document. In addition, HTML styles are much more limited in terms of the parameters you can specify. You may be able to specify the size of text relative to other text on the page (that is, larger, smaller, smallest, and so on) and attributes like bold or italics, but not exact fonts or point sizes. To do that, you need to go behind simple HTML to a relatively new development called cascading style sheets, which give you greater control over these parameters. (Cascading style sheets are beyond the scope of this book.)

➥ **External content.** These are the components that will be shown on the page, or played back when you click a button or link, but aren't included within the HTML text itself. Markup instructions point to where the browser should search for these pieces, whether on the CD-ROM or disk with the HTML page, or somewhere on the Internet. Typical external content includes image files that are displayed on a page, plus audio files, movies, and so on. Often called encoded files, these files are not in plain ASCII text and require a special software module to decode them and play them back. The facility can be built into the browser itself (as is the case with the decoders for the two most common type of image files used on Web pages: JPEG and GIF format files), or included as a plug-in (an external module that becomes part of the browser) or helper application (a module that can be activated by the browser automatically).

➥ **Comments.** The fourth kind of information that may be included on an HTML page is comments. These are just as you might expect: remarks about the page or its author that don't display, don't modify any of the text, or point to an external component. A comment is placed inside tags that include an exclamation point:

```
<! Ignore this line. It's just a meaningless
comment. Thank you.>
```

Like all languages, HTML is an evolving standard. At first, HTML included only a few, limited instructions for formatting text and displaying graphics in a few standard ways. Then, as a way to jazz up sterile Web pages, extensions to the language were developed in somewhat haphazard fashion by vendors like Netscape and Microsoft. At first, these extensions were supported only by a particular browser, so Web sites began sprouting banners that said "Netscape Enhanced" or "Best Viewed with Microsoft Internet Explorer." Finally, a truce of sorts was declared in the browser wars: both Netscape and Microsoft decided to support a more-or-less common set of extensions and adhere to the current release of HTML, which at this writing is HTML Version 3.2.

Links

The final structure you need to understand to create HTML pages with Photoshop graphics is *links*. Links are controls within an HTML document that provide a location for the browser. That location can be one of the following:

➥ Another place on the same page that the browser should jump to

➥ Another page stored elsewhere on that Web site or hard disk

➡ Another page on a different Web site or hard disk (or somewhere on your computer network)

➡ The location of an image, audio file, movie, executable file, or other component, either local or elsewhere on the Web or network, that the browser should download. If the browser has a plug-in, helper, or built-in support for that type of file, it can display or play it. If not (which will probably be the case with executable files), the browser will offer to store the file on your hard disk.

As you can see, links are a powerful feature that enable HTML page browsers to build in jump-off points that visitors can use to navigate through multiple pages, view images, download files, and perform other functions.

URLs and the World Wide Web

Strictly speaking, you don't need to know much about the World Wide Web and URLs to create HTML pages. Many businesses are using internal intranets to provide employees with databases, including access to personnel information through Web-style documents. If you're a photographer, you might want to create a portfolio of images that fits on a CD-ROM or floppy disk and that can be viewed with an Internet browser.

Even so, most readers of this book plan to use Photoshop to create graphics for pages posted on World Wide Web sites. To create Web pages with graphics, however, it helps to understand something about Internet addresses and URLs.

Uniform resource locators, or URLs, are nothing more than a kind of Internet address, just like dbusch@dbusch.com (my e-mail address).

Your Web pages may contain URLs that link to pages or images elsewhere on your Web server's host computer, to pages or images on other computers somewhere else in the world, or even to HTML or image files on a local hard disk, CD-ROM, or network. As long as you include the correct address — either an Internet address or a local path — your browser should be able to find the HTML pages or images you point to.

Your Second Web Page

In Chapter 1, I had you put together a simple Web page using some graphics you created in Photoshop. Now it's time to put together a slightly more complicated set of pages that will give you the opportunity both to learn more about Photoshop's Web-friendly features and how to add graphics to HTML pages. I'm going to divide the project into four separate steps: creating two textures to use as foreground and background effects for a banner; producing an eye-catching banner using a couple of interesting techniques; transforming the banner into a rounded button in transparent GIF form; and creating two actual Web pages that use these graphics and include hyperlink jumps from one page to another.

Creating text for Web pages

HTML pages can include text in one of two ways. First, you can place the text you want to display on a page in the page's text file in ASCII format. You'll want to do that for the majority of the text — the body text and header text — that appears on a page.

However, when you're working with plain ASCII text on an HTML page, there are some severe limitations on the different ways you can vary and enhance the text display. You can choose from only six different relative head sizes (with the actual point sizes on the user's screen determined by your visitor's browser), select bold, italic, or normal text, specify a mono-spaced font, and insert a limited number of bullets, numbers, special symbols, and other characters.

The second way of putting text on a page, as a JPEG or GIF graphic, gives you greater control over how the text is displayed (the exact colors are still up to the user's browser) and opens the door to fancy text effects that Photoshop shines at producing.

As I noted, ASCII text has its limitations — the bottom line being that it's boring. However, there are a few drawbacks to dressing up your page with text in the form of images, too:

⮞ **Length of download time.** Any type of image file, even a small one, takes longer to download and display in a browser than text.

⮞ **Difficulty in editing text.** Text-as-images can't be easily edited without changing the original image file. A misspelled ASCII text name can be corrected in seconds; make the same error in a Photoshop image and you may have to re-create the image from scratch (or maybe not, if you were smart enough to save a copy with all individual layers of an image kept separate).

⮞ **Trade-off between resolution and file size.** Text converted to image form suffers from the same drawbacks of any image you include on a Web page: if the text is sharp and clear, the image file may be too large to download quickly. Make the text image small in file size, and you can lose resolution. Figure 4-2 shows an example of a sharp but humongous image text file (top) and a lithe, slightly blurry version of the same text (bottom).

Figure 4-2: Sharp text (top) and blurry text (bottom) can be produced, depending on the needs of your Web page.

➡ **Hogging screen space.** If you want to place your text on a background other than the browser's background color, the image of the text must fit inside a rectangular block that can hog a lot of screen space. Note that you can make *part* of the block transparent, so that your text appears inside what looks like a triangle, circle, or irregular area, but that rectangular block is still there. No other image or text can intrude on the space it occupies.

Figure 4-3 shows an example of image text as it appears on a Web page (top) and the area it actually takes up (bottom).

Adding texture to text

If you've been using Photoshop for long, you've probably learned how to fill text with a simple color or gradient. You may also have learned how to add a texture to text. In this next section, we'll create our own great texture, and then superimpose it on text to produce an interesting effect. Follow the directions in the steps below to produce your own cool type.

Creating the text's background

First, we'll use a few Photoshop tools to generate a dramatic texture from scratch. For this part you won't need anything except Photoshop itself.

1. **Use File ➪ New to create a new, empty Photoshop document.** Make the Width 560 pixels and the Height 150 pixels, set the Resolution to 72 pixels per inch, the Mode to RGB Color, and Contents to White (shown in the dialog box in Figure 4-4).

Figure 4-3: This irregularly shaped text box (top) actually takes up the space shown in the box on the bottom.

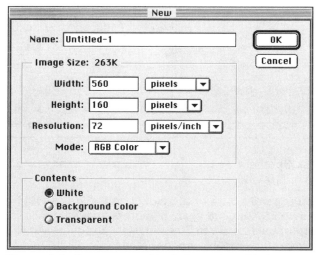

Figure 4-4: Create a new, blank document with these parameters.

2. **In Photoshop's Swatches palette, choose light blue and dark blue as your foreground and background colors.** Move the cursor over to a light blue swatch, and it turns into an eyedropper. Click to set the foreground color. Now, move to a dark blue swatch, hold down the Option key, and click again to set the background color.

3. **Double-click the Gradient tool in the toolbox, and check the Gradient Tool Options palette to make sure Opacity is set to 100**

percent, blending mode is set to Normal, Gradient is set to Foreground to Background, and Type is set as Linear.

4. Drag from left to right in your new document to apply the light-to-dark blue gradient.

5. **Choose Filter ➪ Noise ➪ Add Noise.** Set the options for this filter to Gaussian and Monochromatic, and adjust the Amount slider to a setting of 32. Click OK to add the noise.

6. Now choose **Filter ➪ Render ➪ Lighting Effects** to produce the dialog box shown in Figure 4-5.

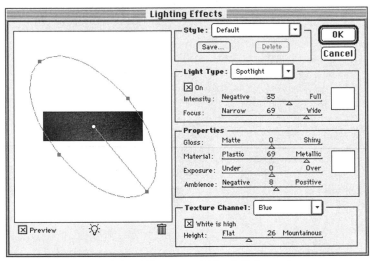

Figure 4-5: Use Lighting Effects to add both light and texture.

7. **Choose Spotlight as the Light Type; set Intensity to 35; Focus to 70.**

8. **In the Properties area of the dialog box, Gloss should be set to 0 so that the texture we apply is neither too shiny nor too matte.** Material should be set to 70 (metallic), Exposure set to 0, and Ambience (the amount of non-directional lighting that bounces around the "room" from other than the main Spotlight light source) should be moved to a value of 8.

9. **Adjust the Spotlight until its center is in the middle of the image and the edges create a shadow effect at the upper-right and lower-left corners, as shown in Figure 4-5, above.**

10. **Finally, to add texture, choose Blue from the Texture Channel pull-down list.** Make sure the White is high box is checked, and set the Height for the texture effect to a flat, unobtrusive value of 26.

11. If you'd like to save this effect to use again later, click the Save button at the top of the dialog box, and give it a name.

12. Now, click OK to apply the lighting and texture effect to the image. It should look like Figure 4-6.

Figure 4-6: *The image so far looks like this.*

13. **Save the file as** `coolback.jpg`. When the JPEG Quality dialog box pops up, choose Maximum as the quality level. We don't want to lose any of our sharpness until we're done with the image.

Creating the text's texture

Now we need to create some texture for the text itself. Just follow these steps:

1. **Use File ➪ New to create a new, empty Photoshop document, as you did above.** Make the Width 560 pixels and the Height 150 pixels, set the Resolution to 72 pixels per inch, set Mode to RGB Color, and set Contents to White.

2. **Press the D key on your keyboard to return Photoshop's foreground/background colors to their default values.** Then choose a different light blue from the Swatches palette for your foreground color.

3. **Apply a gradient using the same options you used in the previous section, only drag from the top of the image to the bottom.**

4. **Choose Filter ➪ Noise ➪ Add Noise.** Set the options for this filter to Gaussian and Monochromatic, and adjust the Amount slider to a setting of 32. Click OK to add the noise.

5. **Now, select Filter ➪ Artistic ➪ Plastic Wrap to pop up the Plastic Wrap dialog box, shown in Figure 4-7.**

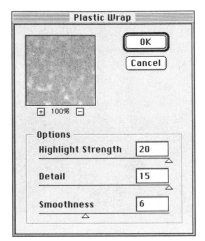

Figure 4-7: Set the options in the Plastic Wrap filter's dialog box.

6. **Make the Highlight Strength 20; Detail, 15; and Smoothness, 6.** Click OK to apply the filter.

7. **Use Filter ⇨ Sharpen ⇨ Sharpen More to produce an icy-looking effect, as you can see in Figure 4-8.**

Figure 4-8: An icy-looking effect is the result.

8. **Save this new texture as** `icytext.tif`.

Adding a texture to the text

Now, we can combine the two textures to produce our finished text.

1. **Load** `icytext.tif` **and** `coolback.tif` **textures into Photoshop.**

2. **Click the Type tool, holding down the mouse button so both the standard type icon and the dotted line, type mask icon are visible.**

Move the mouse to the right to select the type mask icon. You can also hold down the Option key while you click the Type tool, and Photoshop will cycle through the available tools.

3. **Move the cursor to roughly the center of the** `icytext.tif` **image, and click to produce the Type Tool dialog box, as shown in Figure 4-9.** Choose a fat font from the Font menu and enter 72 points for the size.

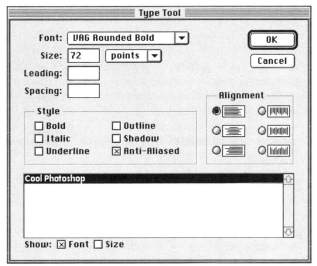

Figure 4-9: You can specify the size of the type and other parameters in the Type Tool dialog box.

4. **Click the horizontal centered alignment button, check the Anti-Aliased box, and type in the following text:**

```
Cool Photoshop
```

5. **Click OK to deposit your text into the image as a selection.** It will be centered around the point where you positioned the mouse cursor and clicked earlier. The image should look like Figure 4-10.

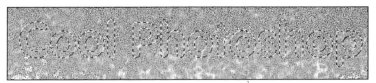

Figure 4-10: The type has been entered into the image as a mask.

6. With any selection tool selected, move the cursor inside the selection and reposition the mask on the background texture until you have a surface showing through the text outline that you like. Then press Command-C to copy the selection.

7. **Move to the** `coolback.tif` **image and press Command-V to paste the characters down into a new layer.** Photoshop 4.0 automatically deposits the text into a new layer.

Inserting a shadow

Our text will be more distinctive if we surround it with a blurry, glowing shadow. Photoshop 4.0 includes a Drop Shadow macro already pre-defined for you in the Actions palette. However, the following steps show you how to add one of your own design, with a new twist using layer masks:

1. **In the Layers palette's fly-out menu, select Duplicate Layer.** Name the new layer Shadow.

2. **Click the Shadow layer so that the paintbrush icon appears (indicating that it is the active layer).** The Layers palette should now look like Figure 4-11.

Figure 4-11: The new Shadow layer is active in the Layers palette, as indicated by the paint brush icon.

3. **Select Filter ➪ Blur ➪ Gaussian Blur and set the radius to about 4 pixels, shown in Figure 4-12.**

4. **In the Layers palette, click the Preserve Transparency box so that only the image portion of the layer will be affected by our next step, which is to fill the blurred text with a hue.** Without this box checked, the entire layer will be filled.

5. **Choose a dark blue color from the Swatches palette.**

Figure 4-12: Using a pixel radius of 4 blurs the Shadow layer dramatically.

6. Use Edit ⇨ Fill to fill the blurred text with the blue hue.

7. Now use Layer ⇨ Duplicate Layer to create a copy of the Shadow layer. Call it Shadow 2.

8. Select a magenta color from the Swatches palette, making sure Preserve Transparency is checked in the Layers palette. Fill the duplicate shadow with the magenta hue.

9. In the Layers palette, grab the name of the layer with the text with the mouse and drag it so that it is stacked above the blue, blurry shadow and the magenta shadow in the Layers palette list. Your image should look something like Figure 4-13.

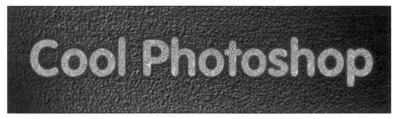

Figure 4-13: The text, blurry blue and magenta highlighting, and background look like this after the layers have been reordered.

Using a layer mask

A layer mask is a special grayscale channel that can be applied to any of the layers of an image and used to control how much of the image shows through. You can learn how the layer mask operates while producing the blended effect between the blue and magenta shadows. You could have just used a blue/magenta gradient to color a single shadow, but doing it this way allows you to save the image in Photoshop format with the two colors separate. You can then easily change the color scheme at a later time.

1. **Select the original shadow image in the Layers palette.** From the Layer menu, choose Add Layer Mask. Two fly-out choices will appear. Select Reveal All, as shown in Figure 4-14.

Figure 4-14: *Photoshop 4.0's new Layer menu includes the Add Layer Mask choice.*

You've just created a layer mask that initially allows everything in its layer to show through, as opposed to Hide All, which covers everything up. Obviously, you'd select one over the other depending on whether you wanted to paint areas that would hide or conceal parts of a particular layer. In the end, it doesn't really make any difference, except for the amount of work you must do. It's easier to add a little to a Reveal All style mask than to remove almost everything from a Hide All mask, for example.

2. **The layer mask should now be active, as indicated in the Layers palette by a mask icon (shown at left in Figure 4-15).** When the layer itself is active, the mask icon will be replaced by the familiar paintbrush icon, as you can see at right in the same figure.

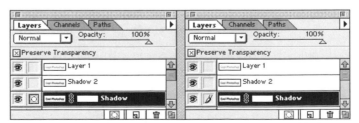

Figure 4-15: *At left, the layer mask is the active, paintable layer; at right, the layer itself is active.*

3. **Choose the Gradient tool, making sure that the standard black/white foreground/background colors are selected.** We're now going to learn how to create a custom, reusable gradient.

4. **In the Gradient Options palette, make sure Linear is checked.**

5. **Apply the gradient to the layer mask by clicking in the left of the window and dragging to the right.**

6. **Select the magenta shadow image in the Layers palette.** From the Layer menu, choose Add Layer Mask.

7. **Apply the same gradient as above to the layer mask by clicking in the right of the window and dragging to the left.** The pair of layer masks will mask off each of the shadows in opposite directions, producing a gradient between them. But, in contrast to using a normal gradient effect, you can edit this one manually at a later time by applying a new gradient or painting on either or both of the two layer masks.

8. **Merge the layers by selecting the Flatten Image choice from the Layer menu.** Your finished image will look like Figure 4-16.

Figure 4-16: The finished image, with the shadows blended, will look like this.

9. **You can now save the file in the JPEG format, and we'll use it later in this chapter.** Call it `CoolLogo.jpg`, and save using Maximum quality.

Changing the image into a button

You can use the same image as both a banner (like we've created above) and a button, with the techniques we'll use in the following section:

1. **Use File ⇨ New to create a new, empty Photoshop document.** Make the Width 600 pixels and the Height 200 pixels, set the Resolution to 72 pixels per inch, set Mode to RGB Color, and set Contents to White.

2. **Go back to your Cool Photoshop graphic and use Command-A to select the whole image.** Then press Command-C to copy it.

3. **Move to your new, empty document and press Command-V to paste the image from the Cool Photoshop graphic.**

4. **Select the elliptical marquee tool (Option-click until the tool appears in the toolbox, if necessary).** Then, select an oval that includes the Cool Photoshop text.

5. **Choose Filter ➪ Distort ➪ Spherize, and make sure Amount is set to 100 percent and Mode to Normal.** You can spherize either horizontally or vertically (producing a cylinder), or in both directions when Mode is set to Normal, producing a spherical effect. Click OK to apply the effect.

6. **Press Command-C to copy the spherized image, then press Command-V to paste it.** Photoshop 4.0 will automatically create a new layer for the oblong, rounded new button, which should look like Figure 4-17.

Figure 4-17: The new oval button has been spherized.

7. **Use Image ➪ Image Size and change the Pixel Dimensions Width pull-down list to Percent, if it isn't set for that value already.** Enter 25 percent as the new size, and click OK to shrink the button.

8. **Use Filter ➪ Sharpen ➪ Sharpen More to add sharpness and contrast to the button.**

9. **Since the button already resides on a transparent layer, we can use the Photoshop GIF89a Export filter to export it as a transparent GIF.** Use File ➪ Export ➪ GIF89a Export. Make sure the Interlaced box is checked and Adaptive Palette is selected. This image has fewer than 128 colors, so you can choose the 128 option from the Colors pull-down list.

10. **Click OK to save the button.** Name the file `CoolButn.gif`.

You now have most of the components you need in hand to construct a more advanced Web page.

Building our page

We'll use a text editor to create our HTML pages so that you can learn how all of the tags work and where they go. When you actually start producing your own Web pages, you may prefer to use an authoring tool. You'll find that what you learn in this chapter will help even when you've switched to more automated techniques. Open SimpleText or your favorite word processor (remember to save your HTML page in Text Only mode if you use something other than SimpleText). Then, follow these directions to assemble a page from the components we have.

Starting the page

As you learned in Chapter 1, every Web page must start out with the <HTML> tag to let the browser know it is looking at an HTML page. You'll place the closing tag, </HTML> at the end of this page, after you've followed the procedure listed below.

Type in the following lines, placing a hard return between them. These tags start out the page and mark the document heading. The first line, with the <!DOCTYPE> tag, is required for all HTML 3.2 compliant documents, as a way to let browsers know that HTML 3.2 tags may lie within. The material between the <TITLE> and </TITLE> tags will be shown in the title bar of the page when displayed in a browser:

```
<!DOCTYPE HTML Public "-//W3C//DTD HTML 3.2 //EN">
<HTML>
<HEAD>
<TITLE>Cool Photoshop Home Page </TITLE>
</HEAD>
```

Copy the file backgrnd.jpg from the Chapter 4 folder on the CD-ROM that accompanies this book, and place it in the same folder you'll be using to store the finished HTML page.

Type in the line below, which instructs the browser to use the file you specify as the background for the entire page. The background will be tiled as often as needed to fill up the entire browser window:

```
<BODY BACKGROUND="backgrnd.jpg">
```

Enter the line below. Use one continuous line, even though the listing may have a line break in it:

```
<CENTER><P><IMG SRC="coollogo.jpg" alt="Cool Photoshop
Logo" HEIGHT=150 WIDTH=560></P></CENTER>
```

There are several components to this line. The meaning of each tag is as follows:

- `<CENTER>` `</CENTER>` The browser will center the lines between these opening and closing tags in the margins of the browser window, regardless of what size it might be.

- `<P>` `</P>`These tags mark the beginning and ending of a paragraph and tell the browser to insert a paragraph break after the last character. You can use them to format text or to insert a break between components.

- `IMG SRC="coollogo.jpg"` This tag tells the browser to place the file coollogo.jpg at this point on the page. Since a uniform resource locator (URL) folder or subdirectory information did not preface the file name, the browser will expect to find the image file in the same directory or folder as the current page.

- `alt="Cool Photoshop Logo"` This is alternate text that will be displayed by browsers that can't show images, or those that have had image display turned off by the user. While an alt description is optional, you'll be doing your graphics-impaired visitors a favor by at least letting them know what they are missing!

- `HEIGHT=150 WIDTH=560` The dimensions of the image in pixels. These parameters are also optional. If you leave them off, the browser can examine an image file as it downloads and allow the right amount of space. However, if you include the size specification, the browser can pre-allocate room for the image file and continue downloading the rest of your page if it takes awhile for the picture to be received. Leave off the height and width, and if there is a problem receiving the image, the browser may hang at that point and never display the rest of the page.

  You can also use these parameters to display an image in a size that is smaller or larger than its actual size. Change Height to 225 and Width to 840, and the browser will blow up the image to 150 percent its actual size — probably with mixed results. You can also display an image smaller than actual size, turning a full-sized image into a button, for example, just by specifying a smaller Height or Width. If you change one dimension disproportionately from the other, the image will be squeezed or stretched horizontally or vertically.

Now, type in the line that follows, which includes text that will be displayed in the Heading 1 (H1) size. The ALIGN parameter that follows the H1 specification tells the browser to center the heading. You can substitute LEFT or RIGHT to align the heading with the right or left margins, instead:

```
<H1 ALIGN=CENTER>Welcome to Cool Photoshop!</H1>
```

The next line to be typed in is just a paragraph of text that begins and ends with the <P> and </P> tags and has no carriage return between the lines. Note the <I> and </I> tags, which format the text between the <P> and </P> tags in italics:

```
<P>Welcome to the <I>Cool Photoshop</I> page. We hope to
provide you with a wide variety of very cool effects that
you can create with Photoshop and incorporate onto your
own Web pages. From time to time, we'll offer updates, new
filters, clip art, and other bonuses for regular
visitors.</P>
```

Now type the following line, which is similar to the one you entered above, only it uses the Heading 3 (H3) tag:

```
<H3 ALIGN=CENTER>Bookmark this page, and return
often!</H3>
```

The next line deposits a horizontal rule on the page. The WIDTH= parameter tells the browser to make the line as wide as the current window. A Width entry of 75 percent would make the rule three-fourths the width of the window. In that case, you'd probably want to make sure you used the ALIGN=CENTER parameter to center that horizontal rule between the two margins. You can also specify a width for the rule in pixels, but that can backfire if you use a width that is wider than what the user's browser window can display:

```
<HR ALIGN=CENTER WIDTH="100%"></H2>
```

There are several other parameters you can use with the horizontal rule tag:

➥ COLOR=color You can use standard color names like Red, Blue, Green, White, or enter a hexadecimal value that represents the red, green, and blue values of an exact color that (you hope) the browser can reproduce. (Hint: Load Photoshop, move the cursor to a color you want to reproduce, then use the Info palette to determine the RGB values for that color. Convert the three decimal values shown by the Info palette into hexadecimal, concatenate them together — producing a value like D466FF — and substitute for *color*. Tricky, and not recommended for beginners.)

➥ NOSHADE Tells the browser not to use an engraved, 3D effect.

➥ SIZE=n Sets the height of the rule in pixels.

Now, add the following line, centered text in the Heading 2 (H2) size:

```
<H2 ALIGN=CENTER>In weeks to come:</H2>
```

The next set of lines produce an unordered list. The beginning and end of the list are set off with <UL> and </UL> tags. Each listed item in between is marked with <LI> and </LI> tags and show up in the browser with bullets in front:

```
<UL>
<CENTER><LI>Learn About HTML with the author, in a series
entitled: </LI></CENTER>
</UL>
```

The next line is an example of preformatted text. You'd use the <PRE>, </PRE> tag pair to mark text which should appear in a monospaced font, which allows you to show simple tables on-screen while retaining the original alignment. Preformatted text also stands out from the rest of the text on the page. We used it here to represent an HTML listing. Because your browser tends to interpret the greater than (>) and less than (<) symbols as tag markers, you need to use the special characters &gt and &lt to represent them (also note the <B> and </B> tags used to boldface the text):

```
<CENTER><PRE><B>&lt;TITLE&gt;What's Next?&lt;/TITLE&gt;
</B></PRE></CENTER>
```

Now, type in the next unordered list below:

```
<UL>
<CENTER><LI>Study Graphics Formats</LI></CENTER>
<CENTER><LI>Create Your Own Web Pages</LI></CENTER>
</UL>
```

Add a horizontal rule:

```
<HR ALIGN=CENTER WIDTH="100%">
```

And add a message to jump to the next page:

```
<CENTER><P>Jump to Page 2 when you're ready:</P></CENTER>
```

Here's our first hyperlink. Type in the line below and then read on for an explanation of what you've just done:

```
<CENTER><P><A HREF="Coolweb2.htm"><IMG SRC="Coolbutton.gif"
alt="Cool Web Button" HEIGHT=48 WIDTH=144></A></P></CENTER>
```

The new tag here is the <A>, </A> tag and its HREF parameter. The target inside the quotes following HREF can be one of two kinds of destinations: an address or a file.

In this case, the destination is an address, specifically another HTML page located in the same subdirectory as the current one. If we'd wanted to, we could have typed some other kind of URL. For example:

```
<A HREF="http://www.dbusch.com/CoolWeb/coolweb2.htm">
```

would have directed the browser to find the next page at the specified address on the World Wide Web. We could have also substituted the name of an image file:

```
<A HREF="myimage.jpg">
```

or

```
<A HREF="http://www.dbusch.com/CoolWeb/myimage.jpg.">
```

In either case, instead of loading a page, the browser would have attempted to find and display the image pointed to on a blank page.

An <A HREF> tag is only the link that makes the browser jump to the new page (or a named location within a page) or image. Users need something to click to activate the jump. The IMG SRC="Coolbutton.gif", because it's located between the <A> and </A> tags, will display as a hot zone in the browser window. A click anywhere on the image will cause the browser to jump to the HREF specified.

You can also provide text as the link's hot zone, and you probably should, so that those who aren't displaying graphics in their browser (or can't) have something to click. Add the following line to provide that option:

```
<CENTER><P><A HREF="Coolweb2.htm">[Take Me to Page
2]</A></P></CENTER>
```

Finally, add these lines to "close" the page:

```
</BODY>
</HTML>
```

Load your finished page into your browser. If you've typed everything in correctly, the page should look like Figure 4-18.

Save your page as `Coolweb1.htm`.

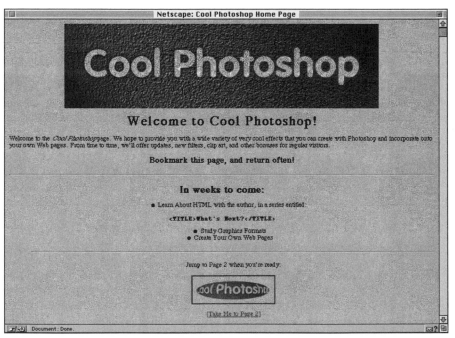

Figure 4-18: The finished first page will look like this.

Providing a page to jump to

As long as we included a page to jump to, it's probably a good idea to create that page, as well. There's nothing new here. Just type in the following lines, as you did before:

```
<!DOCTYPE HTML Public "-//W3C//DTD HTML 3.2 //EN">
<HTML>
<HEAD>
<TITLE>Cool Photoshop Page 2 </TITLE>
</HEAD>
<BODY BACKGROUND="backgrnd.jpg">
<CENTER><P><IMG SRC="coollogo.jpg" alt="Cool Photoshop
Logo" HEIGHT=150 WIDTH=560></A></P></CENTER>
<H1 ALIGN=CENTER>Here's the Second Page of Cool
Photoshop!</H1>
<HR ALIGN=CENTER WIDTH="100%">
<P>By the time you finish this book, you'll have created
pages with lots of great graphic images, all created
inside Photoshop! Just imagine all the tips and tricks
you'd be able to put on this page!</P>
<P><HR WIDTH="100%"></P>
<CENTER><P>Return to Main Page When Finished</P></CENTER>
<CENTER><P><A HREF="Coolweb1.htm"><IMG SRC="Coolbutton.gif"
alt="Cool Photoshop Button" HEIGHT=48
WIDTH=144></A></P></CENTER>
<CENTER><P><A HREF="Coolweb1.htm">[Take Me Back to Page
1]</A></P></CENTER>
</BODY>
</HTML>
```

Moving On

The tags and techniques you learned in this chapter are all the basics you need to get started placing graphics onto Web pages. Later on, I'll introduce a few additional options, which include the following:

➥ Aligning text and wrapping it around graphics

➥ Adding borders to graphics

➥ Using anchors to jump to specific positions within pages

In the next chapter, we'll look at how you can use Photoshop to improve images for your Web pages.

Working with Existing Photos and Images

While Photoshop is a powerful tool for creating images, textures, and backgrounds from scratch, often you'll want to spiff up existing images for use in Web pages. This chapter is devoted to providing an overview of some of Photoshop's best tools for retouching, compositing, and manipulating the images you already have — whether they're scanned, loaded from CD-ROM, from clip art sources, or captured from video sources.

Although this book is targeted to those who already have some experience using Photoshop, I'm not going to just list the program's key image manipulation features and explain how they apply to Web graphics. On the theory that it's better to show you than tell you what I mean, I'm going to build a composite image and explain which tools were used as I go along.

In This Chapter

Adjusting Brightness/Contrast

Simple Color Corrections

Colorizing an Image

Blending Images

Retouching Photos

Manipulating Several Images

I'm going to work with two photos and then combine them into one graphic for a music-oriented Web page. You can copy the same images I'm going to use from the CD-ROM and follow along, if you like. Copy the files `Rockstar.tif` and `BBKing.tif` from the CD-ROM, and open them in Photoshop.

Correcting brightness and contrast

Many of the pictures you'll need to improve for the Web will have some brightness and/or contrast defect. The picture may be too dark, or too light, or it has plenty of dark and light tones, but not enough in-between tones. Both the rock star and B.B. King images we're working with need some improvement. We'll start with the rock star.

1. **Select the** `Rockstar.tif file`, **and choose Image ⇨ Adjust ⇨ Levels from the menu bar.** You'll see the Levels dialog box, like the one shown in Figure 5-1. The main feature of interest is the histogram in the center.

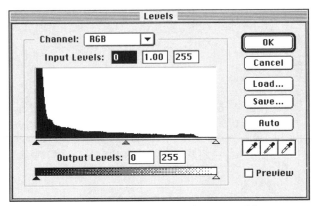

Figure 5-1: The Levels dialog box features a histogram.

A histogram is a kind of bar chart, with 256 lines extending from completely black (represented by the black triangle at the left) to completely white (represented by the white triangle). In the middle is a gray triangle used to represent a number called *gamma* that measures the contrast of the midtones of an image.

In this case, Photoshop displays a histogram that combines the density values of the three red, green, and blue layers of the image. If you adjust the contrast in this dialog box, you'll adjust the contrast in all three layers. That's usually the best route to take when dealing with a color image, since adjusting the brightness and contrast of a color layer is a form of color correction, and fixing color (which I cover in Chapter 12) is best handled in other ways.

Each of the histogram's 256 line positions show how many pixels are represented by the combined color channels' density values, which range from 0 to 255. An average photograph will have a histogram that looks something like a mountain, with some pixels at the black end of the scale, some at the white end, and a peak in the middle, where lots of intermediate tones reside. Few images will fit neatly between the black and white end points, and the mountain frequently has a greater slope at one side than the other.

You can see that our rock star image has a preponderance of tones at the dark end, and the light tones don't even extend to the end of the scale. That means that some of the 256 values available to represent the tonal range of this image are wasted.

2. **We can improve the image simply by moving the white point over to the left so that the 256 tones are distributed over the actual tones in the image.** Move the slider and watch how the preview image on your screen changes to add more detail to the photo. The changes are rather subtle at this point, and wouldn't show up well on the printed page, so I'm not providing a figure as an illustration at this stage.

3. **Now adjust the gamma of the image, using the middle, gray slider.** It's easiest to think of gamma as a kind of brightness indicator that can be adjusted from the normal value of 1.00 to very dark (.10) or very light (9.99). However, the gamma control only changes the brightness of the middle tones. It doesn't affect the lightest and darkest areas. That's why it receives a special name of its own. The Levels dialog box can be used to adjust the brightness and contrast in sophisticated ways. There is even an Auto button that can make some corrections for you.

The Auto button automatically moves the white and black points to locations that Photoshop judges are best for a particular image. You can almost always do a better job making these settings in the Levels dialog box yourself.

4. **When the image's contrast has been improved to your liking, click OK to apply the changes you've made in the Levels dialog box.** Before and after samples are shown in Figure 5-2.

Figure 5-2: Before and after the Levels dialog box has been used to correct this image.

Using variations

We'll explore the Variations facility of Photoshop in more detail in Chapter 12, but a preview here is appropriate. Just follow these steps:

1. **Choose Image ⇨ Adjust ⇨ Variations.** Photoshop displays an interesting arrangement of images (see Figure 5-3) that shows what your original image would look like with various degrees of lightening and darkening applied to the very lightest highlights, middle tones, and shadows, along with various color variations in red, green, blue, magenta, yellow, and cyan tints.

2. **Choose from Shadows, Midtones, Highlights, and Saturation radio buttons at the top of the screen.**

3. **When any of those four buttons are active, you can click in the boxes shown to apply changes to your image.** For example, you can click in the Lighter or Darker boxes at right to adjust brightness, or one of the color-tinged views to add that color to the image.

4. **As you make changes, compare the Original and Current Pick images at the top of the dialog box.** Click OK when you're satisfied with the color balance and brightness of the image.

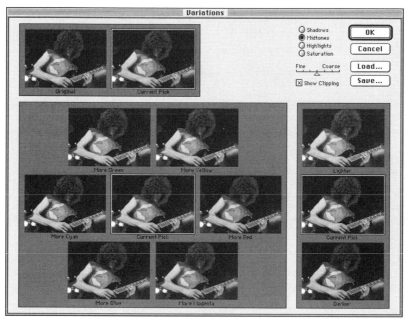

Figure 5-3: The Variations dialog box offers color and density options.

When working with Variations, you can change the Fine…Coarse slider to increase or decrease the amount of change a given adjustment will produce. Set the slider to Coarser if you want more dramatic changes, or to Fine if you'd like to work with subtle modifications. If you're working with several photos that are all shot under the same conditions, you can save the settings you decide upon and then Load them later to apply them to a different image.

Colorizing a monochrome image

We want to add the image of B.B. King to our collage. However, it's a black-and-white image and would fit in better if we colorized it and then changed the size to fit in better with the other picture. To do this just follow these steps:

1. **Practice using the Levels control to adjust the brightness and contrast of this image** (BBKing.tif). Use Image ➪ Adjust ➪ Levels, and move the black, white, and gamma sliders to improve the photo.

2. **From the Mode menu, select RGB Color.** Photoshop instantly converts the picture to a color image. Unfortunately, it still contains only grayscale information. We can fix that.

3. **Choose Image ⇨ Adjust ⇨ Hue/Saturation.** The Hue/Saturation dialog box appears (see Figure 5-4).

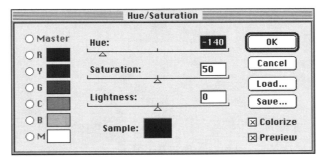

Figure 5-4: The Hue/Saturation dialog box can be used to colorize an image.

4. **Check the Colorize box.** This tells Photoshop to add color to the image, based on the settings of the other sliders.

5. **Move the Saturation slider to the 50 percent level.** This sets the amount, or richness, of the color you're adding. We don't want to overpower our image with color, so we'll use an intermediate setting.

6. **The default Hue value produces a red value that looks more like a deep sepia brown at the 50 percent saturation level.** The slider represents movement around a color wheel, with red at the zero point, green at one end, and blue at the other. We want a "bluesy" look that befits the King of the Blues, so set the Hue slider to -140.

7. **Click OK to confirm your new settings.** We now have a color image to work with.

Changing the size

B.B. King's image is too big, so we can use Photoshop's ability to resample it at a smaller size. Then, we'll copy the photo and paste it into the rock star image. Just follow these steps:

1. **Using Image ⇨ Image Size, change the measurement to percent in the drop-down list in the Pixel Dimensions area, as shown in Figure 5-5.**

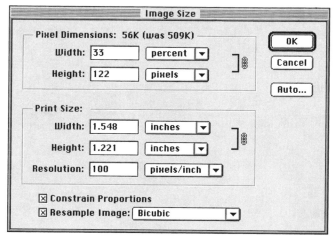

Figure 5-5: *You can change the size of an image using this dialog box.*

2. **Type 50 in the Width box.** Note that Photoshop automatically changes the height to keep the same aspect ratio if the Constrain Proportions box at the bottom of the dialog box is checked. Click OK to apply the change.

3. **Select the entire image (Command-A) and copy it by pressing Command-C.**

4. **Paste the image in** Rockstar.tif **by selecting that window and pressing Command-V. Photoshop will paste B.B. King's image in a new layer.**

5. **Move the pasted image up to the upper left corner of the photo.**

Blending the images

We need to blend in the two images a little. Just follow these steps:

1. **Click the layer holding B.B. King's image in the Layers palette, and click outside the photo itself with the Magic Wand tool.** Everything except the photo will be selected.

2. **Use Select ▷ Feather, and type in 30 for the feathering radius.**

3. **Press Delete three times, or until the border between the two images blurs enough to suit you.** B.B. King's image will be blended into the photo. The image so far will look like Figure 5-6.

Figure 5-6: We've combined and blended the two pictures.

Retouching the image

Photoshop allows you to retouch an image to improve small defects. To explore how this is done, follow these steps:

1. **Activate the layer with the rock star.**

2. **Select the Dodge tool from the toolbox.** Set Exposure to 50 percent and choose Midtones from the drop down list at the top left side of the palette.

3. **From the Brushes palette, choose the 65-pixel brush.** Lighten the rock star's face with a few strokes of the Dodge tool.

4. **Switch to the Burning tool, and darken his right arm.**

5. **Use Filter ⇨ Render ⇨ Lens Flare, and in the dialog box that appears, move the center of the flare to the upper right corner.** Select a Brightness value of 110 percent, and the 105mm Prime as the lens type. Click OK to apply the effect.

6. Select a bright yellow to be your foreground color from the Swatches palette.

7. **Choose the Type tool, and type in Rock & Blues, placing a carriage return after each word (including the ampersand).** Make sure the Centered button is checked in the Text dialog box.

8. **Change the foreground color to blue.**

9. **Use the Type tool to apply the same text as before, using the same parameters.** The text will be pasted into a new layer.

10. **Choose the Move tool, and move the blue text down and to the right.** The image should now look like Figure 5-7.

Figure 5-7: Text has been added to the graphic.

Using the rubber stamp

Frequently, you'll need to remove portions of an image that you'd rather not have in the image. Other times, you'll want to patch defects by copying good portions over the bad spots. You'll find Photoshop's Rubber Stamp cloning tool invaluable. In fact, we can apply it to this image. Our rock star doesn't need to wear any torn clothing since his group's first album hit the charts, so it's a simple matter to repair the rips in our image editor. Just follow these steps:

1. **Select the Rubber Stamp tool.** Make sure Clone (aligned) is showing in the Option field of the Rubber Stamp Options palette.

2. **Move over an area of the rock star's shirt that is undamaged.** Option-Click to define a new source area.

3. **Move the cursor over to the torn area of the shirt, and click a few times.** As you expect, pixels from the source spot, marked with a cross-hair (if you've set brushes and cursors to their precision setting in Photoshop's Preferences dialog box), are copied over the torn area of the shirt. You can stop clicking at any time, and resume at any point. The source location stays the same, and your clicks with the Rubber Stamp always copy pixels in relation to it.

Figure 5-8 shows the rock star's shirt after we "mended" it.

Figure 5-8: The Rubber Stamp tool mended the torn shirt.

With a few simple steps, we've corrected the brightness and contrast of two images, fixed the color in one, colorized the other, then blended the two. After that, we added text, a bright stage light, and fixed a torn shirt. If you'll compare the finished image with the originals we began with, you can see that Photoshop empowers you to create some dramatic images from exist-ing photos. The tools we used in this chapter are basic ones that you'll apply over and over as you create cool Web pages with Photoshop.

Moving On

You won't always be working with pre-existing photos. In the next chapter, we'll see how you can create 3D effects from scratch, and apply them to building interesting buttons, rules, and other components for your Web page.

Creating 3D Imagery in Photoshop

Left to their own devices, graphics created for Web pages tend to just lay there, looking flat and uninteresting. Adding a three-dimensional touch to your images can make your Web page look like a living thing — an object rather than just a flat sheet. This extra touch of realism makes your Web site more inviting and pleasant to look at.

This chapter explores techniques for creating 3D-style images in Photoshop. You won't need a high-end rendering package, or need to devote hours of training to learn how to produce 3D images. The illusion of depth can be synthesized easily if you understand a few things about how humans perceive objects, and apply that knowledge to the tools already built into your favorite image editor.

In This Chapter

How 3D Works

Where Photoshop Fits In

Creating 3D Effects

Experimenting with Filters

How 3D Works

Like ancient Egyptian tomb drawings, 2D images have only height and width with no depth at all. It's difficult to represent real-world objects in this way. Moreover, in 2D drawings and Web pages, every object exists on the same imaginary plane. You can't just draw something that is farther away in a smaller size: there's no way the viewer can identify if the difference is size or distance.

When we view things in real life, we are able to perceive depth because we use two eyes — each with a slightly different point of view — to view the scene. Our brain "knows" that when an object looks identical through both eyes, the object must be farther away, or that when the views are very different it must be close.

A Web page, photograph, or computer printout, on the other hand, is a flat representation of a scene. Everything in a Web page on our screen is the exact distance away from our eyes. It's impossible to produce a true 3D image unless we can give each eye a different view (as is done with 3D pictures and holograms). We can, however, represent depth by including the visual cues that our brain has learned represent distance.

For example, objects appear to get smaller as the distance grows between them and our eyes. If we see two men in a photograph, and one appears one-sixth the height of the other, our brain assumes that they are roughly the same size, and that one is farther away. A single object that extends a great distance into a background, such as a stone wall, will appear to recede or get smaller along its length.

Other visual cues help us discern 3D information. A visual *horizon*, or vanishing point, exists at some point in an image, usually "higher" in the picture than the foreground. Objects that are farther away are both smaller and higher as they approach the horizon. The shading of the light falling on objects (shadows are shorter the farther away the object is), or even extremely subtle things (for example, clear air produces a diffusing or fog effect that is visible over distant objects) also help us recognize distance between objects. Figure 6-1 is a flat Web page that includes a fanciful drawing representing a scanner grabbing a pixelated image of a photographic print. Because of the way the picture is laid on its side, with overlapping light bar and scanner sensor, we can imagine that we are looking at a 3D picture of a print.

Figure 6-1: The pixelated portrait looks as if it were captured in 3D because of the perspective cues.

Artists may understand all of these things, but you and I may find it difficult to create realistic special effects from images we create from scratch.
The objects we create don't have the visual cues that say "3D" to our
brains.

So how do computers generate 3D effects? Ordinarily, special 3D software
is used to create 3D images. These programs can duplicate realistic shadows and reflections through a process called *ray tracing,* in which the path
of the beam of light from the light source(s) illuminating an image are
mathematically calculated, down to the amount of reflection and diffusion
produced by various types of surfaces.

Sophisticated 3D programs can add atmospheric fog, textures, and other
visual cues. Moreover, they can produce a view of a set of objects from any
viewpoint — actually recalculating all of the values that make up the image
for each viewpoint you choose. All this number crunching takes time,
which is why 3D drawing programs often generate rough versions of
images, perhaps showing only the "wire frame" outline, until you're ready
to produce the high-quality final image, which, through a process called
rendering, takes into account all of the mathematical calculations.

Where Photoshop Fits In

Photoshop doesn't have specific 3D tools, but we can still simulate 3D
images by using what we know about "real" 3D. Figure 6-2, for example,
shows a Web page with 3D buttons. Our eyes and minds know that light
most often comes from above and to one side, so when we see buttons like
these, apparently brighter at the top edge than at the bottom, we view them
as three dimensional.

Other ways to make a page look three-dimensional include creating layers
that give the page depth. Figure 6-3 shows a Web page with five distinct
levels. Can you spot them? The bottom-most layer is the one containing
the stopwatch image that makes up the background. The watches are partially obscured by a layer of clouds which, presumably, extends in front of
them. Next comes the layer that holds the larger stopwatch image behind
the "60 Minute" logo, since the logo itself overlaps the watch. There are no
visual cues to tell us where the other lettering and the rules on the page
reside, but they appear to be on the same level as the logo.

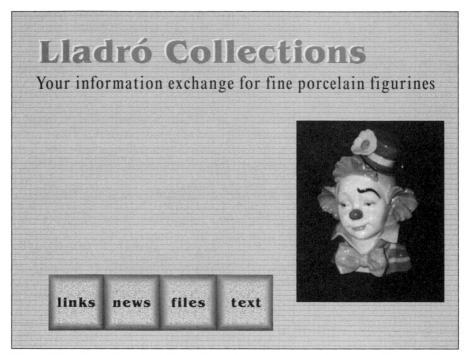

Figure 6-2: The buttons look three-dimensional to our eyes because of the way the edges are shaded.

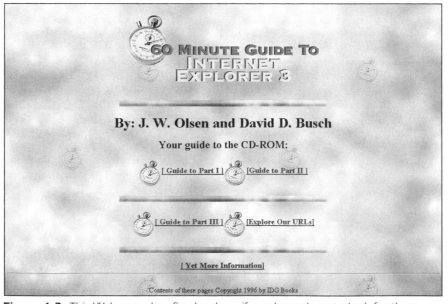

Figure 6-3: This Web page has five levels — if you know how to look for them.

Where's the fifth level? If you look closely at the horizontal rules, you'll see that they are shaded lighter on top than on the bottom, so they, too, appear to be three-dimensional. The rules must extend upward into space, into a fifth, and final level on this page. You can see that even simple techniques can produce the desired depth in a Web page.

We can go even farther if we wish. Figure 6-4 displays a Web page that mimics a white piece of cardboard with holes torn into it. The logo and buttons are all 3D representations of those holes. The lettering appears to be printed on a textured background behind the holes, and drop shadows behind the text reinforces this appearance. We scanned in the holes, of course, but the effect is quite convincing.

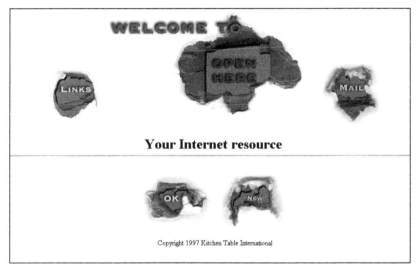

Figure 6-4: The holes in this Web page look realistic.

Creating 3D Effects

We'll create some 3D effects, starting with a simple one based on a spherical button. We'll use this button a few times in this chapter, and then later on in Chapters 9 and 10, which deal with Photoshop filters in a little more detail than we have room for in this chapter.

To create the basic button, follow these steps:

1. **Open a new, blank Photoshop document.** Set the size to 400 x 400 pixels and the background as transparent.

2. **Select the oval selection tool from the toolbox.**

3. Place the cursor roughly in the center of the image, then hold down the Option and Shift keys and drag a perfect circle centered around the point you click.

4. Using the Swatches palette, set the foreground to a dark green hue.

5. Now, Option-click in a lighter green to set the background to that color.

6. **Double-click the Gradient tool in the toolbox to bring the Gradient Tool Options palette to the foreground.** Set the type of gradient to Radial, and make sure Gradient is Foreground to Background and Opacity is 100 percent. Blending mode should be Normal.

7. **Drag from the lower right to upper left to apply the gradient to the circle you just created.**

8. **Use Filter ⇨ Render ⇨ Lighting Effects to produce the dialog box shown in Figure 6-5.**

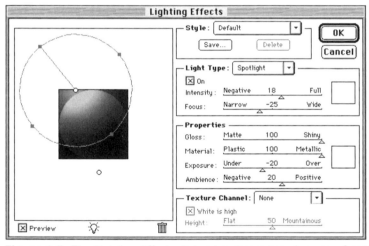

Figure 6-5: The Lighting Effects dialog box has a broad range of options.

9. **In the dialog box, set the Light Type to Spotlight and drag it to the upper left corner of the preview window, as you can see in Figure 6-5 above.** Set Intensity to 18, Focus to -25, Gloss and Material to 100, Exposure to -20, and Ambience to 20. This gives us a shiny metal spherical effect, with a highlight in the upper left of the sphere.

10. **Now, grab the light bulb icon at the bottom of the preview window, and drag a second light, placing it below the center of the window.** Set Light Type to Omni, and make the coverage as shown in Figure 6-6. Leave the other settings the same as for the first light.

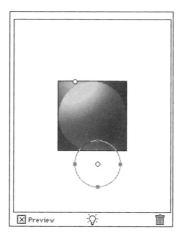

Figure 6-6: *Set a second light with omnidirectional illumination.*

11. **Click OK to apply the lighting effect. Your basic button will look like Figure 6-7.** Save the button as `Basic.psd`, using Photoshop's native format.

Figure 6-7: *The basic spherical button we'll use for this chapter's projects looks like this, on a transparent background.*

Basic instructions

For all of the examples that follow, make duplicate copies of Basic.psd as required, and save each effect in a file name of your choosing if you elect to keep it. Note that we'll make all the buttons in a large size. You can use Photoshop's Image Size command to reduce them to a size that best fits your own Web page.

Making screw heads

We're going to produce two different screw heads first. They lend themselves to any mechanically- or hardware-oriented Web page as lively 3D buttons. Note that simple dark-medium-light stripes produce the illusion of three dimensions.

Follow these directions to create two different screw heads:

1. Load Basic.psd into Photoshop.

2. Choose the rectangular selection tool from the toolbox.

3. **Select a thin rectangular section across the width of the button, make it about half the thickness of the slot that would appear on a screw.** Center the selection so it is positioned at the "equator" of the button.

4. **Some of the selection will extend beyond the width of the button.** Use Command-click in those sections to deselect them so that the selection only extends across the button itself.

5. **Press the cursor Up arrow four times to move the selection upwards.**

6. **Press D to make sure your foreground color is the default black, then press Option-Delete to fill the selection with that color.**

7. **Press Command-C to copy the current selection, then Command-V to paste it.**

8. **Choose a very light green from the Swatches palette, and fill the pasted selection with this hue.**

9. **Press the cursor Down arrow eight times to move the pasted selection downwards.**

10. **Press Command-V again to paste the selection once more, and select a medium green from the Swatches palette.** Fill the newly pasted selection with this color.

11. **Press the cursor Up arrow until the medium green selection is centered between, and partially covering up, a thin black strip of the first section you created, and the light green strip of the one you created in Step 8.** You'll now have a horizontal line that has a 3D appearance, as shown at left in Figure 6-8.

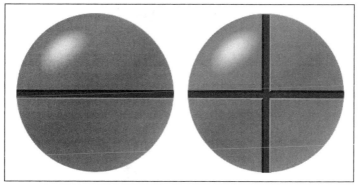

Figure 6-8: *The dark-medium-light strips appear to be a three-dimensional slot, making the button look like a screw head.*

12. **Select the whole strip, copy it, paste it down, and then use Layer ➪ Transform ➪ Rotate 90 CCW to create a vertical slot.**

13. **Use the Pencil, as necessary, and the black and green colors to retouch the overlap of the horizontal and vertical slots, as shown at right in Figure 6-8.**

A real button

Would you like a Web page button that looks like a real button? That's easy to accomplish. Just follow these directions:

1. **Load a copy of** `Basic.psd`.

2. **Select the area outside the button using the Magic Wand, then invert the selection with Select ➪ Inverse.** Now, only the button itself is selected.

3. **Choose a very dark red and a very light red as the foreground and background colors.**

4. **Replace the colors already contained in the button with a radial gradient using your new red tones.** Drag from the upper right to lower left, so the upper right corner is dark and the lower right is light, as shown in Figure 6-9.

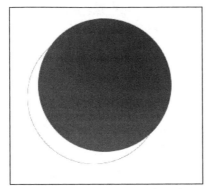

Figure 6-9: The radial gradient has been applied.

5. **Use Select ⇨ Modify ⇨ Contract to reduce the size of the selection.** Enter 16 as the value. The selection will shrink, as shown in Figure 6-10.

Figure 6-10: The selection has been moved inward by 16 pixels.

6. **Now, fill the new, inner selection with the same gradient as before, only reversed.** Start at the lower left, and drag to the upper right. You'll end up with a button that looks like a push-button. The effect shows up best in color, as you can see in Color 3-1 in the color insert. A monochrome version is shown in Figure 6-11.

7. **Let's add some buttonholes and make it a real button!** Use the oval selection tool, and hold down Option and Shift to create a perfect circle approximately where a button's hole would be found.

8. **Fill the circle with black.**

Figure 6-11: The new button
looks like a push-button.

9. Copy the circle using Command-C, then paste it down into a new layer using Command-V.

10. Fill the pasted copy with yellow.

11. Select the Move tool, and move the yellow circle down and to the right a few pixels so that the black circle underneath is visible.

12. Choose Layer ⇨ Defloat to lay down the yellow floating selection.

13. Choose Layer ⇨ Merge Layers to merge the button, black shadow, and yellow hole.

14. **Press D to make sure the default colors are black and white again, then press Delete.** The yellow circle is removed, leaving a "hole" with a black shadow.

15. **Repeat Steps 7 to 14 to create a second hole underneath the first.** Your button should look like Figure 6-12.

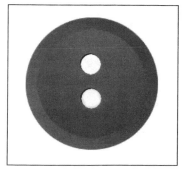

Figure 6-12: The finished button
with two holes.

Experimenting with filters

We'll look at all the tricks you can do with filters in Chapters 10 and 11, but several of Photoshop's most useful plug-ins produce interesting 3D effects and deserve to be mentioned here. We'll create some interesting buttons with textures in this section. Use a fresh copy of Basic.psd for each effect.

1. **Load** Basic.psd **into Photoshop, then apply the Filter ⇨ Texture ⇨ Craquelure filter. Use a Crack Spacing of 12, and Crack Depth of 9. Click OK to apply the filter.**

2. **Use Filter ⇨ Distort ⇨ Spherize at 100 percent to make the cracked surface into a spherical button, as shown in Figure 6-13.**

Figure 6-13: The Craquelure filter produces this rough, 3D effect.

3. **On another copy of** Basic.psd, **apply the Filter ⇨ Stylize ⇨ Extrude filter. Set Type to Blocks, Depth and Size to 30 each, and make sure the Random button is checked.**

4. **Use Filter ⇨ Distort ⇨ Spherize again to give your button a rounded surface, as shown in Figure 6-14.**

5. **On another copy of** Basic.psd, **apply the Filter ⇨ Distort ⇨ Glass filter. Set Distortion to 7, and Smoothness to 3. For Texture, choose Tiny Lens. Your finished button will look like Figure 6-15.**

Figure 6-14: Extrude produces this button that looks as if it were carved out of wood.

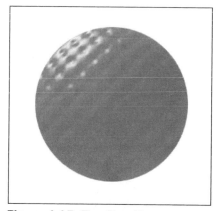

Figure 6-15: The Glass filter creates a golf ball effect.

Twisting buttons

If you're creating your buttons as transparent GIFs, there's no reason why they have to be circular, square, or any particular regular shape. In this section, we'll create a few buttons in odd shapes. Just follow these directions:

1. **On a new copy of** Basic.psd, **apply the Filter ⇨ Distort ⇨ Polar Coordinates filter.** Make sure the Rectangular to Polar radio button is

checked. Polar Coordinates wraps your image around a central point, making it look as if you were viewing it from above a globe that it has been pasted onto. Your new button will look like Figure 6-16.

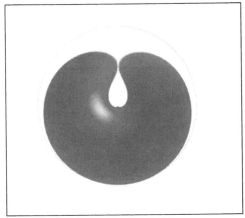

Figure 6-16: Applied once, the Polar Coordinates filter transforms the button into this shape.

2. **Apply Polar Coordinates two more times to create the strange shape shown in Figure 6-17.** You can see that applying the same filter a few times can produce more intense results.

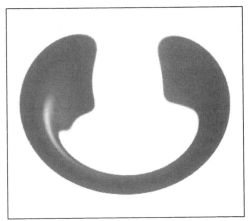

Figure 6-17: Applied two more times, the Polar Coordinates filter produces this odd shape.

3. Using a new copy of Basic.psd, use Polar Coordinates as you did above, only apply the filter just twice.

4. Cut off the top half of the resulting U shape by selecting it and pressing Delete.

5. Select the lower half, copy it by pressing Command-C, then paste it immediately by pressing Command-V.

6. Flip the pasted selection vertically using Layer ⇨ Transform ⇨ Flip Vertical, then move it so it mates with the bottom half to form a donut shape, as shown in Figure 6-18.

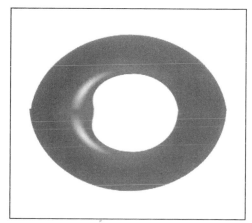

Figure 6-18: Matching two halves can create this 3D donut shape.

Flipping some disks

Ready to do a little more than just create endless textures with a round button? In this next section, we're going to build some buttons and graphics for a music-oriented Web page. We're going to travel back in time to an age when phonograph records were the only way to collect music. Just follow these steps:

1. Use Basic.psd, and apply the Filter ⇨ Distort ⇨ Zig-Zag filter. Set the Mode to Pond Ripples, Amount to -13, and the Ridges slider to 20. Click OK to create the circular disk shown in Figure 6-19.

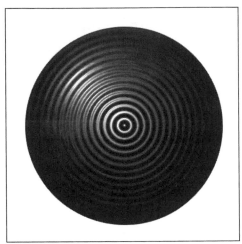

Figure 6-19: The Zig-Zag filter forms the basis of our stacks of tracks.

2. **Use Image ⇨ Adjust ⇨ Hue/Saturation and change the color of the disk to blue-black to resemble a phonograph record (if you've ever seen one).**

3. **Choose the rectangular selection tool and position it in the center of the disk.** Drag to the upper right to select the upper left quadrant of the disk.

4. **Press Command-C to copy the quarter-disk, then Command-V to paste it.**

5. **Press Layer ⇨ Transform ⇨ Flip Horizontal to flip the quarter-disk, then move it so it covers the upper right quadrant of the disk.**

6. **Press Command-V to paste another copy, then use Layer ⇨ Transform ⇨ Flip Vertical to flip it.** Move it so it covers the lower left quadrant of the disk.

7. **Press Command-V one final time, and use Layer ⇨ Transform ⇨ Flip Vertical, followed by Flip Horizontal to create a piece to cover the lower right quadrant.**

8. **Now, choose the oval selection tool and place the cursor in the center of the disk.** Hold down the Shift and Option keys and drag a circle from the center that's about the size of a record label.

9. **Choose a color for the label (I used Red) and fill in the label, using an 80 percent Opacity setting in the Edit ⇨ Fill dialog box.**

10. **Using the oval selection tool again, create a hole in the center of the record. Your finished disk should look like Figure 6-20.**

Figure 6-20: The finished disk looks like this.

You can use this graphic as a button or as a decoration on a music Web page, enlarging or reducing it as required. However, there are several other things we can do to it. Photoshop makes it easy to tilt the disk on its side, for example. Just follow these directions:

1. Use the rectangular selection tool to select the disk

2. Choose Layer ⇨ Transform ⇨ Perspective. Manipulate the handles to produce a sideways view of the disk, as shown in Figure 6-21. Press Return to apply the perspective change.

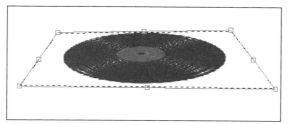

Figure 6-21: The Perspective control creates an on-edge view of the phonograph record.

3. Select the new disk and use Command-C and Command-V to create copies of the disk. Stack them on top of one another, as in Figure 6-22, or show them tumbling through the air, as in Figure 6-23.

Figure 6-22: Stacks o' tracks are easy to create in Photoshop.

Figure 6-23: Tumbling disks can provide a background graphic or other illustration for your Web page.

Basic Control Design

By this time you've probably absorbed enough of the 3D concept to create your own custom controls and buttons on your own. I'll lead you through a couple quick exercises to make sure you've got the idea nailed. Follow these directions to create a few controls. We'll make the buttons extra large, so they'll be easy to work with. You can reduce them using Image ⇨ Image Size, or redo them at the appropriate size once you've practiced.

1. Create a new, empty Photoshop document measuring 200 x 200 pixels in RGB mode.

2. Use the Swatches palette to select a light blue as the foreground color, and fill the box with it by pressing Option-Delete.

3. Use Command-A to select the entire image, then press D to return the default colors to the foreground and background.

4. Use Edit ⇨ Stroke to stroke around the edge of the image using a two-pixel setting, placing a black border all around. Make sure the Inside button is checked. Click OK to apply the stroke.

5. Swap the foreground and background colors so that white is now the foreground hue.

6. Use Edit ⇨ Stroke again, only with an 8-pixel setting, and Opacity set to 50 percent. Click OK. This adds a lighter blue border around the image.

7. Use the Magic Wand and click inside the new light blue border to select it. Your image will now look like Figure 6-24.

8. Use the Lasso and hold down the Option key to deselect the border from lower left to upper right, so that only the right side and bottom of the border are selected. Cut a diagonal corner.

9. Use Image ⇨ Adjust ⇨ Brightness/Contrast, and slide the Brightness control all the way to the left to darken the lower and right edge of the button. Press OK to apply the change. Your finished button will look like Figure 6-25. You can add directional arrows or other artwork to complete it.

Figure 6-24: The image with the light blue border selected.

Figure 6-25: The finished button looks like this.

You can modify this basic button to serve a variety of needs. Figure 6-26 shows two variations, both created by editing the original button. You can also apply textures to buttons.

Note that our 3D perspective is highly dependent on the direction of the light. Simply flipping the button we just created horizontally and vertically changes the orientation of the light, and the button now looks like a depression rather than a raised object, as you can see in Figure 6-27.

Figure 6-26: Two variations of the original button.

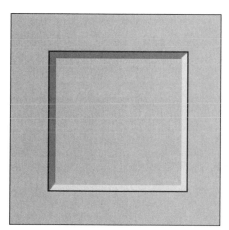

Figure 6-27: Now the button looks like a depression, rather than a raised object.

You can use this to good effect to create depressed icons and images within your buttons, as in Figure 6-28.

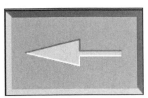

Figure 6-28: Adding lighter and darker lines makes the arrow look like a depression, too.

Moving On

We used quite a few different techniques in this chapter to create 3D graphics. You'll learn more about filters and other tricks for creating stand-out buttons and images in Chapters 9 and 10. In the next chapter, however, we'll look at some of the things you can do with transparent GIFs.

Creating Transparent GIFs

Not every image you create for a Web page will fit neatly into a square or rectangular frame. Sometimes you'll want to include images that fit best into circles or ovals. Perhaps you're doing a Web page on the pyramids of Egypt and would love to have some pyramid-shaped buttons and other images. Unfortunately, browsers, like image editors such as Photoshop, work only with rectangles.

Don't lock yourself into a four-walled prison, yet. If you can't get around the requirement for rectangular images, it is possible to simulate odd shapes by making everything else in the picture — except for the exact image shape you want — transparent. That's the secret behind transparent GIFs. In this chapter, I look at exactly how transparent GIFs are created, and show you how to avoid the pitfalls associated with them.

In This Chapter

What's a Transparent GIF?

3D Effects with Transparent GIFs

Alternate Methods

Minimizing Colors

Interlacing

What's a Transparent GIF?

The most recent specification for the GIF format, GIF89a, includes a provision that allows a single color to be designated as invisible, or transparent. When a browser displays such an image, it ignores that particular color and, instead, substitutes pixels representing the underlying background for the pixels of that color. The background can simply be a background color, or a background image that is tiled to cover a page's window in the browser. You can see the effect in Figure 7-1.

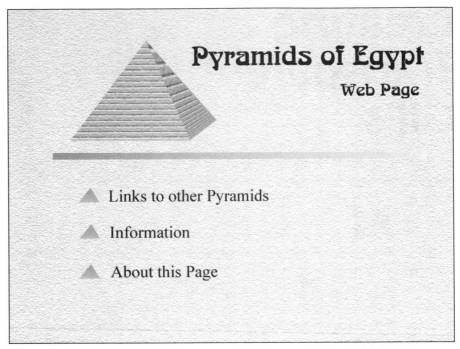

Figure 7-1: A Web page using transparent GIFs to represent pyramid shapes.

In Figure 7-1, the sand-like background is a JPEG file, but the large pyramid, the main text, and the smaller pyramid buttons are all transparent GIFs. The horizontal rule is another JPEG file. As you can see, the GIFs merge smoothly into the background, with nary a clue that they are actually rectangular in shape. Figure 7-2 shows you the real shapes of the graphics on the page. Note that the title text and large pyramid are included in a single image. That's because the text overlaps slightly into an area that would have been covered by the large pyramid's square GIF, had they been separate. Just because GIFs are transparent doesn't mean you can stack them on top of each other.

The advantages of transparent GIFs are as follows:

- You can place odd-shaped graphics on the background of your choice.

- Transparent GIFs are a good way to use text styles not supported by browsers. Just create the text as an image and place it on the page as a transparent GIF.

- By combining several images and making the area between them transparent, you can compose and arrange graphics on your page in any way you like.

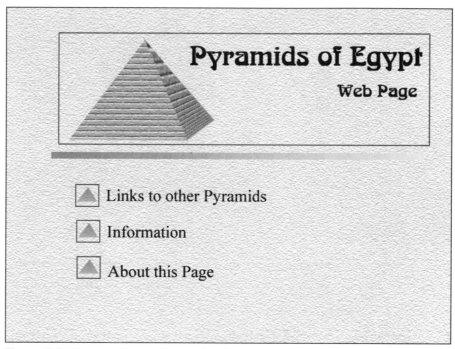

Figure 7-2: The actual area taken up by the graphics is shown here.

And the disadvantages:

➡ GIFs support only 256 or fewer colors. You cannot create a good-quality transparent GIF of a full-color image that requires more colors.

➡ Covering large portions of your page with transparent GIFs will increase the download times dramatically. For that reason, you should always interlace these images so visitors at least have a clue about what is being downloaded.

➡ Only one color can be transparent, and all instances of that color become see-through. You must take some care to insure that everything you want to be transparent is represented by that color — and nothing else.

The pros and cons will become clearer as we work through an example. I'm going to show you how to create a Web page like the one shown in Figure 7-3, which you first saw used as an example in Chapter 6.

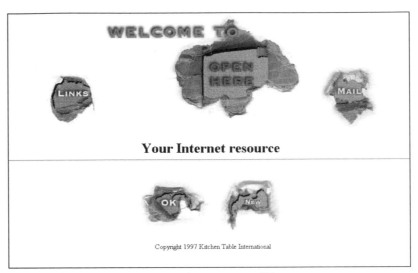

Figure 7-3: This page uses several transparent GIFs.

Creating a 3D Hole

I created this page to demonstrate some cool 3D effects you can achieve with Photoshop and transparent GIFs. If you want to follow along, load `Tear5.psd` from the CD-ROM, then carry out the following directions, which you can also apply to your own projects:

1. **The first step is to decide on a background color or graphic for your Web page, since the transparent portions of the GIF must be compatible.** If you're using a textured background, the edges where transparency begins must be unobtrusive. For this page, I decided to use a white background for the page to simplify things.

2. **Scan or create the odd-shaped graphic you want to turn into a transparent GIF.** I tore some holes in white-painted corrugated cardboard, and scanned the images at 300 dpi, producing images something like the one shown in Figure 7-4.

3. **Next, I painted around the perimeter of the hole using a large brush and white, with the opacity set to about 25 percent.** The goal was to gradually fade the off-white surrounding the hole into a pure white at the edges of the image. That pure white would actually blend in with the page's white background, but I can also make it transparent to achieve an even better match. Figure 7-5 shows the blended image.

Figure 7-4: The original scanned holes looked like this one.

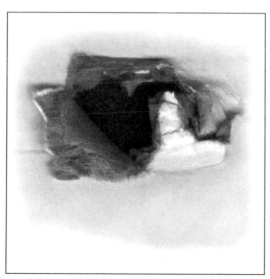

Figure 7-5: The edges of the image have been blended out to pure white.

4. I want to insert type into the hole in the center of the cardboard, so the next step is to select that dark area with the Magic Wand. Set the Magic Wand's tolerance level to 32, and make sure the

Anti-Aliased check box is marked. Click in a dark area in the center of the hole. If some pixels remain uncaptured, use Select ➪ Similar to grab them. The selected area should look like Figure 7-6.

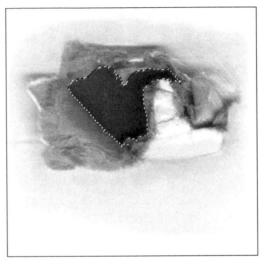

Figure 7-6: The center hole has been selected.

5. Next, I copied the background layer and deleted the center hole, so the image now looks like Figure 7-7.

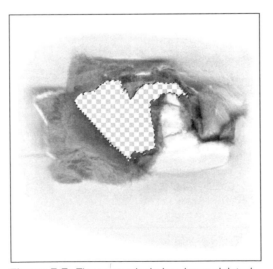

Figure 7-7: The center hole has been deleted.

6. Next, I used Layer ⇨ New ⇨ Layer to create an empty layer, which was filled with a light blue selected from the Swatches palette, then textured using the Filter ⇨ Texture ⇨ Texturizer dialog box. Texture was set to Canvas from the drop-down list, Relief to 4, and the Light Direction to Top Left.

7. Move the copy of the original hole image above the new textured background on the Layers palette, so the texture will show through the section removed from the hole.

8. Next, add some text Using the Text tool and a font of your choice, enter the letters OK. I used Copperplate Gothic Bold, in 28 point size, using black as the foreground color to fill the type. Photoshop automatically places the text in a new layer of its own.

9. Drag the text to position it, if necessary.

10. Select the layer containing the text if you need to. Make sure the Preserve Transparency box is not checked.

11. Now, use Gaussian Blur to blur the black text and create a shadow. I used a radius of 9 pixels. The image will look like Figure 7-8.

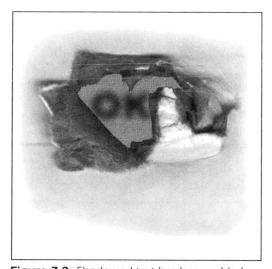

Figure 7-8: Shadowed text has been added.

12. Select the Text tool one more time, and change the foreground color to yellow.

13. Apply the same text as before (OK) and position it so that it floats above the shadow we just created. The image should now look like Figure 7-9.

Figure 7-9: *The completed text is shown in the hole in the cardboard.*

14. Return to the original background-with-hole layer, and select the hole that had been cut out with the Magic Wand.

15. Use Layer ➪ New ➪ Layer to create a new layer.

16. **Make the foreground color black (press D to return to the default colors), and stroke the selection.** Specify Outside for Location and a width of 5 pixels. Press OK to apply the stroke in the new layer.

17. **Use the cursor arrow keys to move the stroked line down and to the right a few pixels, creating a shadow.** The image will now look like Figure 7-10.

18. **Save a copy in Photoshop's original PSD format, in case you want to make changes to the image or its layers at a later date.**

Figure 7-10: The completed image looks like this.

Saving the image as a transparent GIF

Now we can save our image as a transparent GIF. Just follow these steps:

1. First, use Layer ⇨ Flatten Image to combine all the layers into one.

2. Double-click the Magic Wand, and set its tolerance to 1.

3. Click on the outer edge of the graphic. All of the pure white pixels will be selected.

4. Inverse the selection (Shift-Command-I) so that everything except the white pixels is chosen.

5. Press Command-C to copy the selection, and then Command-V to paste it in a new layer. Your image will look like Figure 7-11.

6. Choose File ⇨ Export ⇨ GIF 89a Export. The dialog box shown in Figure 7-12 will appear.

Figure 7-11: The image border has been deleted.

Figure 7-12: The GIF89a Export dialog box is used to create transparent or interlaced GIFs.

7. **In this case, because we made the area we wanted to be transparent the same as the transparent area on the layer that was active when we accessed the GIF89a dialog box, the process is automatic.** The filter will make the transparent areas of the image transparent in the GIF. Just click OK to produce the transparent GIF.

Another method

You may want some control over exactly which colors are made transparent, or need a preview of how the graphic will look in 256 colors. Here's an alternative method that gives you a little more control over the process. Just follow these steps:

1. Load another copy of the graphic into Photoshop.

2. **Convert the graphic to indexed color by using Image ⇨ Mode ⇨ Indexed Color.** The Indexed Color dialog box, shown in Figure 7-13, appears.

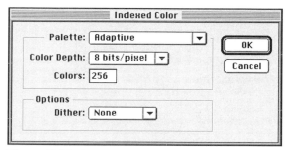

Figure 7-13: The Indexed Color dialog box gives you control over the palette used to create your GIF.

3. **Choose Adaptive from the Palette drop-down list, and make sure None is showing in the Dither drop-down list, then click OK.** You do not want any dithering to take place in an area that you might want to make transparent.

4. **Just for fun, let's make the "OK" transparent in the graphic instead of the border.** Choose File ⇨ Export ⇨ GIF89a Export. Because no transparent area has been specified — as we did before by pasting into a transparent layer — the dialog box shown in Figure 7-14 appears, giving you the opportunity to select the transparency color manually.

5. **Click with the cursor (which now has an eyedropper shape) in the yellow OK.** All yellow hues that match in the image will change to gray in the preview window, indicating that they will be used for transparency.

6. **Click OK to save your GIF.**

Figure 7-14: The GIF89a Export dialog box appears when no transparent area has been specified, giving you control to select the transparency color manually.

Now that you've gone through all the steps needed to create a transparent GIF, here is a review of the main points:

➡ You can create a transparent GIF directly from a 256 or 16.8 million color image. Select the portion you want to be non-transparent, and paste it into a new, transparent layer. If you like, you can select and delete other portions of the image (such as "holes") and make them transparent as well. With only that layer active, use the GIF89a Export filter. The transparent areas will be made transparent in your final image, and the other parts of the graphic will be reduced to 255 (or fewer) colors, because one of the 256 colors has been set aside for transparency.

➡ You can also reduce your image to 256 colors yourself with Photoshop's Mode command by selecting the color you want to be transparent. One good way to see exactly what colors will be affected is to use Photoshop's Select ➪ Color Range command. Choose the color you plan to make transparent, and all of the other colors in the image that match will be selected as well. You might need to enter Quick Mask mode (press Q) to make the selection(s) more visible and obvious.

➡ When converting to 256 colors, don't use dithering, which can confuse the color issue. Photoshop will combine available colors to simulate others, and may use the hue you had planned to make transparent. When that happens, spots and speckles will show through your image.

Examples and Tips

In this section, I offer examples of how interlaced GIFs can be used, along with tips for making their creation a bit easier.

Minimizing your need for colors

The example in Figure 7-15 was created to deliberately reduce the need for colors in the final graphic, so that the 216 colors available on the Web page would be plenty. It's shown with the background image showing through.

Figure 7-15: *This image used few colors.*

True-color images don't always convert well to 256 or fewer colors. For this image, which consists of the stopwatch and some lettering, only the watch itself requires a long tonal range, and that is confined to blacks, whites, and grays. As you have noticed, a grayscale image can look great with only 256 tones, while a full-color image will look posterized. I only had to "rob" two colors from those used for the watch — red and yellow — which are used for the lettering (although you can't see that in the black-and-white figure). Instead of a blurry shadow, as we used in the example above, I elected for a 3D black shadow with hard edges, since only black and not a range of grays were required. Blurs, transitions, gradations, and other image components that require many colors should be avoided when making GIFs that are limited to 256 or fewer colors.

Minimizing your need for transparency

Figure 7-16 shows an example of how to make choices that will reduce your need for a transparent GIF. The example rule at the bottom of Figure 7-16 certainly looks cool, but its irregular shape means it could only be shown on a page as a transparent GIF. The example rule at top is similar, and not quite as eye-catching, but it fits neatly into a rectangular image box and can be shown on any page as a tiny JPEG file in full color, with no transparency required.

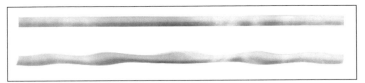

Figure 7-16: Two rules: the one at top can be shown as a JPEG file; for the one at bottom, a transparent GIF is required.

3D wizardry

I created the example in Figure 7-17 for a Web page I developed that dealt with digital photography and scanners. I wanted a graphic that represented the iris of a lens, and perhaps a lens surface itself. It was simple to create the iris in Photoshop and place a spheroid in the center. You can't see it in the black-and-white figure, but the leaves of the iris/shutter are represented in red/green/blue and cyan/magenta/yellow in a way that duplicates a standard color wheel.

Figure 7-17: This graphic represents the iris of a camera lens.

These strong colors can be represented with only 256 hues. By making this a transparent GIF, I could use the image as a logo, as buttons on the Web page, and as a background graphic.

Multiple choice

For Cosmo's Ammo Emporium, shown in Figure 7-18, I used several transparent GIFs. The bullet-holes in the glass are a great example of how transparency can be used. The black-and-white impact cracks show up well with only a few colors, making a small, quick-to-download GIF. Cosmo's logo is also a transparent GIF. It's large, but uses only two colors: green and black, so it also downloads quickly. Using the GIF gave me the freedom to use any typestyle, and not just one supported by browsers.

Figure 7-18: Even large GIFs can download quickly if they contain few colors.

Interlacing

Interlacing is also available from the GIF89a Export dialog box, so I'll address that capability here. Interlacing is a way of relieving the tedium of downloading by allowing the browser to receive alternating lines that it can display immediately, rather than wait until the entire image is received, line by line. Visitors to your Web page can see a rough image very quickly, which gives them something to do as well as an idea of what the page will look like when finished. Interlaced graphics also let them decide whether to stick around or move on, so make sure your images are interesting enough to capture their attention.

Interlaced images are actually a tiny bit larger than their non-interlaced counterparts, but the trade-off is usually worth the slight extra size. With large images, even interlaced graphics can take forever to download, so the lesson is to avoid large graphics. You also wouldn't want to interlace an image used as a background, since the background won't display at all until the entire graphic has been received.

While interlaced GIFs were the first format of this type for Web pages, Photoshop also supports the latest version of JPEG, which allows *interleaved* images. Not all browsers can display interleaved JPEGs, however.

Moving On

Transparent GIFs are a great way to break up the blocky, rectangular world of Web pages, and this chapter provided some good examples of how you can use them. In the next chapter, I explore the world of image maps, and see how they can make your pages even more interactive.

Building Interactive Image Maps

The best interactive software contains *hot spots* scattered throughout each window or screen. Pass your cursor over one of the zillions of buttons in a program like Microsoft Word, for example, and a *tool tip* pops up explaining that button's function. Click on the image of a mailbox in a children's CD-ROM, and the door may pop open, revealing a bee or some other surprise inside.

You can include *clickable* graphics on your Web page, too, although all I've talked about so far have been stand-alone graphic elements that provide access to an individual URL linked to that graphic. As you move beyond simple pages, you'll want to explore the more advanced capabilities at your disposal with image maps. Like a geographic map, these images are divided into regions. Clicking within the boundaries of a particular region invokes the hypertext link or URL associated with that portion of the image map. In essence, instead of embedding a whole collection of images on your page — one for each link — you can combine bunches of links in one or more clickable image maps.

This chapter explains how image maps work and how you can use Photoshop to create them. I go a bit deeper in my discussions of HTML than I have in previous chapters, but you need to know some basics on setting up image maps on your pages just to get started in your experimentation.

What Are Image Maps?

When it comes to clickable image maps, the name says it all. As I already said, they are pictures divided into separate areas that can be clicked with the cursor in a browser window. Each region can be associated with its own hyperlink or URL, so visitors can navigate throughout your site or connect to other Web pages just by clicking the appropriate portion of the map. Figure 8-1 shows a real map of Australia that could easily be converted into an image map. If you wanted to learn more about any particular region of Australia, you could click that part of the image map and jump to a page that contains the information you were looking for.

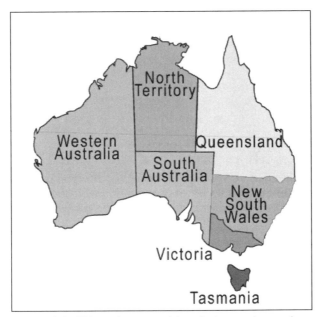

Figure 8-1: This real map could easily be used as an image map.

The basics for creating and setting up image maps are easy to understand. The HTML tags for an image map simply define the image that will be used as the map, list the coordinates within that image that describe each region on the map, and associate a URL with each set of coordinates. If you've taken a geometry class, or worked with charts, nothing could be simpler.

For example, a region measuring 100 × 100 pixels, starting at the upper left corner of the image, could be defined by a set of four numbers representing the x and y coordinates within the image: 0,0; 0,100; 100,100, and 100,0. That would set the four corners of the region at the 0,0 (upper left) 0,100 (upper right), 100,100 (lower right), and 100,0 (lower left) positions.

Tell the browser to load a specific URL whenever a visitor's mouse clicks within that area, and you're all set.

Of course, things get slightly more complicated if you want to use a region that's not a rectangle, but the concept is the same — and just as easy to understand. A circle could be defined by specifying the x and y coordinates of its center, plus the number of pixels in its radius. An irregular polygon could be described just by listing the coordinates of its connecting points.

Unfortunately, nothing is quite so simple in the real world of the Web. To create and use image maps, we have to deal with concepts like server-side image maps, client-side image maps, and at least two different ways of describing them.

Server-Side Image Maps

Although it seems like ancient history, until fairly recently an alarming number of Web cruisers were still using text-only browsers that couldn't display image maps at all, while others were using one of a plethora of graphical browsers with varying sets of capabilities. Because so many different kinds of browsers were in use, the only viable way to use image maps at all was to have the Web server take care of all the work, and let the browser display whatever images and pages the server spoon-fed it.

Thus, server-side image maps were born. These maps consist of a labeled image or map that is downloaded to your browser. The only thing your browser has to supply the server is the coordinates of the mouse when you click on one of the labeled areas. The coordinates defining a hot spot are stored on the server, along with the URL to be accessed when a region is clicked.

However, the ability to handle requests from a clickable image map is not built into the basic software used on World Wide Web servers. Interpretation of clicks, and the resulting instructions to deliver a new URL must be handled by a CGI script on the server, which has some unpleasant side effects.

One of these is the inevitable wait while the server processes your request and begins to initiate sending the URL you requested. Your computer may be nearly idle and wasting clock ticks, but if the server is overloaded, you'll wait and wait while your request and all the others hitting the site at that time are processed.

Another side effect is that you can't see what URL you are requesting when you pass your cursor over a region. You'll notice that your browser displays the link in its status bar when you move the cursor over any other kind of hyperlink. When you're accessing a server-side image map, however, all you see are the current mouse coordinates, which is not very useful.

To make things even more interesting, there are two different ways to describe an image map on your Web page, depending on what kind of software your server is running. Your server may support the image map definitions set up by CERN, or it may use the definitions described by NCSA. While the way the definitions are set up is similar, one mode won't work on the other kind of server. That means you need to set up your Web pages for the specific server you'll be using, and you can't easily transport a Web page written for one type to the other without editing all of the HTML pages that include image maps.

Finally, to use server-side image maps at all, your Web page host account must have access to the server's cgi-bin subdirectory. That privilege is not automatic if you're sharing Web space with others. You may have to ask your provider for access.

For all of these reasons, server-side image maps have not been used as extensively as they could have, and have actually become less popular as other alternatives emerged.

Client-Side Image Maps

The advent of client-side image maps solved some of the problems found in the original implementation of clickable images on Web pages. The key to the growing acceptance of this alternative has been the overwhelming preference of Web users for either Netscape Navigator or Microsoft Internet Explorer. Both of these browsers support client-side image maps, and once the pair grabbed more than 90 percent of the installed base among frequent World Wide Web users, Web authors could use such maps with the confidence that most of their visitors would be able to access them. If you happen to own the server being used, you probably like client-side image maps because of the load they take off of your system, too. The number of hits on a server for a particular page is significantly reduced.

To use a client-side image map, a browser must support the HTML extensions that make them possible. These are tags that define the image being used as a map, much as the <IMG SRC> tag associates a graphic with a URL, and define what areas are matched with each hyperlink you want to use. You don't need CGI capability: all of the work is handled by the browser, which determines which URL you have requested, and passes your request on to the Web server.

The other advantages of client-side maps are clear. Perhaps the biggest one is that you can test your image maps locally on your computer, using just your Web browser. With server-side image maps, you must upload the map and revised page, and test it while online. Client-side maps are more portable, since they work on any server and with any browser that supports them. Visitors like being able to preview URLs as they move the cursor around your map, too.

Creating an Image Map

The first step in creating an image map is to build the graphic itself, and then determine the coordinates that will be used to define your links. Luckily, Photoshop has all of the tools you need for this step built in. We'll create a simple image map and find the coordinates in this section. Just follow these steps:

1. **Find the file** `Australia.gif` **on the CD-ROM, and open it in Photoshop.** This is the same map first shown in Figure 8-1.

2. **Make sure the Info palette is displayed.** If necessary, open it from the Window menu. The Info palette is shown in Figure 8-2. Notice that the coordinates of the mouse cursor are shown in the lower left corner.

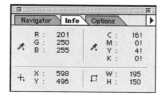

Figure 8-2: The Info palette shows the coordinates of the mouse cursor.

3. **You must set Photoshop's default measurements to pixels for the coordinates to be shown in that unit.** Click the plus sign to the left of the X and Y in the Info palette, and choose pixels as the unit of measurement, if you have not already specified that value earlier.

4. **Activate the rectangular selection tool, and select an area that includes the island of Tasmania and the text label, as shown in Figure 8-3.** It's not mandatory to select the area that you are defining, but this does make it easier to see the region as you find the coordinates.

Figure 8-3: Select the area to be defined.

5. **Now, move the cursor to the upper left portion of the selection and write down the coordinates shown.** In our case, this is X-245, Y-355.

6. **Repeat for the upper right, lower right, and lower left corners.** Our values were 385, 355; 385,420; and 245,420, respectively. If you do this step correctly, you'll find matching pairs of values, since either the X or Y values will be the same for corners on the same edge of the rectangle. If you're not as mathematically challenged as I am, you can simply take readings from opposite corners of the rectangle, and use them to determine the values for the other two corners.

7. **Choose the irregular polygon selection tool, and select an area representing Victoria and its text label, as you can see in Figure 8-4.**

8. **Move the cursor to each point you marked, and write down the coordinates.** Starting at the upper left and moving around clockwise, I got 201,331; 281,339; 281,283; 359,334; 294,357; 198,358.

9. **Repeat steps 7 and 8 for each of the other areas of Australia, recording the coordinates as you go.**

That's all there is to determining the coordinates for your image map. If you want to define a circular area, you need to write down only the center point, plus the number of pixels in the radius.

Figure 8-4: Irregular regions are marked off using multiple sides.

Adding the Image Map to Your Web Page

Placing the image map on your HTML page is a bit tedious because of all the information you have to type in, but not really complicated. Follow these steps to define the map itself and some URLs. Use your favorite HTML text editor — as in earlier chapters, SimpleText (on the Mac) or Notepad/Wordpad (on Windows machines) works fine.

1. **Enter the tag below as your first line for the image map.** This tells the browser that an image map is being set up, and the name of it is "australia":

    ```
    <MAP NAME="australia">
    ```

2. **Now, type in the tag below, which defines Tasmania's region:**

    ```
    <AREA SHAPE="rect" COORDS="245,355 385,355"
    HREF="tasmania.htm">
    ```

The elements of this tag are as follows:

➡ AREA tells the browser that a new region is being defined.

➡ SHAPE specifies that a rectangle is being defined. (Other allowable values include polygon and circle.)

➡ COORDS provides the coordinates for the upper left and lower right corners, which are all the browser needs to define a rectangle. I had you write down the coordinates of all four corners so you could see their relationship, and because you need to record all of the coordinates for non-rectangular polygons.

➡ HREF is the HTML hyperlink accessed when this region is clicked.

3. **Next, type in the tag that defines the irregular polygon around Victoria:**

```
<AREA SHAPE="polygon"
COORDS="201,331,281,339,291,283,359,334,294,357,198,
358" HREF="victoria.htm">
```

4. **If you were creating a real-world image map, you'd repeat Step 3 or Step 2 for each of the other regions in the map.** You can do so now, if you like, using the information you gleaned from the previous exercise.

5. **Add the closing tag to end the map:**

```
</MAP>
```

6. **Finally, define the image that will be used on your Web page, and tell the browser the name of the image map:**

```
<IMG SRC="australia.gif" BORDER=0 ALT="Australia
Image Map" USEMAP=#australia">
```

Staying Compatible with Server-Side Image Maps

I'm not going to delve into server-side image maps extensively, because this is, after all, a Photoshop book and not an HTML guide. Instead, I'll cover some of the differences you should be familiar with, and some paths for optimizing compatibility.

Given the advantages of client-side image maps, why would you want to use server-side maps at all? The chief reason is one that is difficult to justify: to remain compatible with the dwindling number of browsers that can't view client-side maps. If it's of overriding importance to you to be compatible with every possible graphical browser, you'll want to stick with a server-side map, or possibly with an HTML page that can be accessed with both kinds of maps.

Creating a Server-Side Map

To create a server-side map, you need the same basic information as with client-side maps — that is, a list of coordinates defining the regions for a given image file. However, the information is stored in a file uploaded to the server, and is not included on your Web page itself. A typical file, using our Australia example, might be named australia.map and include lines that look like these:

```
rectangle (245,355)(385,355) tasmania.htm
polygon
(201,331)(281,339)(291,283)(359,334)(294,357)(198,358)(201,
331) victoria.htm
```

CERN and NCSA files look similar, except that the URL is placed last in a CERN map file, and first in an NCSA file. Also, NCSA uses shorter names, like "rect" and "poly." Once you've created your map file, you need to upload it to the directory required by your server (check with your provider's administrator to get permission and instructions on how to do this).

Finally, you'll need to add tags to your HTML page that point to the file containing the map on the server and the image file itself, which is likely to be in a different location on the same server. The tags might look like this in our simplified example:

```
<A HREF="/bin/cgi/mapprog/maps/australia.map">
<IMG SRC="australia.gif" ISMAP>
</A>
```

The subdirectories used and names will vary. Several of the Web hosting sites I've used have helpful documents you can download that tell exactly how to set up a server-side image map on their particular server. Check with your own provider for more information.

Creating Double-Duty Maps

You can create an HTML page with a client-side image map that can also function as a server-side map with browsers that require them. Simply create the client-side map on your page as described earlier. Then wrap a server-side map description around the URL reference, like this:

```
<A HREF="/bin/cgi/mapprog/maps/australia.map">
<IMG SRC="australia.gif" BORDER=0 ALT="Australia Image
Map" USEMAP=#australia" ISMAP>
</A>
```

As always, the server-side parameters will vary, depending on your own server's requirements. A browser that can read client-side image maps will read the HTML lines and use that map; a browser that can't interpret the instructions for a client-side map will instead use the server-side instructions.

Moving On

Image maps are a useful tool for linking your pages to others in flexible ways. In the next two chapters, I show you some of the most versatile tools in your Photoshop arsenal: filters. In Chapter 9, you'll learn about Photoshop's built-in filters, while in Chapter 10, I introduce you to third-party products such as Kai's Power Tools.

Photoshop's Native Filters

Photoshop's built-in filters are easily the most powerful tool in your arsenal for creating cool Web pages. Whether you are modifying an eye-catching graphic to be the centerpiece for a page, or developing a seductive button that will lure visitors to another page on your site, filters can help provide a distinctive look for every component.

I've been using filters extensively in this book, but a chapter or two devoted to some more effects, plus a little background material, is well worth the time. I look at dozens of different effects you can put to work with the 100 or so filters included in Photoshop. In Chapter 10, I look at some more great techniques, using some add-on filters, while in Chapter 15, I discuss some of these add-on packages in a more general vein.

In This Chapter

What Are Filters?

Filters by Function and Category

Using Filters

What Are Filters?

Image processing filters sift through pixels of an image, holding some back, letting others through, changing some pixels here and there, and in some cases, moving little bits of your image to new and more interesting locations. Filters are actually mini-applications that operate on your entire image or just a selection of it. Table 9-1 that follows shows some filters and their function.

Table 9-1	Image Processing Filters
Filter	**Description**
Sharpen filter	Looks at each pixel and its tonal relationship with the pixels that surround it. Where it finds groups of pixels that differ in brightness with other nearby groups of pixels, the sharpen filter decides that an edge has been located. It then increases the contrast of the pixels at the edges, so that the image looks sharper.
Blurring filter	Reduces the contrast between edges and lowers the sharpness of an image.
Color correction filter	Examines the color values of each pixel and adjusts the amount of each hue according to settings you specify.
Distortion filters	Relocate filters using their own sets of algorithms: a Twirl filter, for example, might move pixels in a clockwise or counterclockwise direction, with the amount of movement dependent on the distance of the pixel from a defined center point. Pixels farther from the center would move a greater distance, producing a distinct whirlpool effect in your image.

Because they are mini-applications, filters operate somewhat in a world of their own. That is, they receive information about the pixels in an image or selection through a window built into Photoshop called an application programming interface (API). The filter then performs its modifications on the pixels, then reports back to Photoshop what it has done, through that same API window.

Photoshop applies the effect and then closes the filter. However, the program keeps a copy of the image or selection in its unaltered form, so you can immediately adjust the percentage of the effect on the original using the Filter menu's Fade Filter sliders, shown in Figure 9-1. This facility is one of the most useful additions to Photoshop 4.0, as it gives you unprecedented control over the degree of filter effects that are applied. Prior to the Fade command, you had to add the filter to a copy of the image layer you wanted to apply it to, then manually adjust opacity.

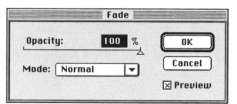

Figure 9-1: The Fade dialog box allows you to specify how much of an effect to apply.

Filters are installed into a folder called Plug-ins (and its subfolders), which Photoshop looks for every time it loads. Information within these plug-ins tells Photoshop how to arrange them in the Filter menu, and you can activate any of the dozens of filters included with the program (or those that you've added from third parties) by selecting an image, then activating the desired filter from the menu. All of the dirty work is handled by the dialog box that pops up in response; although, some filters have fixed parameters and do their work without input from you as soon as they are activated. A typical filter dialog box is shown in Figure 9-2.

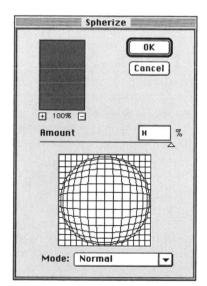

Figure 9-2: Most filters operate through dialog boxes such as this one.

The hardest thing about using filters is sorting out all of the different types, and remembering exactly what they do. Adobe doesn't help much, because it has arranged Photoshop's 100 plug-ins into sometimes arbitrary categories. For example, you'll find Dry Brush and Watercolor under Artistic effects, and filters like Dark Strokes under a category called Brush Strokes. Diffuse Glow, Grain, and Film Grain, which all add a grainy effect to an image, are located in Distort, Texture, and Artistic categories, respectively. And why are Texture Fill and Texturizer under separate submenus?

Filter Types by Function

To help you sort out all of the filter options, I've grouped their functions into nine major categories, so you can approach them by what they do. Once you're clear on that, you can examine another list I've put together, which groups them in Photoshop's own categories.

Acquire/import/export modules

Found in the File menu under Import and Export, these filters include TWAIN scanner modules, export filters such as the GIF89a plug-in we've used previously, and the Quick Edit module that allows you to work on small portions of images.

Production filters

These specialized filters are intended for pre-press tasks, such as making color separations or producing files for high-resolution film output equipment. You generally won't use any filters of this type for producing Web graphics.

Image enhancement filters

These filters improve the appearance of images, making them sharper so details stand out more dramatically, or softer, so that defects are blurred. Others of this type improve the brightness or contrast of an image, or make other changes that improve a graphic without making significant changes to its content.

Distortion filters

These are the filters that stir up the pixels in your image, twisting them onto a spherical surface, embroiling them in ripples, waves, or whirlpools, or attenuating the image as if you were viewing it through a bubbly glass sheet.

Texturizing filters

These filters add random textures, like Photoshop's Noise and Grain filters, or overlay an image with familiar rough surfaces, like canvas, sandstone, or frosted glass.

Pixelation filters

These filters take texturizing to the next logical step. Instead of simply adding a texture overlay, pixelation filters make their effects part of the image, as if the graphic were brushed on with thick strokes, or broken down into crystal shards.

Rendering filters

Rendering filters give you something from nothing, adding star-like lens flares, misty clouds, or shimmering layers of plastic and chrome to your images.

Contrast enhancing filters

These filters operate on the variations in contrast at color or edge boundaries, increasing these variations so that edges are lighter, brighter, or otherwise emphasized, as you'll find in Photoshop filters like Glowing Edges, Ink Outlines, or Emboss.

Other filters

Photoshop also includes some miscellaneous filters, such as Offset, which moves all of the pixels in an image or selection a specified number of pixels in the direction you indicate. Also in this category is the NTSC Colors filter, which converts an image into a palette of hues used as a standard in the television industry.

You'll learn more about these categories of filters and how Photoshop's near-100 plug-ins fit into them in the sidebar I included in the next chapter.

Photoshop's Filter Categories

Photoshop's main filter categories are grouped at the top of the Filter menu, shown in Figure 9-3, with any third-party filters grouped at the bottom of the list. For Photoshop 4.0, Adobe completely re-arranged its Filter menu, merging its original filter set with those in Adobe Gallery Effects, previously offered as a separate product.

Figure 9-3: Photoshop's Filter menu includes nearly 100 different effects.

Artistic

This selection of 15 filters adds an artistic effect to images, as if they were daubed with a brush, sponge, or knife. My favorites in this group include:

Dry Brush   Fresco

Paint Daubs   Palette Knife

Sponge   Watercolor

A second, more dramatic group includes:

Colored Pencil	Cutout
Rough Pastels	Smudge Stick
Underpainting	

Other filters in the Artistic group simulate graphic arts and photographic methods, such as:

Film Grain	Neon Glow
Plastic Wrap	Poster Edges

Blur

This section contains six filters that de-sharpen your image dramatically:

Blur	Radial Blur
Gaussian Blur	Motion Blur
Blur More	Smart Blur

Those in the first column create standard blurring effects, while Motion Blur smears your image as if it were captured while in motion by a camera with a slow shutter speed. Radial Blur duplicates the image you get when you zoom in on a subject during an exposure. Smart Blur is an update of Gaussian Blur, with additional parameters you can set, such as image quality and edge/overall blurring.

Brush strokes

Adobe broke out these eight painterly filters into a category of their own, even though they have effects similar to some of those in the Artistic category. They include the following:

Accented Edges   Angled Strokes

Crosshatch   Dark Strokes

Ink Outlines   Spatter

Sprayed Strokes   Sumi-e

Distort

These 12 filters — with the exception of Diffuse Glow, which is a blurring/ grain filter — generally move pixels around in your image dramatically. They include:

Diffuse Glow   Displace

Glass   Ocean Ripple

Pinch   Polar Coordinates

Ripple   Shear

Spherize   Twirl

Wave   Zig-Zag

You can tell what most of these filters do by their names, although Zig-Zag is actually a better water-type filter than Wave, Ripple, or Ocean Ripple. You might want to experiment with the strange Polar Coordinates filter, which takes an image and wraps it around a central point.

Noise

The following four filters either add random noise, or remove it from your image:

Noise   Despeckle

Dust & Scratches   Median

Pixelate

Adobe obviously wanted to break up the large number of painterly filters found in Gallery Effects into as many categories as possible. In this sub-menu you'll find seven more, differentiated from the Artistic and Brush Strokes categories by a reliance on dots rather than strokes. They include:

Color Halftone	Crystallize
Facet	Fragment
Mezzotint	Mosaic
Pointillize	

Render

These five filters should be your first stop when you have experimentation on your mind. Lighting Effects, for example, puts a photo studio on your monitor, giving you the capability of adjusting multiple light sources in spot, fill, flood, and nondirectional varieties. These filters include:

Clouds	Difference Clouds
Lens Flare	Lighting Effects
Texture Fill	

Sharpen

Three of the four sharpening filters — Sharpen, Sharpen Edges, and Sharpen More — are so-called single step filters: there's no preview window — you just apply them. The fourth, Unsharp Mask, allows you to specify the amount and kind of sharpening to apply.

Sharpen	Sharpen Edges
Sharpen More	Unsharp Mask

Sketch

Yes, there are even more painterly or artistic filters, such as:

Bas Relief	Chalk & Charcoal
Charcoal	Chrome
Conté Crayon	Graphic Pen
Halftone Pattern	Note Paper
Photocopy	Plaster
Reticulation	Stamp
Torn Edges	Water Paper

Stylize

Stylize filters are hybrid filters, which do things like find the edges or contours within an image, break it up into tiles, or cast its pixels to the wind. They include:

Diffuse	Emboss
Extrude	Find Edges
Glowing Edges	Solarize
Tiles	Trace Contour
Wind	

Texture

Adobe tucked in six filters in this submenu that offer some variations on other filters listed elsewhere. For example, the Mosaic Tiles, Texturizer, and Film Grain filters all have their counterparts elsewhere in the Filter menu. My favorite of this group is Patchwork, but you may find that the Stained Glass and Craquelure filters offer unique effects of their own.

Craquelure	Grain
Mosaic Tiles	Patchwork
Stained Glass	Texturizer

Video

You probably won't have much need for these two filters. De-interlace removes odd or even lines, corresponding to the two video fields in video captures, while the NTSC Colors filter modifies an image palette to correspond with the National Television Standard Code standard.

De-Interlace   NTSC Colors

Other

You can create your own filters with the Custom plug-in, offset an image to generate a seamless Web page background, or filter out pixels with brightness or darkness values you specify.

Custom   High Pass

Maximum   Minimum

Offset

Using Filters

This section will be a whirlwind tour through a large group of Photoshop filters, showing you some of the great effects you can achieve. First, we'll create some interesting buttons, using the same basic button we created in Chapter 6.

Find Basic.psd and load it into Photoshop. Make duplicates of that file as required to experiment with the following effects. Use File ➪ Export ➪ GIF89a Export to save any of your favorite buttons as transparent GIFs you can drop onto a page.

Motley trio

To create the three buttons shown in Figure 9-4, follow these steps:

1. Duplicate Basic.psd three times.

2. To one copy, apply the Filter ➪ Artistic ➪ Sponge filter, with Brush Size set to 1, Definition to 24, and Smoothness to 4. Click OK to create a motley button.

3. To the second copy, apply the Filter ➪ Brush Strokes ➪ Spatter filter, using a Spray Radius of 25, and a Smoothness of 1, then

click OK to give us a large, rough surface, which you can see in Figure 9-4.

4. **To create an asteroid-like surface, apply the Filter ⇨ Pixelate ⇨ Mezzotint filter to the third copy.** Choose Fine Dots as the texture. Click OK to apply the texture. Your three buttons should look like Figure 9-4.

Extra texture

We can apply some texture to our buttons using three more filters. Just follow these directions:

1. **Make three more copies of** Basic.psd.

2. **To the first copy, apply Filter ⇨ Noise ⇨ Add Noise, and set the Amount to 50, Distribution to Gaussian, and mark the Monochromatic check box.** Click OK to produce a fuzzy, grainy button, shown in Figure 9-5

3. **To the second copy, apply Filter ⇨ Texture ⇨ Texturizer.** Choose the Canvas texture, set Scaling to 75 percent to reduce the relative size of the texture, and from the Light Dir drop-down list, select Upper Left to correspond with the main light source we used when we created the basic button. Click OK to create a canvas-textured button.

4. **Apply Filter ⇨ Sketch ⇨ Halftone Pattern to the third copy.** Set Size to 1, Contrast to 5, and choose Line as the pattern type from the drop-down list. Click OK.

5. **Apply Filter ⇨ Distort ⇨ Spherize, set at 100 percent, to this same button to give it more of a curved look.** All three finished buttons are shown in Figure 9-5.

A twirling vortex

Now we're ready to apply some more advanced effects to the same basic button. You'll be surprised at how different these Web page components look, thanks to a few simple filter transformations. Just follow these directions:

1. **Create another copy of** Basic.psd.

2. **Apply Filter ⇨ Distort ⇨ Twirl.** Set the angle to -999 degrees, which produces almost three full rotations, as you can see in Figure 9-6.

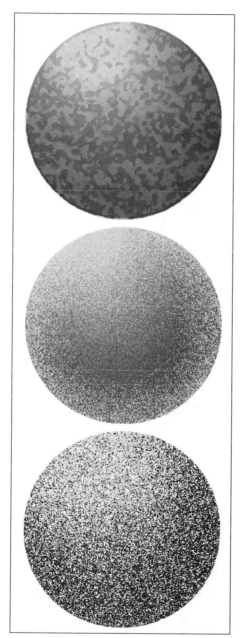

Figure 9-4: Three filters provide three very different effects.

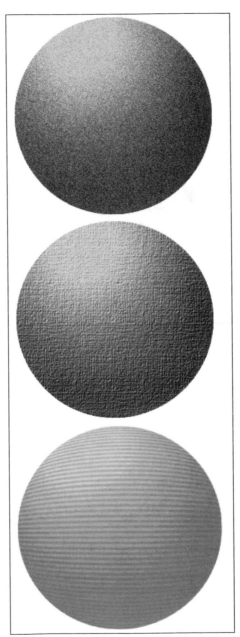

Figure 9-5: The Noise, Texturizer, and Halftone Pattern filters produce these effects.

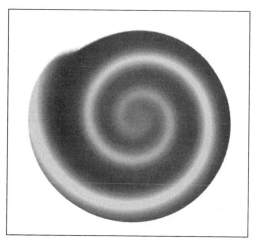

Figure 9-6: The Twirl filter with -999 degrees of rotation applied to the button produces this effect.

3. **Now, apply the same filter four more times.** Our button is starting to get interesting, as you can see in Figure 9-7.

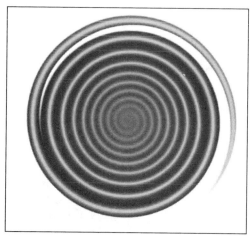

Figure 9-7: Four more applications of the Twirl filter produce this effect.

4. **Apply the same filter four more times, to produce a hypnotic spiraling vortex.**

5. **Choose the oval selection tool, and position the cursor in the center of the vortex.**

6. Hold down the Option and Shift keys to drag a circular selection centered around the point where you clicked.

7. **Invert the selection using Shift-Command-I, then press Delete.** All the area outside the circle you created will be removed, producing a neatly trimmed vortex like the one shown in Figure 9-8.

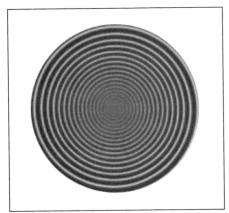

Figure 9-8: Trimming the excess produces a hypnotic vortex like this one.

A galaxy of effects

If you're doing a sci-fi or astronomy-oriented Web page, you'll love the outer space effects you can achieve with Photoshop with very little work. Follow these directions to create a galaxy in less time than the Big Bang:

1. **Using the Swatches palette, Option-click in a deep blue area to make that color the background hue.**

2. **Create a new, blank Photoshop document measuring 600 x 600 pixels.** Check the Background Color radio button so the new document will be filled with the deep blue you just selected.

3. **Choose Filter ⇨ Render ⇨ Lens Flare to produce the dialog box shown in Figure 9-9.** Drag the center of the flare to roughly the middle of the image, and choose 105mm Prime as the lens type. This will give us a good, basic "milky way" type cloud to work with. Click OK to apply the flare.

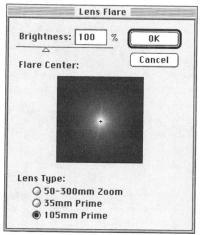

Figure 9-9: The Lens Flare filter produces a star-like effect.

4. **Apply the Twirl filter twice, using the -999 degree setting you used in the last exercise.** Your "galaxy" will appear as if you are viewing it from above the plane of the ecliptic — as you can see in Figure 9-10.

5. **Use the Layer ➪ Transform ➪ Perspective control, and drag on the control handles to distort the galaxy image as shown in Figure 9-11, producing an edge-on view.**

6. **Place a "star" at the edge of the galaxy using the Lens Flare filter once again.** Use the same 105mm Prime lens, but change the Brightness to 80 percent, to tone it down a little. One happy result of these settings is that some "planets" are created, as you can see in Figure 9-12.

7. **Although we can use this image as is, there are a few more effects we can apply.** Save your galaxy as Galaxy.psd to keep this version intact.

8. **Make a duplicate of** Galaxy.psd.

9. **Use Filter ➪ Noise ➪ Add Noise, and add some monochromatic noise with an amount of about 38.** The image will look like Figure 9-13.

Figure 9-10: The Galaxy looks like this from above.

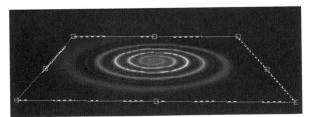

Figure 9-11: The Perspective control gives us an edge-on
view of our galaxy.

10. **Make another copy of** `Galaxy.psd`, **and apply the Filter ⇨ Render ⇨ Difference Clouds filter to it.** You'll get the eerie effect shown in Figure 9-14.

11. **Make another copy of** `Galaxy.psd`, **and apply the Filter ⇨ Render ⇨ Lens Flare filter a few more times, varying the brightness value to generate some extra galaxies and nebulae, as shown in Figure 9-15.**

Figure 9-12: Our galaxy now has a bright supernova and some out-of-scale planets.

Figure 9-13: A little noise adds a fuzzy starfield to the galaxy.

Figure 9-14: The Difference Clouds filter sinks our galaxy in a hazy miasma.

Figure 9-15: Extra galaxies make the image look even more realistic.

Some more effects

Once you've started working with a particular graphic, don't give up until you've tried out every possible permutation with filters. Here are three more examples of effects you can achieve with the same `Basic.psd` button image we've been using since Chapter 6. Just follow these directions:

1. Make three copies of `Basic.psd`.

2. Paint one of them with contrasting colors in wavy lines, as shown in Figure 9-16.

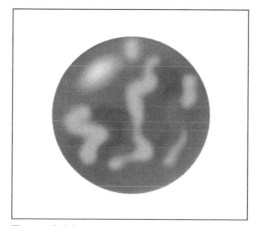

Figure 9-16: Add some wavy lines to the button.

3. Now, use Filter ➪ Distort ➪ Zig-Zag, and choose **Pond Ripples, Amount: 67, and Ripples: 5.** You'll get a button like the one shown in Figure 9-17.

4. Take another copy and use the same filter, this time specifying **Out From Center, 11 ridges, and an amount of 100.** You'll end up with a button like the one in Figure 9-18.

5. Finally, with the third copy of `Basic.psd`, use the **Around Center mode, 5 ridges, and an amount of 100.** The finished button will look like Figure 9-19.

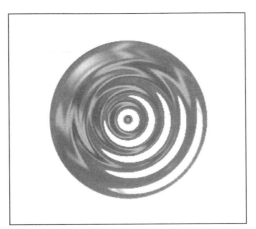

Figure 9-17: This abstract button was produced using Zig-Zag's Pond Ripples option.

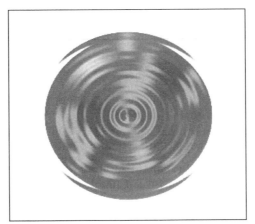

Figure 9-18: The same filter with different options produces this effect.

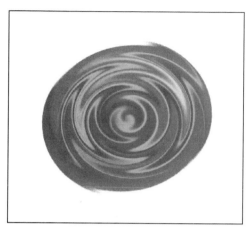

Figure 9-19: A few more changes produce this effect.

Working with edges

Filters are a great way to create fuzzy edges and other edge effects that can free your Web page from blocky squares and rectangles. This section will show you how to create interesting edge effects using the filters built into Photoshop, and other kinds of graphics using only the edges. Generally, you select the edge of your graphic, and apply a filter of some sort to it. To see how this works, just follow these directions:

1. **Load the file** Edges.psd **from the CD-ROM.** This is a plain rectangle you can use to see how the edge effects look. Note that the rectangle rests on a transparent background, so you can save the edge effect as a transparent GIF that will blend in with the rest of your page's background.

2. **Make a copy of** Edges.psd**.** Then select the area outside the rectangle with the Magic Wand.

3. **Choose Select ⇨ Modify ⇨ Expand, and type in 10 for the value.** The selection will creep in on the rectangle by a value of 10.

4. **Use Filter ⇨ Blur ⇨ Gaussian Blur with an amount of 4 to create the blurred edge shown in Figure 9-20.**

Figure 9-20: Gaussian Blur has smeared the edges of this graphic.

5.   **Repeat Steps 2 and 3 above.**

6.   **Now, apply the Filter ⇨ Distort ⇨ Ripple command.** Set Amount
     to 500, and Size to Medium. You'll get an effect like Figure 9-21.

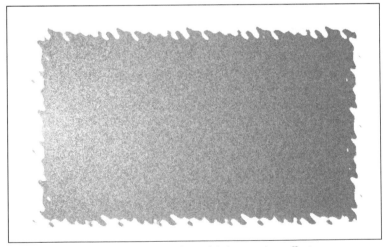

Figure 9-21: Rippled edges produce this interesting effect.

7. Repeat steps 2 and 3 above.

8. Now use Select ➪ Invert to invert the selection.

9. Press Delete, which removes the center part of the rectangle, leaving only the border.

10. Select All by pressing Command-A.

11. Use Filter ➪ Distort ➪ Twirl, with the Angle set to +999.

12. Click OK, to produce the effect shown in Figure 9-22.

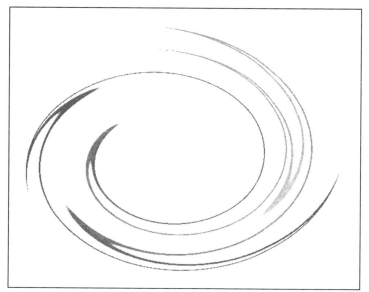

Figure 9-22: Swirling only the border produces an abstract effect.

13. Repeat Steps 2 and 3 one more time.

14. **Apply the Filter ➪ Distort ➪ Wave filter.** Use a value of 5 for the number of generators, a wavelength of 10 to 120, amplitude of 5 to 35, a Type of Triangle, and make sure the Repeat Edge Pixels button is checked. Click the Randomize button until you get an effect you like, then Click OK to apply the change. Your edge will look something like Figure 9-23. The cool part about this effect is that you get a new — but related — edge every time.

Figure 9-23: The Wave filter produces edges like these.

Moving On

This chapter provided you with a good look at how Photoshop's built-in filters can be used to create interesting graphics for Web pages. I explored variations of a broad range of filters so that you could see how even small changes in filter parameters can produce dramatically different results. In the next chapter, I look at more filter effects using some useful third-party filter add-ons.

Cool Effects with Add-on Filters

If you think the 100 filters built right into Photoshop exhaust all the possibilities for creating cool Web graphics, you probably haven't used any of the stellar add-on packages available that give you even more effects. Plug-ins such as Kai's Power Tools, KPT Convolver, Squizz, Terrazzo, and other accessory packages available from third parties, offer extra capabilities that you'll want to add to your arsenal.

A general discussion of some of these tools is included in Chapter 15. If you want some information on how they work, and what they can do, check there.

NOTE This chapter assumes you already have Kai's Power Tools, and concentrates on practical techniques and tricks without bogging you down with background. You can achieve great effects with any of the add-ons discussed in Chapter 15, but because Kai's Power Tools is virtually a must-have purchase for any serious Photoshop user, I concentrate here on effects you can achieve with that product, especially those that are difficult or impossible to realize with an unadorned copy of Photoshop.

In This Chapter

Building Better Buttons

Building Better Backgrounds

Strange Effects

Building Better Buttons

Spherical or hemispherical buttons are a basic effect any Web page designer will want to exploit. As you've seen in previous chapters, you can build PGB (pretty good buttons) using Photoshop's Spherize and Lighting Effects filters, but KPT does spheres better, faster, and offers more flexibility. For a quick test drive of some useful techniques, read through the directions that follow.

Using Glass Lens

You'll find that the Glass Lens filter is one of the most flexible tools KPT offers. Check it out with these steps:

1. Load the file `Spain2.tif` **from the CD-ROM that accompanies this book.**

2. **Choose the oval selection tool, hold down the Option and Shift keys, and drag to create a perfect circle anywhere in the sky area, as shown in Figure 10-1.** It doesn't really matter what portion you use, or even what file you use. We're just trying to grab some interesting tones and colors to create an abstract hemisphere.

Figure 10-1: First create a circle in a portion of the sky area with interesting tones.

3. **Choose Filter ⇨ KPT 3.0 ⇨ Glass Lens, and the dialog box shown in Figure 10-2 appears, with a preview of the effect you will be applying shown in its window.**

4. **There are three key controls at the left side of the Glass Lens dialog box.** At the top is the Mode button. Click it to switch from Normal, to Soft, to Bright. We want a bright glass lens, so change the mode to Bright.

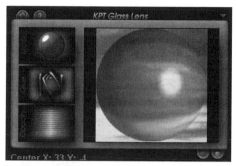

Figure 10-2: The KPT Glass Lens dialog box shows a preview of your effect.

5. **The Glue control is similar to Photoshop's blending modes.** Both Normal and Procedural+ look good. You can select the one you prefer.

6. **Opacity controls how much of the underlying image shows through the shiny surface of the glass lens.** For this example, I set opacity at 80 percent.

7. **Notice the spectacular highlight on the preview sphere? KPT Glass Lens allows you to change the position of the light source and thus, move that highlight.** Just click on the light with the cursor, and drag to the position you like. The coordinates of the bright spot, relative to the center of the sphere, are shown in the lower left of the dialog box, as you can see in Figure 10-3.

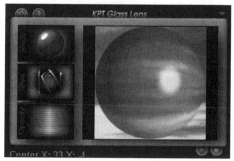

Figure 10-3: When the highlight is moved, its coordinates are shown in the lower left corner of the dialog box.

8. **When you get the effect you want, click the green button at lower right; or, click the red button to cancel.** Click green now to apply the Glass Lens filter.

9. **The circular area you've transformed is still selected.** You can press Command-C to copy it, then File ⇨ New to create a new file to paste it into. Select Transparent as the background of the new file.

10. **Press Command-V to paste the button into the new file.** Resize the button to the size you want with Image ⇨ Image Size, then save it as a transparent GIF, using the techniques you learned in Chapter 7. Figure 10-4 shows just a few of the buttons you can extract just from this one image. KPT's Glass Lens is a great way to create spheres from existing images, whether they are abstract or incorporate an image appropriate to your Web page.

Figure 10-4: These four buttons were created with KPT's Glass Lens filter.

This filter works equally well with abstract originals. In Figure 10-5, I just took a gradient, applied some random scribbles to it with the Airbrush, then added a bit of monochromatic noise before applying the Glass Lens filter. You can perform filtering effects first, and then apply the Glass Lens filter to transform the modified image into a round button. Add some text, as in Figure 10-6, and you have a fine, attractive button.

Creating a Seamless Background

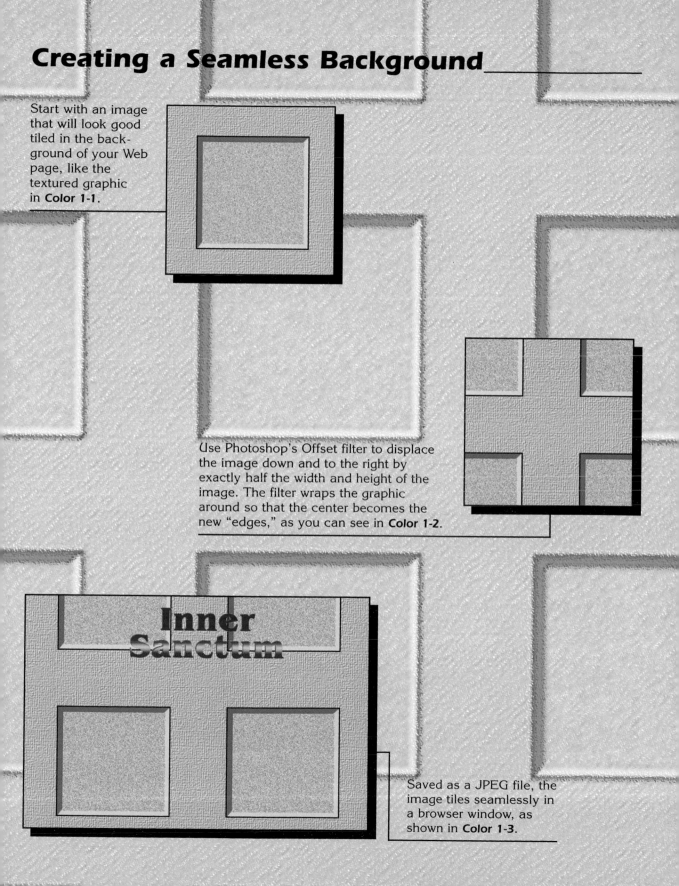

Start with an image that will look good tiled in the background of your Web page, like the textured graphic in **Color 1-1**.

Use Photoshop's Offset filter to displace the image down and to the right by exactly half the width and height of the image. The filter wraps the graphic around so that the center becomes the new "edges," as you can see in **Color 1-2**.

Inner
Sanctum

Saved as a JPEG file, the image tiles seamlessly in a browser window, as shown in **Color 1-3**.

Special Effects with Kai's Power Tools

Kai's Power Tools is an essential add-on for any serious Web graphics worker. You can develop glossy buttons, like the one in **Color 6-1**, using the KPT Glass Lens filter,

or build custom gradients and effects like those shown in **Color 6-2**.

Several KPT filters are excellent for creating interesting backgrounds, like the tiled, perspective-altered image in **Color 6-3**.

Sheet Aluminum

Even hackneyed filters like Page Curl can be used imaginatively, as you can see in the sample page in **Color 6-4**.

- Industry Update
- New Plant Openings
- Other Rolled Metal Sites

Color Correcting with Variations

Photoshop's Variations dialog box gives you a preview of lightening, darkening, color correction, and saturation modifications you can make by selecting the best image from a set of samples.

Finished Web Pages

Your cool Web pages can be simple, like the one shown in **Color 8-1**;

Pennie Pincher

Online Rare Coin Catalog

Contents:

[U.S. Coins-18th Century]

[U.S. Coins-19th Century]

[U. S. Coins-20th Century]

[Foreign Coins]

David D. Busch

Online Portfolio

To check out my photographs, select a category:

[Fashion Photography]   [Scenics]

[Celebrities and Entertainers]

serve as a gateway to other pages on your Web site, like the one in **Color 8-2**;

or make a bold statement about your own sense of style, like the page in **Color 8-3**.

Figure 10-5: *Random scribbles and some monochromatic noise were the basis for this button.*

Figure 10-6: *Some text turns this into a functional button for your Web page.*

More spheres

If extreme is your scheme, you'll want to use KPT's Spheroid Designer, which allows you to create the wildest spherical objects in creation. Just how radical KPT is in this mode will be evident from the interface/dialog box, shown in Figure 10-7, sometimes described as the dashboard from a Martian flivver.

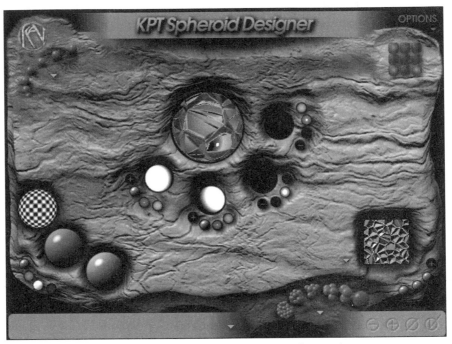

Figure 10-7: Spheroid Designer has a daunting array of controls.

It doesn't really matter what base image you use to create your spheroid, although you can specify enough transparency that the underlying image does show through, if that's what you're after. It's likely that once you've explored Spheroid Designer's controls, however, you'll end up with something that bears no resemblance to your original graphic. Some of the adjustments you can make include the following:

➥ **Amount of Curvature.** Tweak the uppermost of the large spheres at the lower left corner to adjust the amount of curvature in your spheroid.

➥ **Ambient/Diffuse Light.** Drag the mouse over the middle large sphere at lower left to change the amount of diffuse light shining on the spheroid.

➥ **Transparency.** Drag up or down on the bottom large sphere at lower left to increase or decrease the transparency of your spheroid.

➥ **Diffusion/Diffuse Hue/Ambient Intensity/Ambient Hue.** Drag on the four small marbles at lower left to fine-tune the amount and color of the diffuse and ambient light falling on the spheroid.

➥ **Four Light Sources.** Click the four spheres immediately surrounding the preview window in the center to turn on and off four different light sources, which you can position and color independently with the marbles next to them.

➥ **Adding Bump Textures.** At lower right is a square preview window showing any bump texture map you may have activated. Choose a bump texture from the drop-down list indicated by the down arrow next to the preview window. Add or subtract to the bump amount using the four marbles to the lower right of the bump preview window. Click on the clusters of spheres to control how many spheres are created within your selection.

➥ **Saving Your Work.** At upper right are Memory Dots that can be clicked to save your current settings. You can also click the plus sign at the lower right edge of the dialog box to save your current settings to disk. Settings can be retrieved from the drop-down list that pops up when you click the down arrow at the lower center edge of the dialog box.

➥ **Mutations.** At upper left are mutation controls: seven marbles that let you activate random changes in your spheroid, based on attributes that you chose from a drop-down list next to the marbles.

Spheroid Designer's controls take some practice, but once you've mastered them, you can easily create stunning buttons like the one shown in Figure 10-8.

Figure 10-8: A button like this one is easy to create with Spheroid Designer.

Twirl away

Some very cool effects can be achieved with some of KPT's pixel-moving filters. We'll play with them a bit in this next section. Just follow these steps:

1. Load `Spain03.tif` from the CD-ROM.

2. Select a circular section anywhere you like, as shown in Figure 10-9.

Figure 10-9: We'll use a circular section of this image for our effect.

3. **Choose Filter ⇨ KPT 3.0 ⇨ KPT Twirl to produce the dialog box shown in Figure 10-10.**

4. **Set the Mode control at upper left to Normal.**

5. **Place the cursor in the preview window, and twirl.** Click OK to apply the effect. You can see the dialog box and the effect in Figure 10-10.

Figure 10-10: The KPT Twirl effect generates a different look than Photoshop's own Twirl filter.

6. If you like, click the Mode control and change to Kaleidoscope, to produce the effect shown in Figure 10-11.

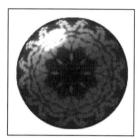

Figure 10-11: The Kaleidoscope mode creates symmetrical abstract effects. We added the Glass Lens filter here to give the button a 3D look.

Building Better Backgrounds

If the kaleidoscopic image created in the last exercise had you thinking about interesting abstract seamless backgrounds, Kai's Power Tools has a lot of other cool effects that can make building those backgrounds easier. I provide a quick example of several of them, as a preview.

Perspective tiling

KPT's Planar Tiling's Perspective option is a quick way to create a great 3D effect that would take quite a while to duplicate in Photoshop using conventional tools such as Free Transform. I created an interesting background — a little garish for actual use, but distinctive enough to show up well on the printed page — by following these steps:

1. **Create a light-to-dark gradient (I used yellow to red) and place an object you want distorted with a perspective effect on the gradient.** In this case, I used the logo of Kitchen Table International, the world's leading fictitious supplier of computer hardware, software, firmware, and limpware. I made the image wider than it was tall to leave some extra room at the sides. The original graphic is shown in Figure 10-12.

2. **KPT's Planar Tiling filter, in Perspective mode, created the tiled, tilted version shown in Figure 10-13.**

Figure 10-12: This logo can be transformed into an interesting Web page background.

Figure 10-13: After Planar Tiling, the image looks like this.

3. I cut out a square section of the distorted image (inset in Figure 10-14), increased the brightness and reduced the contrast to convert it into a more subdued background image, then used Photoshop's Filter Í Other Í Offset filter to produce a seamless background for tiling, as you can see in Figure 10-14.

Gradient Designer

KPT's Gradient Designer is much more flexible than Photoshop's new gradient editing capabilities, since you can choose from more than a dozen different gradient patterns (not just linear and radial, as in Photoshop) with names like Radial Sweep and Rectangular Burst. You may select the hues used for the gradient, select brightness, contrast, and other parameters, and specify a repeating gradient, as I did for the sample shown in Figure 10-15.

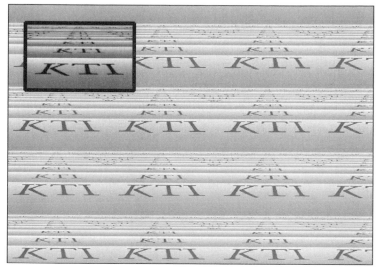

Figure 10-14: The finished image makes a garish, yet eye-catching background.

Figure 10-15: A gradient, repeated seven times, produced this hypnotic background.

Texture Explorer

Kai's Power Tools' Texture Explorer is a treasure-trove of great background effects for Web pages. There are 200 inventive preset textures supplied that you can browse through and arrange around the perimeter of the preview window, shown in Figure 10-16. You can "mutate" colors, brightness, texture, and other parameters a little at a time, or instruct the filter to show you a cavalcade of interesting effects, one after another, until you find one you like.

Figure 10-16: Texture Explorer offers a treasure-trove of effects.

For a musical theme page, I created a Notes-oriented background, then applied a texture from the KPT library, as you can see in Figure 10-17.

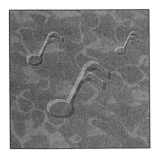

Figure 10-17: A background texture brightens up this musical motif.

Strange Effects

Other KPT filters can be used to produce one-of-a-kind special effects that can give a unique look to your Web graphics. Here are a few examples.

Vortex Tiling

The KPT Vortex Tiling filter sends your image down a whirlpool, spinning off duplicate pixels as it goes, creating rather dramatic effects. An ordinary image of Segovia, Spain's Roman aqueduct, shown in Figure 10-18, was transformed into a stunningly original image in seconds. I fiddled with the filter's vortex radius control, and produced several quite different looks before settling on the version shown in Figure 10-19.

Figure 10-18: A Roman aqueduct in Segovia, Spain, before processing.

Figure 10-19: The same aqueduct after processing through Kai's Power Tools' Vortex Tiling filter.

Figure 10-20: The photograph has been transformed into a painting, using KPT's Pixel Effects filter.

Painterly effects

Photoshop's built-in filters aren't the only ones that can create painterly effects. KPT's Pixel Effects filter, applied to the Roman aqueduct, turns the sharp photograph and its distracting background into a fuzzy piece of art, as you can see in Figure 10-20.

Corner curl

Don't give up on KPT's most over-used filter, the Page Curl. Even if you're sick of seeing images with their corners coyly curled up, you can still find some interesting uses for this filter. Figure 10-21 is an example.

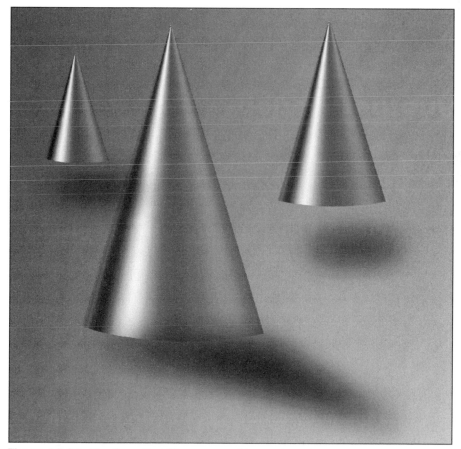

Figure 10-21: The Page Curl filter was used to produce these cones.

In this case, I used Page Curl as a quick way to create a set of metallic cones, simply by curling one corner of a page, and then rotating the points to an upright position. The oval selection tool then snipped off the upper sections of the cone, which could then be resized as needed. In Figure 10-22, the Page Curl filter was applied several times to create a rolled sheet metal look for a Web page.

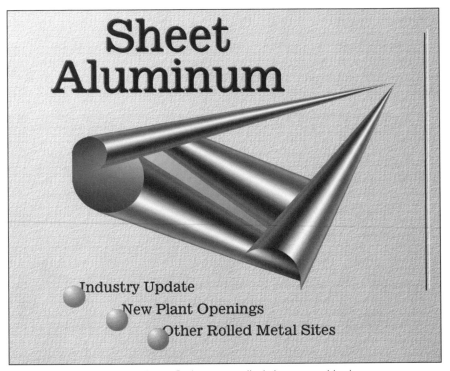

Figure 10-22: This time, Page Curl gave a rolled sheet metal look.

Moving On

Now that you have a good feeling for how add-on filters can help create outstanding Web graphics, we'll move on to look at some text effects you can achieve with filters and other Photoshop facilities.

Great Text Effects in Photoshop

If you are doing desktop publishing instead of Web page building, Photoshop is not your best tool for creating text. It lacks text editing capabilities, and the sophisticated and automated tools for leading (line spacing), kerning (letter spacing), tracking, and other typographic fine points that you find in programs like Adobe PageMaker or QuarkXPress.

However, for most HTML pages, fancy text must be treated as graphics, anyway, and that's the realm in which Photoshop excels. This chapter shows you some interesting effects.

In This Chapter

Choosing a Graphic Format

Producing Textured Text

Twisting and Distorting Text

Some Quick Text Effects

Choosing the Best Graphic Format for Text

You'll recall that GIF and JPEG, the two most important graphics file formats used on Web pages, have some significant differences. You should keep these in mind when selecting a destination format for fancy text you're creating for a Web page. The key points are the following:

➡ Use GIF if you want to create a transparent image in which the text seems to float on the background of your page.

➡ GIF is best when the text has small elements that you want to appear as sharp as possible. GIF's compression scheme produces reasonably small files without losing any image detail.

➡ Use JPEG when your text or its surrounding background includes subtle gradients or other graphics that can benefit from full-color rendition. For example, if you want a smooth, blurry drop-shadow behind the text, JPEG will reproduce it more accurately. If you want a drop-shadow behind a GIF image, use a solid shadow. Figure 11-1 offers a comparison between JPEG and GIF when a soft, blurry shadow and background gradient is used.

Figure 11-1: The image at top was saved as a JPEG file, and includes a full range of tones. At bottom, the image was saved as a 256-color GIF file, and displays banding in the gradients.

Smooth gradients almost always require a rectangular, non-transparent image. Figure 11-2 shows the same text as above with a solid drop shadow, saved as a transparent GIF so that the image can be displayed on a textured background.

Figure 11-2: The same text looks good as a transparent GIF with a solid drop-shadow.

The best way to dream up new text effects is to play with some like those in the next section, and branch out from there.

Grabbing Textured Text

Copy the Oldwood.tif and Oldstone.tif files from your CD-ROM, and follow these steps to learn a quick way to add texture to text.

1. **Select the Type Mask tool by holding the Option key and clicking on the Type tool until the dotted-line Mask icon appears.**

2. **Move the cursor to roughly the center of the Oldwood.tif image, and click to produce the Type Tool dialog box.** Choose a fat font, and enter 32 points for the Size, and 20 points for Leading. A leading setting less than the height of the font will compress the two lines of type together more closely.

3. **In the Alignment box, click the horizontally centered alignment button.** In the Style box, check Anti-Aliased, then type in the text that follows. Be sure to press Return between the words to place the text on separate lines.

```
Medieval
Life
```

4. **Click OK to deposit your text into the image as a selection.** It will be centered around the point where you positioned the mouse cursor and clicked earlier. The image should look like Figure 11-3.

Figure 11-3: The type has been entered into the image as a mask.

5. **With any selection tool active, move the cursor inside the selection and reposition the mask until you have a surface showing through the text outline that you like.** Then press Command-C to copy the selection.

6. **Open** Oldstone.tif **and press Command-V to paste the characters into a new layer.**

Creating a Glow

Let's add a blurry glow behind our text, using the following steps:

1. **In the Layers palette's fly-out menu, select Duplicate Layer and name the layer, Shadow.**

2. **Select Filter ➪ Blur ➪ Gaussian Blur and set the Radius to about 7 pixels.**

3. **In the Layers palette, check the Preserve Transparency box so that only the image portion of the layer will be affected by our next step, which is to fill the blurred text with a hue.**

4. Choose a bright yellow color from the Swatches palette.

5. Now, use Edit ⇨ Fill to fill the blurred text with the yellow hue. You can also use the Option-Delete key. Where Delete removes a selection and replaces it with the background color, Option-Delete replaces a selection with the foreground color.

6. In the Layers palette, grab the layer with the woody text with the mouse, and drag it so that it is above the yellow, blurry shadow. Your image should look something like Figure 11-4.

Figure 11-4: The text and foliage background look like this after the layers have been reordered.

Backlit Text

Backlighting black letters against a black background produces a dramatic effect, especially on a Web page that has a black background. Here's a fast way to create a great-looking backlit effect. Just follow these directions:

1. Create a new, empty document 400 × 300 pixels in size.

2. Press D on your keyboard to set Photoshop's foreground and background colors to their default value of black and white.

3. Press Option-Delete to fill the document with black, your foreground color.

4.   **Select the Type Mask tool.** In the Type Tool dialog box, select a font of your choice, such as Times Roman Bold, set Spacing to 2, Size to 72, and enter BACKLIGHT in the text box.

5.   **Choose Selection ⇨ Save Selection from the menu bar to save the mask you produced.**

6.   **Choose Selection ⇨ Feather from the menu bar, and specify a 4-pixel radius to feather the selection.**

7.   **Choose a purple color as the foreground from the Swatches palette and Select Edit ⇨ Fill from the menu bar to fill the feathered selection with a bright purple.** Make sure the Preserve Transparency box is not checked. Your text should look like Figure 11-5.

Figure 11-5: The blurry text on a black background has a fluorescent effect of its own.

8.   **Reload the selection you saved in step 5. Fill it with black.** You'll produce the vivid back-lit effect shown in Figure 11-6.

Figure 11-6: The whole image is black, except for the blurry shadow we created.

9.   **Next, select Layer ⇨ New ⇨ Adjustment Layer from the menu bar, and use the default Hue/Saturation choice.** The new Adjustment Layer will appear at the top of the Layers palette, as shown in Figure 11-7.

10.   **Use the sliders on the Hue/Saturation dialog box that appear to adjust the colors displayed by the background layer you created earlier.** Even though you used a purple shade for the backlighting, with the Adjustment Layer you can change the hue to red, green, or any other shade, and modify the saturation level and brightness as well. When you get an effect you want to save, store the file on your hard disk using File ⇨ Save As.

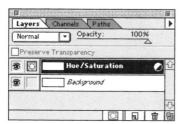

Figure 11-7: The circular black/white icon at right designates an Adjustment Layer.

Adding Perspective to Text

We covered basic 3D techniques in Chapter 6. Now it's time to examine in a little more detail some of the ways Photoshop can add perspective to images. Photoshop's Transform and Free Transform tools can perform six different transformations of this type on 2D objects: scale, rotate, skew, distort, perspective, and flip (horizontal or vertical).

Rotating the text

Load the file Collect.tif from the CD-ROM, and make copies of it as required to try out these effects. Then, follow these steps to see what you can do with Photoshop's Transform tools:

1. **Select the Collectibles Corner text with the lasso tool.**

2. **Select Layer ➪ Transform ➪ Rotate, and selection handles will appear around the image.**

3. **Move the cursor to the upper left corner handle again.** The cursor changes into a pair of curved arrows. You can rotate the selection by dragging the handles.

4. **Drag any handle — any of them can be used to rotate the image around its center point.** Hold down the Shift key to constrain rotation to 15 degree increments.

5. **Press Return to accept the change.** You can use this technique to create rotated text for a Web page, as shown in Figure 11-8.

Figure 11-8: Rotated text was used to create this Web page.

Skewing the text

Skewing slants a selection in one way or another. To see how it works, follow these steps:

1. Select the text using the Lasso tool, as before.

2. Choose Layer ➪ Transform ➪ Skew, and the selection handles will appear.

3. Next, drag the handle in the upper left corner. Corner handles can be dragged horizontally or vertically, but not both ways at once, producing a slanting effect, as you can see in Figure 11-9.

4. Grab another corner handle and drag it to one side to produce an interesting effect, like the one shown in Figure 11-10.

5. Press Escape to cancel the transformation, or press Return to make it permanent and save the file to disk (if you'd like to save the effect).

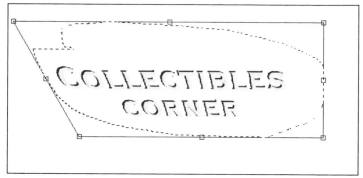

Figure 11-9: Skewing produces a slanted effect.

Figure 11-10: Several changes can produce a slanted effect like this one.

Distorting the text

Distortion is like skewing, but with some added features, as you'll see in the following steps:

1. **Select the text using the Lasso tool.**

2. **Choose Layer ⇨ Transform ⇨ Distort, and the selection handles will appear again.**

3. **Grab the upper left selection handle, and drag it.** Notice that when Distort is active, you can drag the handle freely, vertically, horizontally, and diagonally, while the other corner handles remain in place. You can even drag the handle inward, toward the interior of the original selection (which isn't possible with Skew) to produce an effect like the one shown in Figure 11-11.

Figure 11-11: The Distort tool lets you twist the selection freely.

Changing perspective

The Perspective tool creates a 3D effect by moving two of the selection handles in opposite directions, making the outer borders of your selection converge on an imaginary vanishing point somewhere else in the image. We used this tool in Chapter 6 to create an edge-on view of the phonograph records. To learn how perspective can be used with text, try these steps:

1. **Select the text using the Lasso tool.**

2. **Choose Layer ⇨ Transform ⇨ Perspective, and the selection handles appear.**

3. **Grab the upper left selection handle, and notice how the upper right handle moves in the opposite direction when you drag horizontally.** When you drag one way, the opposite handle moves in the other direction.

4. **Press Return to accept the change. Create a drop-shadow under the page, and add a gradient behind both, using techniques you learned earlier in this book.** Your image will look something like what you see in Figure 11-12. This is a great technique for producing images that look as if they were printed on a piece of paper that is laid out in front of the viewer.

While you can rotate an image freely using Transform or Free Transform, Photoshop also enables you to rotate in fixed increments of 180 degrees, 90 degrees clockwise, and 90 degrees counterclockwise, and to flip a selection horizontally or vertically. You can use Numeric Transformations to apply sets of transformations to selections using fixed amounts, since you can "dial in" the exact movements you want. The latter facility can apply several different effects at once, as you can see in the dialog box shown in Figure 11-13.

Figure 11-12: Dragging any corner handle produces a perspective effect.

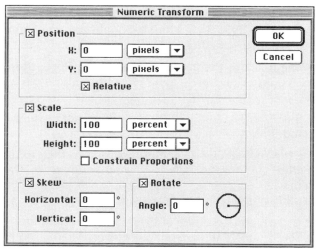

Figure 11-13: The Numeric Transform dialog box enables you to perform several transformations at once, using specific values for each.

Text Effect Quickies

Here are some quick recipes for achieving cool text effects that will enhance the look of your Web page. I'm going to show you how to simulate the look of metal, ice, stone, and other textures from scratch without the need for special texture files. Each recipe will include only general instructions; I'll assume that by this time you know how to use basic Photoshop features.

Creating a metallic sheen

If your Web page has a futuristic or industrial look, you'll want to apply a metallic sheen to text or other objects. Here's a fast way to simulate that look:

1. **Open a new, blank Photoshop image, using Transparent as the contents.**

2. **Select the Type Mask tool and enter the text you want to metallicize. I used a font called Copperplate Gothic.** Click OK to place the text mask in your image.

3. **Make sure the default foreground/background colors are active, and then fill the type area with black, with an opacity of 50 percent, to produce a medium gray.**

4. **Add some noise to the gray text. I used the Photoshop Noise filter, set to Gaussian Noise, and Monochromatic, with a value of 45 pixels.**

5. **Apply the Filter ⇨ Sketch ⇨ Chrome filter, using values of 10 for detail and smoothness.**

6. **Choose the rectangular selection tool, and in the Options palette, set Feather to 5 pixels.** Make sure that the Preserve Transparency box in the Layers Palette is checked. Then select the upper half of the first line of the text you've typed in.

7. **Select a dark and light pair of colors (I used dark and light blue) as the foreground and background colors.** Then apply a linear gradient with an opacity of 70 percent to the selection, dragging from top to bottom.

8. **Select the lower half of the line of text and apply the same gradient, this time dragging from bottom to top.**

9. **Repeat steps 6 through 8 for any additional lines of text you may have typed.**

10. **Use Image ⇨ Adjust ⇨ Levels to provide the brightness and contrast you want for the image.** The gray Gamma slider offers the best control.

11. **Export the image as a transparent GIF, or save it to your hard disk to incorporate in another image.** My finished image looks like Figure 11-14.

Figure 11-14: A metallic sheen is easy to achieve using Photoshop's Chrome filter.

Tin-snips

Here you get two effects for the price of one. I wanted a rough look, almost as if the characters were cut out of metal with tin snips. One of the intermediate steps looked pretty good on its own. So, you can learn two different type effects with a few simple steps.

1. **Open a new, blank Photoshop image, using Transparent as the contents.**

2. **Select the Type Mask tool and enter the text you want to process.** I used a font called Charlesworth. Click OK to place the text mask in your image.

3. **Save the selection.**

4. **Apply Photoshop's Clouds filter to the text.** The clouds end up looking like metallic reflections rather than actual clouds. It makes the text look like uneven metal.

5. **Copy the text you've just filled with clouds to the Clipboard.**

6. **Use Select ⇨ Feather and specify a setting of 8 pixels to feather the selection.**

7. **Fill the feathered selection with 100 percent black (Edit ⇨ Fill).**

8. **Now, load the selection again, and press the Delete key.** This cuts out the area occupied by the original text, but leaves the feathery shadow, as shown in Figure 11-15. This actually makes an interesting effect on its own, something like the overspray left behind when you airbrush a block stencil.

Figure 11-15: This intermediate step looks like overspray left behind when you airbrush a stencil.

9.   **Paste down the cloud-filled text you copied earlier, then use the cursor arrow keys to move the text slightly so some of the white underneath shows through.** The finished effect looks like Figure 11-16.

Figure 11-16: The finished effect looks like letters cut from sheet metal.

Frozen rock

Now let's create an icy frozen rock look. Just follow these directions:

1.   **Open a new, blank Photoshop image, using Transparent as the contents.**

2. Select the Type Mask tool and enter the text you want to process. I used a sans-serif font called Arial Black. Click OK to place the text mask in your image.

3. Save the selection.

4. Fill the selection with a medium gray, as you did earlier.

5. Apply a sandstone texture to the letters, using Photoshop's Filter ➪ Texture ➪ Texturizer filter. I used a Relief setting of 35 to make the texture stand out sharply.

6. Using the Lasso tool, select the upper part of the characters. Create a wavy boundary to simulate snow caps.

7. Make sure the Preserve Transparency box for this layer is checked, then select a light blue as the foreground color, and apply a light blue-white fill at 30 percent to the remaining tops of the characters to simulate snow.

8. Create a new layer, and load the text selection.

9. Use Select ➪ Feather and a setting of 8 pixels, then fill with black. Then, as you did in the last example, reload the original selection and delete it to produce a drop shadow with a cut-out.

10. Select the rock-text layer, and use the cursor arrow keys to nudge it to allow the cut-out background to show through.

11. Flatten the image, which should look like Figure 11-17.

Figure 11-17: This text has an icy rock look to it, topped with snow.

Wrapping text around a sphere

If your Web page has international pretensions, sooner or later you'll want to wrap text around a globe. Here's a cool way to do it:

1. **Open a new, blank Photoshop image, using Transparent as the contents.**

2. **Create a perfectly circular selection.** Choose the elliptical marquee tool, then hold down the Option and Shift keys while you drag to create a perfect circle.

3. **Save the selection.**

4. **Type in your text in a size that fits inside the selection.**

5. **Make sure the Preserve Transparency box is not checked for the text layer, and then use the Filter ⇨ Distort ⇨ Spherize filter at 100 percent to mold the lettering onto a sphere created from the circular area.** Your image will look like Figure 11-18.

Figure 11-18: The text has been wrapped around the sphere.

6. **Make sure the text layer is still selected, and check the Preserve Transparency box.** Now fill the text with a color of your choice. I used bright yellow.

7. Create a new layer, and load the circular selection you saved in Step 3.

8. Fill the circle with a radial fill, using colors that will contrast with the text. I used dark blues.

9. If you have Kai's Power Tools, you can make the globe a shiny orb using the Glass Lens filter in Bright mode.

10. Create another layer and load the circular selection. Then, using the Line tool, draw several evenly-spaced horizontal and vertical lines, to simulate lines of latitude and longitude.

11. Apply the Distort ➪ Spherize filter once more to bend the lines around the globe.

12. Make sure the layers are stacked so that the background color is on the bottom of the Layers palette, the latitude/longitude lines next, and the text on top. Then flatten the image to produce a globe like the one shown in Figure 11-19.

Figure 11-19: The finished globe looks very corporate.

Plated elegance

Nothing beats the plated look to impress visitors to your Web site. While there are text manipulation tools like Pixar Typestry that can add this look, Photoshop has all of the tools you need. Try out the following technique and see for yourself.

1. Open a new, blank Photoshop image, using Transparent as the contents.

2. Enter the text, using a font of your choice.

3. Duplicate the layer.

4. **Choose two colors to be used to apply the plated look.** I selected a dark gold and light gold for the foreground and background.

5. **With the Preserve Transparency box checked for each layer, apply a linear gradient to each, but in opposite directions.** One layer will have a left-to-right, dark-to-light gradient, while the other layer will have a light-to-dark gradient.

6. **Select the bottom layer in the Layers palette, choose the Move tool, and then nudge the image using the cursor arrow keys upwards and to the right.** This gives the dark areas of the text a light-colored drop shadow, while the light areas have a dark-colored drop shadow. The effect is a pronounced plated look, as you can see in Figure 11-20.

Figure 11-20: Placing a contrasting gradient in the drop shadows produces a plated look.

7. **Enhance the effect with a gradient.** Create a new layer, choose a medium color as the foreground color, then double-click the gradient tool to bring the Gradient Options palette to the front.

8. **Choose Transparent to Foreground as the gradient, and Radial as the type.** Then position the cursor in the center of the image and drag to any corner.

9. **Flatten the image, and then add a Lens Flare to the center.** The text will look as if it is backlit by the sun, as you can see in Figure 11-21.

Figure 11-21: The gradient and lens flare make this logo appear to be backlit by a glowing sun.

Moving On

The last three chapters gave you dozens of examples of cool Web graphics you can create using Photoshop's filters and other facilities. Next, I'm going to show you how to color correct images so they'll look their best on the World Wide Web.

Color Correction

Correcting the color of an image should be easy, right? If an image looks too blue, you just fire up Photoshop, move a few sliders, and subtract that excess hue to make the photo perfection itself. Oops, you say. That's not quite right. Now the image looks a little too cyan. Better remove some of that, too. No, that didn't fix it either.

What's wrong with this picture? As you probably already know, perfecting color is a little like trying to level a chair by sawing a little bit from the legs one at a time, without taking any measurements. Work at it long enough, and you'll end up with a seat a leprechaun might find comfortable.

But don't panic. We're not going to overcomplicate the color correction process just so that you'll be relieved you purchased this book. All you need is a firm understanding of the requirements for color on the Web, and some basics of how to use Photoshop's correction tools. In this chapter, I'll describe five different ways to change the color balance of an image. You'll find that by implementing these methods you can make bad images look their best on the Web.

What's Color Correction?

When applied to images intended for display on the World Wide Web, the term *color correction* is something of a misnomer. In other circumstances, your goal in modifying the color balance of an image is to make the colors and tonal range resemble the original subject as closely as possible, before the vagaries of the photographic and scanning process make their inevitable modifications.

Ordinarily, the goal is a realistic one because you already know the ultimate destination for the image, whether it's an offset press or a monitor screen for a desktop presentation. Even if your job is to make the color of an image unrealistic (for example, extra blue and very dark to make it appear to have been taken under moonlight), you at least have a firm target to shoot for if you've properly calibrated Photoshop for your scanner, monitor, and output device.

Many of the rules go out the window when the Web is your image's final stop. As you learned in Chapter 4, the only control you may have over how an image is displayed is its size in pixels on the destination screen, and whether it's centered or placed at the left or right side of the page. The colors used to display the image may be far out of your purview.

A visitor to a Web page may be using a 256-color screen or a screen capable of displaying millions of colors. A monitor may be badly calibrated so that it shows your images much darker than you intend them to be. If you happen to like colors a little on the warm side and your visitor prefers cooler images, your carefully adjusted image may look wildly off-color.

I'm going to assume that you already have a basic understanding of color theory — at least the portion that uses the RGB color model for images manipulated by Photoshop and displayed on Web pages. Other color systems, including the CMYK (cyan/magenta/yellow/black) model used for the printed page, don't apply in the same way to Web graphics.

For our purposes here, color balance is the relationship between the three colors used to produce your image: red, green, and blue. You need to worry about only three different factors:

➥ **How much your image contains of red, green, and blue.** If you have too much of any color, the image will appear too red, too green, or too blue, respectively. Other color casts are produced by too much of *two* of the primary colors, when compared to the remaining hue. That is, too much red and green produce a yellowish cast; red and blue tilt things toward magenta, and blue and green create a cyan bias. The color wheel shown in Figure 12-1 can help you remember the relationships of these colors.

➥ **The saturation of each color**. That is, how much of the hue is composed of the pure color itself, and how much is diluted by a neutral color, such as white or black. Think of a can of red paint and white paint. Pure red paint is fully saturated. As you add white paint, the color becomes less saturated until you reach various shades of pink. Color can also become desaturated by adding *black* paint, making it darker. Your image editor can help you adjust the saturation of a color by removing these neutral white or black components.

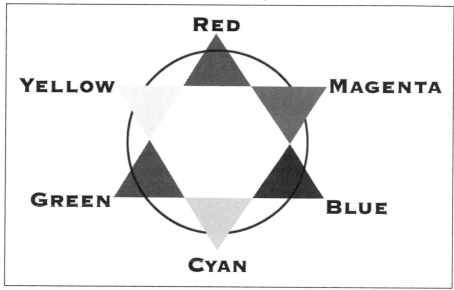

Figure 12-1: RGB colors represented as a wheel.

➡ **The brightness and contrast of the image.** Brightness and contrast refer to the relative lightness/darkness of each color channel and the number of different tones available. If, say, there are only 12 different red tones in an image, ranging from very light to very dark, with only a few tones in between, the red portion of the image can be said to have a high contrast. The brightness is determined by whether the available tones are clustered at the denser or lighter areas of the image. Pros often use something called a histogram to represent these relationships, which I'll discuss later in this chapter.

Where Does Bad Color Come From?

If you're consistently getting bad color, you might want to explore some of the reasons why. Most of the time you'll be working with images captured from color transparencies or prints, and then scanned. Most of your color problems can be traced back to the photographic or scanning steps. I describe potential trouble spots in the sections that follow.

Incorrect illumination

Color films have their own internal color balance, created under the expectation that the film will be exposed under a particular color of light. You may know from experience that daylight at high noon is much bluer than the illumination at sunset. Scientists characterize this changing proportion of colors using something called color temperature, a property measured on a scale derived from heating a mythical "black body radiator" and recording the spectrum of light it emits at a given temperature in degrees Kelvin. Daylight at noon has a color temperature in the 5500- to 6000-degree range. Indoor illumination is around 3400 degrees.

Hotter temperatures produce bluer images (think of a blue-white hot object) while cooler temperatures produce redder images (think of a dull-red glowing ember). Humans don't think quite so logically, however, and tend to call bluer images cool and redder images warm.

If a photograph is exposed indoors under warm illumination using film balanced for cooler daylight, the image will appear much too red. If you were using a daylight-balanced slide film, you'd get reddish slides. The photo-processing lab can add some blue while making prints from daylight balanced color negatives exposed under this warm light, though, giving you well-corrected prints.

Some professional film is balanced for interior (tungsten) illumination. If this film is exposed under daylight, it will appear too blue. Again, prints made from tungsten-balanced color negatives can be corrected at the lab, but the photofinisher may not always do a good job of fixing the images.

Fortunately, you can often make corrections for reddish or bluish images digitally with Photoshop. But that is not the best approach. If an image is very blue or very red, it may not have enough of the missing color to look good. Think about it: you can't add red that isn't there. Remove the excess blue, and all you may be left with is a muddy blue-gray. To avoid the need for this kind of correction, use the correct film, or use a filter over the camera lens to compensate for the incorrect light source. Color negative film is forgiving enough that you may be able to skip this step, but you'll certainly want to take preventive measures with slide film.

Fluorescent light sources

The chief difference between the tungsten and daylight sources we discussed in the previous section is the *proportion* of red and blue light. Some types of fluorescent lights lack particular shades of a color entirely. If you looked at the spectrum of colors produced by such a light source, it would contain black bands that represent the missing wavelengths of light. The normal procedure of adding some color, either with a camera filter or digitally, doesn't always work, because all of a particular hue isn't necessarily missing — only parts of it.

Instead, you need a filter available from your photo retailer that is designed for particular kinds of fluorescent lamps, and that adds only the amount and type of color needed. Since it's difficult to correct for fluorescent lights digitally, you'll want to investigate this option if you shoot many pictures under fluorescent lights and are getting greenish results.

Improper photofinishing

Automated printing equipment sometimes doesn't differentiate between indoor and outdoor pictures properly, or may be confused by images that contain large areas of a single color. Photograph Little Red Riding Hood against a black backdrop for your Web page, and you're likely to get an off-color picture back from your lab.

You'll generally only encounter these problems with color prints, as the processing of color slides won't have any effect on the color balance or density of the transparencies, unless the finisher's replenishment or regeneration systems are malfunctioning. If you often get bad color that you can trace back to your finisher, change labs. You may also ask that your prints be reprinted. You can often make corrections digitally after you've scanned the prints if the bad color is not too bad.

Mistreatment of film

Store your camera in the glove compartment or trunk of your car, or leave a roll sitting in a camera for a few months, and you're likely to end up with pictures that have an awful purple cast or some rainbow-colored flares. When you expose a picture, sensitized grains of silver in the emulsion are changed by the photons of light that strike them. If you don't develop the film right away, both the exposed and unexposed grains can be affected by chemical reactions within the film that are accelerated by heat and aging. Some exposed areas won't develop as they should, and unexposed areas may act as if they were struck by light. You end up with fogged images.

It's impossible to correct this effect in the lab or in Photoshop, so your best solution is to avoid the problem in the first place. Keep your camera in a cool place, and develop the film promptly. Keep in mind that professional and amateur film is similar internally, but that amateur film is intentionally aged to minimize the effects of the typically long time between exposure and processing. Film for professional use is fresher and provides more consistent results, but tends to suffer more from heat and latent image-keeping effects. Don't use professional film at all unless you plan to keep it at reasonable temperatures and process it promptly.

Mixed light sources

Not all pictures are exposed with a single light source. Something as simple as an indoor, window-lit portrait can introduce mixtures of blue daylight and reddish indoor light. Or, if you try to soften light by bouncing it off of a colored wall or ceiling, you'll get images with mixed colors. There's no easy way to correct for this kind of lighting, so either avoid the situation entirely or consider turning the image into an artistic black-and-white shot.

Faded colors

Sunlight can fade more than the carpet next to your patio door. No dyes are truly stable, and will undergo chemical reactions that break them down over time. The reactions are accelerated by ultraviolet light and heat, so color photographs exposed to bright illumination or a hot environment will fade or discolor quickly (usually in less than five years). Even if you keep a print, slide, or negative in the dark, it will still discolor after 5 to 20 years or more. The various color layers of the photographic product don't fade at the same pace, either, so you'll end up with a magenta or other color cast even before the image is noticeably lighter.

While you can often add the missing colors in Photoshop, you might try making a new print from the original negative — if you can find it and it isn't hopelessly scratched. Negatives often last longer than prints, even when stored under identical conditions.

Color Correction: Take 1

There are many ways to fix bad color, and I explore several of them in this chapter. I'll start out with some simple procedures.

Color balance, brightness and contrast, and saturation are all closely related; you can rarely make a change to one of these without affecting the others. Remember that color correction techniques can't *add* detail or color that isn't there. This sort of color correction works well with photographs that have too much of one hue or another. The extra color can be *removed*, leaving a well-balanced picture behind. Or, you may be able to enhance the other colors so that they are all in balance once again. Photoshop can do this by changing some pixels that are relatively close to the color you want to increase to that exact color.

Using color balance

The first way we'll color correct an image is through Photoshop's Color Balance controls. You can work with the file, Badcolor1.tif, in the Chapter 12 folder of the CD-ROM that accompanied this book. Then just follow these steps:

1. Open the Badcolor1.tif file in Photoshop.

2. Select Image ⇨ Adjust ⇨ Color Balance (or press Command-B) to produce the dialog box shown in Figure 12-2.

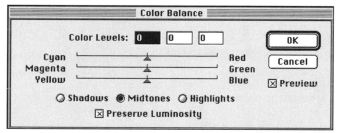

Figure 12-2: Photoshop's color balance sliders let you change only red, green, and blue values, or include cyan, magenta, and yellow as well.

3. **Make sure the Midtones button is selected.** Photoshop lets you set color balance separately for shadows, midtones, and highlights. What we're interested in at this point are the color sliders, which let you adjust the proportions of a particular color, from 0 percent to 100 percent. You may add one color, or subtract its two component colors (the colors on either side of it on the color wheel in Figure 12-1). For example, moving the Cyan/Red slider to +20 (sliding it toward the red end), has the same effect as moving both the Magenta/Green and Yellow/Red sliders to the -20 position (to the left). If you want to add pure red (or green or blue), you can move the relevant control to the right. If your needs lean a little more toward one of the component colors than the other, move those sliders to the left, instead.

4. **This photo has a strong reddish cast.** Remove this red tone by simply sliding the Cyan/Red control towards Cyan, using a value of -36. Cyan is the opposite, or complementary color of red (note that it's on the other side of the color wheel in Figure 12-1). Because Photoshop lets you preview the results, it's just a matter of subtracting red (adding cyan) until the picture looks right. In this case,

a value of -36 applied only to the middle tones of the photo (those other than the highlights or shadows) would make the picture look just about perfect. In most cases, this is all you'll need to do.

NOTE You can see that it is possible to remove red in one of two ways:

➡ Add cyan (thereby subtracting red)

➡ Add green and blue (thereby subtracting magenta and yellow)

This may be a little confusing without looking at the color wheel, but the basic rules are simple. Reduce a cast of a particular color by the following:

➡ Adding the color that is opposite it on the color wheel

➡ Subtracting the color itself

➡ Subtracting equal amounts of the adjacent colors on the color wheel

➡ Adding equal amounts of the other two colors on its color wheel triangle

If you keep the color wheel in mind, you won't find it difficult to know how to add or subtract one color from an image, whether you are working with red-green-blue or cyan-magenta-yellow color models.

Color Correction: Take 2

When color casts are not pure, it's not possible to make corrections just by adding or subtracting a single color. If your image looks a bit too red and has a slight magenta cast to it also, you'd want to manipulate several colors to make the correction. Try it for yourself with Badcolor2.tif on the CD-ROM.

1. **Open the** Badcolor2.tif **file in Photoshop.**

2. **Select Image ➪ Adjust ➪ Color Balance (or press Command-B) to produce the Color Balance dialog box again.** The biggest challenge here is deciding in exactly which direction you need to add/subtract color. Magenta may look a lot like red, and it's difficult to tell cyan from green. You may need some correction of both red and magenta, or be working with a slightly cyanish-green. Your photo retailer has color printing guide books published by Kodak and others that contain red, green, blue, cyan, magenta, and yellow viewing filters. Use them to view your image until you find the right combination of colors.

3. **This image has too much red and magenta.** Instead of adding cyan (subtracting red), we'll subtract magenta and yellow (adding green and blue, a bit more heavily on the green side). Adjust the sliders with +36 green, but only +30 blue. This has the effect of subtracting more magenta than yellow.

Color Correction: Take 3

You can also color correct an image using Photoshop's Hue/Saturation/Brightness controls. The advantage of correcting color this way is that you can change the saturation of individual colors, or of all the colors in an image, without modifying the hue or lightness/darkness of those colors. The Color Balance method changes only the relationships between the colors.

For this example, we'll use an image that has only a minor color cast problem, but which suffered from serious desaturation of its colors. The photo looks weak and lifeless. Copy Badcolor3.tif from the CD-ROM, and follow these directions:

1. **Open the** Badcolor2.tif **file in Photoshop.**
2. **Select Image ⇨ Adjust ⇨ Hue/Saturation (or press Command-V) to produce the dialog box shown in Figure 12-3.**

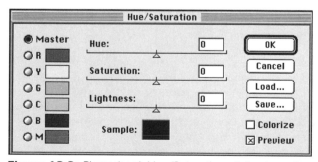

Figure 12-3: Photoshop's Hue/Saturation dialog box allows you to modify saturation and individual hues.

The Hue/Saturation/Lightness dialog box of Photoshop lets you change the richness of the colors in an image without modifying the individual colors, if you prefer. You do this by applying Saturation changes to the main, or Master, channel or layer of an image. If you need to enhance just one color, you can do that, too. The Hue control enables you to change the overall balance of the image (or one individual color layer, if you wish) by rotating the palette one direction or another around the perimeter of the color wheel.

3. **Because our sample picture has such poor saturation, we'll adjust all of the colors first.** Change the Saturation value until the picture gains, in preview mode, the richness of color you are looking for. I used a setting of +50 for our sample picture.

4. **This color is slightly off, too.** Experiment with the Hue control to find a setting that corrects any imbalance. In this case, I entered a value of -20, which moved the color balance clockwise around the color wheel away from magenta and toward pure blue. When you adjust hues for the master channel of an image, no colors are lost or removed: they are simply moved around the color wheel en masse. When you adjust the hue, saturation, or lightness of a particular channel, only that channel is affected, in contrast to the global changes you make on the combined, or master channel, which includes all of them.

5. **Now, make adjustments to the brightness of the image by moving the Lightness (or Brightness, depending on your image editor) slider.** This varies the relative darkness or lightness of all the colors in the image. If you want to change the contrast at the same time, you should use your application's Brightness/Contrast control.

Adjusting hue/saturation/brightness for one color

You may encounter images that can be improved by changing the hue, saturation, or brightness of one color only. For example, you might have a holiday picture that needs to have its reds and greens enriched and its blues muted. Perhaps the green grass and foliage in another picture picked up an undesirable color cast and you want to shift all of the green values one way or another to improve the color. Or, you may want to darken or lighten just one color in an image (rather than all of them, which is done through the conventional Lighten/Darken controls).

All of these corrections are possible with the Hue/Saturation dialog box. Just select the Color channel you want to work with and move the sliders to get the effects you want. In the next chapter I'll provide examples of images that have been modified in this way.

Color Correction: Take 4

You can play with the color balance of an image for hours at a time and never quite achieve what you are looking for. There's no guarantee that, after a lot of work, you won't decide that an earlier version looks better.

Photoshop added a Variations feature with Version 3.0, which is a take-off on the photo lab's "color ring around" service. Photoshop generates several versions of an image and arranges them in an array so that you can view a small copy of each version and compare them. Photoshop's Variations mode is especially useful, so I'll use it to illustrate a fourth way to color correct problem photos. Copy `Badcolor4.tif` from your CD-ROM, and follow these steps:

1. **Load** `Badcolor4.tif` **into Photoshop.**

2. **Choose Image ⇨ Adjust ⇨ Variations from the menu bar.** The Variations window, shown in Figure 12-4, appears.

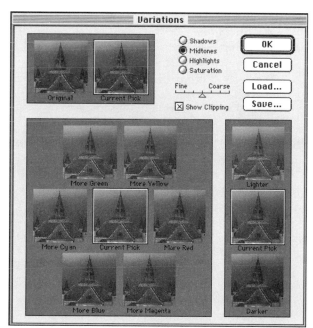

Figure 12-4: Photoshop's Variations dialog box gives you a selection of images to choose from.

There are several components to the Variations dialog box:

➟ To the upper left, you'll find a thumbnail of your original image paired with a preview of the image with the changes you've made. As you apply corrections, the Current Pick thumbnail will change.

➟ Immediately underneath these thumbnail images is another panel with the current pick surrounded by six different versions of the image, each biased toward a different color: green, yellow, red, magenta, blue, and cyan. These show what your current pick would look like with that type of correction added. You can click any of them to apply that correction to the current pick.

➟ To the right of this ring is a panel with three sample images: the current pick in the center with a lighter version above and a darker version below.

➟ In the upper right corner of this window is a group of controls that modify how the other samples are displayed.

3. **If the Midtones button is not depressed, click it.** You also want the pointer in the Fine...Coarse scale to be in the middle, and the Show Clipping box checked. The purpose of each of these controls is as follows:

➟ The radio buttons determine whether the correction options are applied to the shadows, midtones, or highlights, or the image — or only to saturation characteristics. You must make adjustments for each of these separately.

➟ The Fine...Coarse scale determines the increment used for each of the variations displayed in the two lower panels. If you select a finer increment, the differences between the current pick and each of the options will be much smaller. A coarser increment will provide more dramatic changes with each variation. You may need these to correct an original that is badly off-color. Because fine increments are difficult to detect on-screen, and coarse increments are often too drastic for tight control, I recommend keeping the pointer in the center of the scale.

➟ The Show Clipping box tells the program to show you in neon colors which areas will be converted to pure white or pure black if you apply a particular adjustment to highlight or shadow areas (midtones aren't clipped).

➟ You may Load or Save the adjustments you've made in a session so they can be applied to the image at a later time. You can use this option to create a file of settings that can be used with several similarly-balanced images, thereby correcting all of them efficiently.

4. **Our image is too red, so the More Cyan thumbnail will look bet**ter. Click it to apply that correction to the current pick. In fact, we needed to click twice, since the original image is very red.

5. **The image is also too dark. Click the Lighter thumbnail.**

6. **Click the OK button in the upper right corner of the dialog box when finished.** In this example, we worked only with the midtones. In most cases, the shadows, midtones, and highlights will need roughly the same amount of correction. In others, though, the shadows or highlights may have picked up a color cast of their own (say, reflected from an object off-camera). Variations lets you correct these separately if you need to.

Color Correction: Take 5

Although you can use Variations to manipulate the shadow-midtone-highlights to improve the appearance of images that have too-dark shadows or washed-out highlights, you'll soon find that this isn't the best way to do it. Nor will you get good results using Photoshop's Brightness/Contrast controls, which generally affect all of the colors equally. If you've been using Photoshop for any length of time, you will have found that the Levels control can be the fastest way to correct the brightness and contrast of both grayscale and color images. We'll work with the Levels control in this next section. Find Badcolor5.tif on your CD-ROM, and then follow these directions:

1. **Open** Badcolor5.tif **in Photoshop.**

2. **Use Layer ⇨ New ⇨ Adjustment Layer to produce the dialog box shown in Figure 12-5.** If you're using a version of Photoshop prior to Version 4.0, you can skip ahead to step 4. Adjustment Layers are just a way of applying certain kinds of changes without making them permanent.

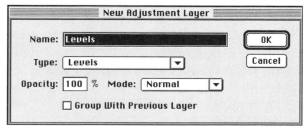

Figure 12-5: Create a Levels Adjustment Layer in this dialog box.

3. **Choose Levels from the Type drop-down list, and click OK to create the Levels Adjustment Layer.**

4. **If you skipped Step 3 because you're using Photoshop 3.0x, choose Image ⇨ Adjust ⇨ Levels to produce the Levels dialog box like the one shown in Figure 12-6.** Photoshop 4.0 users should see this box as soon as they create the new Adjustment Layer.

5. **The key component of this dialog box is the histogram in the center.** As you learn from the sidebar, "What's a Histogram?" found later in this chapter, the vertical lines represent the tones in the image. Because there are no lines representing tones at either the white or black ends of the scale, some tones are being wasted. That is, some of the 256 shades available are allocated to areas where no tones exist. Fix this by sliding the black triangle to the area where the black tones begin, and the white triangle to the area where the important white tones start, as shown in Figure 12-6. Now, the 256 available tones will be allocated in the area where image information actually exists.

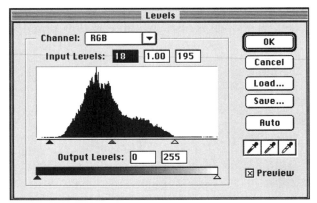

Figure 12-6: The black and white sliders have been adjusted to better represent the actual tones of the image.

6. **Now, move the gamma slider to the left.** Notice how the midtones become lighter, while the dark tones remain relatively unchanged. Stop moving the slider when the image begins to look good to you. Click OK to finish.

7. **Save this file in Photoshop format if you want to play with it again later.** The Adjustment Layer remains intact, and can be modified at any time by clicking the layer in the Layers palette.

What's a Histogram?

A histogram is a kind of bar chart, with 256 lines extending from completely black (represented by the black triangle at the left) to completely white (represented by the white triangle). In the middle is a gray triangle used to represent gamma, which measures the contrast of the midtones of the image.

A 24-bit color image can have 256 different tones for each of the red, green, and blue channels. When the Levels dialog box has RGB shown in the Channels drop-down list, the histogram represents a grayscale composite of all the tones in the image.

There are 256 lines on the histogram, one for each of those tones. The fewer tones used, the higher the contrast of the image. A typical histogram will be shaped something like a mountain, with some pixels at the black and white ends, and a peak of midtones in the middle.

Converting to 8-bit Color

Once you've corrected the color of a photograph with a full range of tones, you can save it in JPEG format and trust that the visitors who will be viewing that image at your Web site have a 16- or 24-bit display, and that their browsers will do a good job of portraying the image you've slaved over for so long. That may be all you can do in the case of photographs.

However, if you have an image that lends itself to 8-bit, 256-color display, you might want to convert the image to a 256-color GIF. As I noted in Chapter 3, GIF format is inherently sharper than JPEG, and if you perform color reduction shrewdly, even photographic images can look good. The trick is to not just change to 256 colors, but also convert to the *right* 256 colors.

Indexed color is based on the notion that many color images can be represented by far fewer than 16.7 million hues. Indeed, many can be displayed with 100 percent accuracy using only 256 different colors and produce a file size that is somewhat smaller — and one that can be easily viewed on systems that have only 256-color displays. Other images may have more colors than 256, but still look good when similar colors are combined and represented by one of the 256 in an indexed color palette.

The key is to create an optimized palette. What you don't want is an equal representation of all the colors in the spectrum. That might give you far too many blues, but not enough greens to represent a given scene. Think of a portrait of a man wearing a brown suit and a solid green tie. You may need only 10 to 20 different greens to encompass all of the subtle shades of green in the tie. Another 50 or so browns might be required for the suit. Only a few blues, yellows, or other hues would be needed. The bulk of your tones might fall into the pinks or browns that make up flesh tones. By carefully selecting the most frequently-used 256 tones in an image, you can often accurately represent a 24-bit file using 8-bit color.

Choosing a palette

Photoshop offers you a choice of methods for choosing the palette to use to convert an image to indexed color. Figure 12-7 shows Photoshop's Indexed Color dialog box.

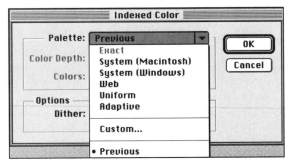

Figure 12-7: Photoshop's Indexed Color dialog box lets you choose a method to convert a 24-bit image to 8 bits.

You need to specify the three parameters used to build the color look-up table (CLUT) that will be used to convert all of the colors in your image to one of the colors in the palette. Photoshop offers eight different choices. They are as follows:

➡ **Exact.** If your image already contains 256 colors or fewer, choose Exact to get a rendition of your image that will be perfect anytime you load it into Photoshop or another application. This palette will probably look good on a Web page, too, although if all the colors in the Exact palette aren't available, there can be some variation.

➡ **System (Macintosh)** or **System (Windows).** These two choices use the default colors used by the Macintosh and Windows operating systems, respectively. They are a uniform sampling of all available RGB colors, and are likely to look good only if the colors just happen to be evenly distributed in your image (which is unlikely).

➡ **Web.** This choice uses a palette of the 216 colors most often used by Web browsers. If your image looks good using this palette, you stand a better chance of having your image look the same from browser to browser, and platform to platform. Multiple images on the same page using this same palette will all look good, too. However, if your image uses a particular set of colors (say, it's heavily laden with browns or other earth tones) you may not be able to get an accurate rendition using the standard Web palette. In that case, the Adaptive palette may be your best choice.

➡ **Uniform.** Photoshop creates a palette based on a uniform sampling of colors, depending on the color depth chosen.

➡ **Adaptive.** If this choice is selected, Photoshop will analyze your image and then build a palette using the most frequently used colors in the image. This is a good choice for photos that have colors that fall into a similar range.

➡ **Custom.** This choice lets you load a previously saved CLUT (so you can share color palettes between similar images, or apply one CLUT to a new image). You may also select the colors you want to use from a set of swatches, as you can see in Figure 12-8. You can click any of the swatches, and choose a new color from the Photoshop Color Picker. When the Color Picker is on the screen, you can also move the cursor to any image area, and select a color from there. You'd use this method if you wanted to include a particular set of colors, as you can dial in exact values in the Picker, select a color from the Picker, or grab a hue from an existing image.

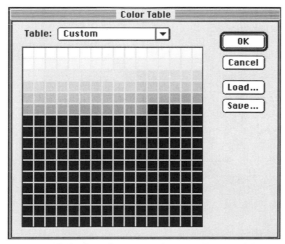

Figure 12-8: The Custom palette option enables you to choose the colors you want to use.

➥ **Previous.** This choice applies the last CLUT you used in this session. You'd use it to apply the exact same palette to a group of images, thereby ensuring that they would be represented in the same way on-screen.

Other indexing options

The Indexed Color dialog box has several other options you can set before you convert your image:

➥ **Color Depth.** This allows you to specify from 3 to 8 bits per pixel (8 to 256 different colors), if you're using the Adaptive palette.

➥ **Dither.** This parameter tells the software how to simulate colors that don't have a direct equivalent in the CLUT palette that is built. Choose None, and the software selects the closest color in the CLUT. Pattern can be used to create odd geometric arrangements of colors. You might like the special effects that result, but avoid this choice if you're looking for realistic color. Your best choice is usually Diffusion, which distributes the extra colors randomly and naturally.

Editing an existing color table

If you load an Indexed Color image into Photoshop, you can modify its CLUT by using the Image ⇨ Mode ⇨ Color Table command. The Color Table dialog box appears. You can load a new CLUT, or edit the colors by clicking the swatches and choosing a new hue for each. Built-in color tables like the ones shown in Figure 12-9 can also be loaded to replace the image's current CLUT.

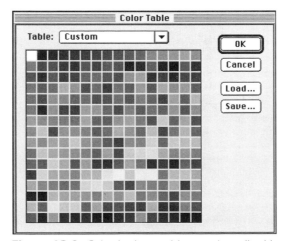

Figure 12-9: Color look-up tables can be edited later on.

Moving On

In this chapter, I've covered what you need to know to modify images and create graphics, buttons, rules, and other components for Web pages. The final section of this book will deal with related topics, including, in the next chapter, how you can best acquire images with scanners, digital cameras, and other image capture devices.

Acquiring Additional Images

One of the most challenging parts of creating cool Web pages is obtaining material to work with in Photoshop — namely, original images. Unless you're an artist, you won't want to create all of your Web images from scratch in painting mode. Unless you're a professional photographer, you may not look forward to going out and taking a snapshot every time you need a graphic.

In this chapter, I look at the two most common routes to obtaining images for Web page construction. First, I'll explore ways you can get your own images digitized and ready for manipulation by Photoshop, using digital cameras, video capture boards, and scanners.

In This Chapter

Digital Cameras

Scanners

Video Options

Sorting Out Options

As you've learned in previous chapters, images acquired for use on Web pages have special requirements that are somewhat different from those for other applications for Photoshop. You need to have a firm handle on what those requirements are before you start shopping for image acquisition hardware. The key points to keep in mind are the following:

➡ **Speed.** If you're maintaining a Web site that can benefit from frequent updates and want to keep your graphics as current as your text, the speed with which you can capture images and get them into Photoshop for tweaking can be a major consideration. In such cases, a digital camera or video capture board might make more sense than a desktop scanner, because the latter can work only with images taken with a conventional camera and then processed. Images captured as digital originals, in contrast, can be edited moments after they are taken.

➡ **Portability.** A scanner is tied to your desktop computer, so you can acquire only those images that you are able to transport to your office for scanning. However, you can capture an image with a camcorder or digital still camera almost anywhere.

➡ **Flexibility.** If you want the most photographic flexibility, you'll want to use a conventional camera, and take advantage of the vast array of options available for these traditional imaging devices. Film cameras have better, longer, faster, and sharper lenses; action-stopping shutters; and tons of accessories for in-camera special effects. Even digital cameras built around Single Lens Reflex (SLR) camera bodies aren't quite as flexible, because film cameras have the advantage of a choice of film stocks. When you need a high-speed film, ultra-sharp film, an infra-red or false color emulsion film, you have no other choice but to use a conventional camera. The flexibility of electronic capture devices, such as scanners and digital cameras, comes after the image has been grabbed in Photoshop.

➡ **Sensitivity.** If you'll be capturing images in low light conditions, make sure your digital camera is up to the task. Otherwise, use a film camera and high-speed film.

➡ **Resolution.** Since Web page images will invariably be smaller than 640 × 480 pixels, electronic cameras almost always have enough sharpness to provide more than acceptable pictures. However, if you plan to enlarge small sections of images, you'll find digital camera pictures don't blow up very well. In such cases, you'll want a conventional camera, coupled with a scanner.

Next, I explain specific hardware options in more detail, and expand on some of the advantages and disadvantages of each type of gear.

Acquisition Hardware

One of the difficulties of writing about specific hardware and software problems for a book like this is that the products change so frequently — with several upgrades usually cascading one on top of another — during the life of a particular edition of the book. In this chapter, I concentrate on specific types of gear as well as the leading vendors, and not on a particular scanner or camera model. You can use this information to get up to speed on image acquisition technology, and then make your own purchase decisions based on what you've learned.

Virtually all hardware used to digitize images can be used directly from within Photoshop, using the File ⇨ Acquire menu command, or a plug-in that can be deposited in the Filter menu. Each scanner, camera, or video capture board is furnished with its own acquisition module, often a TWAIN-compatible driver that situates itself into the File ⇨ Acquire menu automatically. TWAIN (reputedly standing for "technology without an interesting name") is a program interface that sits between Photoshop (and other TWAIN-compliant applications) and the hardware. Photoshop doesn't need to know anything about how the hardware works: it can just send the necessary commands to the TWAIN driver, which includes its own pop-up dialog boxes to handle the fine details of image acquisition. You'll find such drivers included with digital cameras and scanners, while video capture boards may interface with stand-alone applications. The following discussion introduces you to all three, and explains how they can be used as Photoshop tools.

Digital cameras

At first glance, digital cameras seem like a terrible deal. For $500 to $1,000 you get a box with less resolution and fewer features than a $100 point-and-click snapshot camera. Your electronic "film" may run out after as few as five shots, and even some pricey models are limited to a fixed field of view.

Look a little deeper and you'll find that digital cameras may have been designed with Web page crafting in mind. When you're in a hurry to update your page, forget about trotting down to the local photofinisher to develop those point-and-click snapshots. Digital images can be downloaded from a camera directly to your computer in as little as 10 to 90 seconds each, edited, squeezed down to Web-sized bites, and posted within minutes. Avoid buying a $6 roll of film and a $14 bill for finishing at the drug store a few times, and that $500 you paid for a camera with infinitely-reusable silicon "film" may look like a wise purchase. Unless your Web page requires huge numbers of images, the five to 32 or so exposures a digital camera can handle at one time should be plenty.

Digital image sharpness is nothing to be ashamed of, either. The typical 640 × 480-pixel resolution of a digital camera is a lot more than you're likely to need for a Web page image. Often, you'll crop a 128 × 128-pixel-sized section from a full digital image, or resample the picture down into a thumbnail version that can sit comfortably in one corner of a page. Even if you want to make a larger image available (for example, a visitor clicks the thumbnail in order to download a higher resolution version), 640 × 480 pixels is still more than adequate: such files make pretty good 3 × 5-inch prints on a near-photo-quality 720 dpi ink jet printer.

With almost no moving parts, digital cameras are also rugged and reliable. All digital cameras capture images focused on a charge-coupled device (CCD) similar to the imager in your camcorder, and distantly related to the RAM chips in your Mac. The CCD consists of more than 300,000 separate sensors, arranged in a 640 × 480 (or larger) array. Each tiny sensor is doped with chemicals, then covered with a red, green, or blue filter to make it sensitive to one of the primary colors of light. Photons that are focused through the camera's lens and strike the surface of the sensors change their electrical conductivity, and provide analog color and density information that can be digitized to represent the original picture. Each image is downloaded to RAM storage right in the camera. This may take five or six seconds before you can make another exposure, which is why some digital cameras are unsuitable for rapid-fire picture-taking.

Most reasonably-priced digital cameras have a fixed amount of internal RAM. Even with 1MB available, you might be limited to five to 16 high-resolution 640 × 480 images and 32 to 88 or so low-resolution 320 × 200-pixel snapshots. You'll find such a broad range in capacity because some vendors use compression to squeeze more images into RAM, while others opt for a bit more internal memory. Chinon, Kodak, and Epson are blazing a new trail with sub-$1,000 cameras that use removable PC card memory. You'll also find some digital cameras for as little as $299.

With any of these, you still need to download the images from the camera to your computer; the swappable PC cards may not be compatible with your machine even if you have a PC card-equipped PowerBook or notebook PC. These cards are handy, but you really better need the extra capacity — a 16MB card can easily cost more than the camera.

Digital images are ported from the camera to your computer through a serial cable and acquisition software provided by the vendor. As you might expect, sending a 24-bit image through a serial connection one bit at a time can be extremely slow. It can take 10 to 90 seconds to download each image. Expect some companies to introduce image card readers that attach to your computer through a SCSI port. Remove the card from the camera, slip it in the reader, and you can download images up to eight times faster than without it.

Once in your computer, digital camera images can be retouched, cropped, edited, and stored in a format suitable for page-building. Figure 13-1 shows a digital image I captured with a high-end Kodak digital camera.

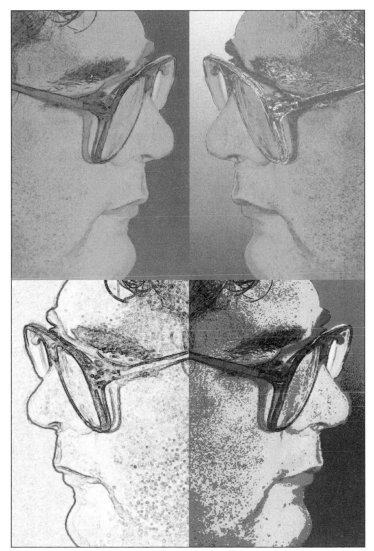

Figure 13-1: Digital cameras can capture sharp images, but are much more expensive than snapshot cameras with equivalent image quality.

What's available

Web architects should avoid both the low and high ends of the digital camera field. Megabuck cameras like those from Kodak, Canon, and others that are built on a professional, interchangeable lens, such as a Canon lens or

Nikon SLR frame, can cost as much as $28,000! However, they boast up to 3,000 × 2,000-pixel resolution (good enough for making 11 × 14-inch enlargements) and other features that are overkill when all you need are mini-pix for a Web page. Digital cameras for specialized applications — such as scientific documentation and photojournalism — are priced from $3,000 to $16,000 and also include features that Web page graphics don't need.

At the low end, the $99 eyeball-on-a-stalk cameras may not have enough resolution and, worse, only grab images in black-and-white. Stick to cameras that can snap pictures in 24-bit color (which you can reduce down to 256 colors for Web use) at 320 × 240 to 640 × 480 pixels.

What to buy

Although there are fewer than a dozen digital cameras on the market that are priced less than $1,000 and are practical for capturing images for the Web, expect to see many more offerings in the coming months as the technology matures. The following are some key points to consider when shopping for a digital camera:

1. **Resolution.** While 320 × 240 may actually be a higher resolution than required for moderately-sized images on HTML pages, resolutions of 640 × 480 pixels and up are far from wasted. Very coarse images are difficult to touch up, and you may have little latitude for cropping. A big, generous image gives you lots to work with in an image editor like Photoshop, as well as the ability to use small portions of the image without losing details in a swarm of pixels. You can always resample an image that is too big down to a smaller size for efficient Web posting — going the other way is difficult.

2. **Storage space.** Look for a camera that can handle the number of images you expect to collect between downloads to your computer. If your desktop system or a laptop will be close at hand most of the time, a camera that can store only five to 16 pictures will do the job nicely. If you expect to wander far afield before you can dump the images, favor a camera with a lot of storage space, or one that uses replaceable PC cards.

3. **Compression scheme.** Cameras that use JPEG or other compression utilities to squeeze more images into available RAM may inadvertently cost you some image quality. You can always compress images later before they are embedded in your Web page, so consider cameras that let *you* decide when and how much to compress the raw pictures.

4. **Lens/Exposure options.** Fixed-focus cameras with a single field of view are okay for grabbing shots. But if you want the most flexibility in subject matter and the best quality over a variety of shooting conditions, look for a camera with adjustable focus or an optional macro attachment; a wide range of shutter speed and aperture combinations (even if they are set automatically); and, possibly, a zoom lens. The latter feature isn't an absolute necessity, however. In most cases, you can always take a few steps back, or move in closer to your subject.

The video option

Video capture devices are another option — even for those who only want still images for their Web pages. Video capture devices enable you to grab stills with your camcorder or retrieve a choice image from any existing videotape, videodisc, or television broadcast. The down side is that video captures are often a little too fuzzy for use on a Web page, as video shot indoors may have been exposed using a relatively slow shutter speed, accentuated by a shaky-handed photographer. At 30 frames-per-second on a television monitor the images can look okay, but may not be up to snuff for still use. Hi-8 camcorders, which have higher resolution CCD sensors, when mounted on a tripod give the best results. I've been very happy with the video captures I've grabbed from a Sony camcorder and have used quite a few in this book. Figure 13-2 shows a sample of an image captured with a camcorder imported into a PC with Minolta's Snappy capture hardware, and manipulated in Photoshop.

Most PCs can have video capture added, and some older AV Macs as well as newer high-end Power Macs and Performas have video capture built in. Just plug in a composite video or S-video connection from your video source, run the acquisition software (Apple is currently supplying a program from Avid), and go. Other, more fully-featured video capture devices fit inside your computer, and there are still more that function as external modules that can be used with any desktop or laptop computer equipped with a serial port and the right software.

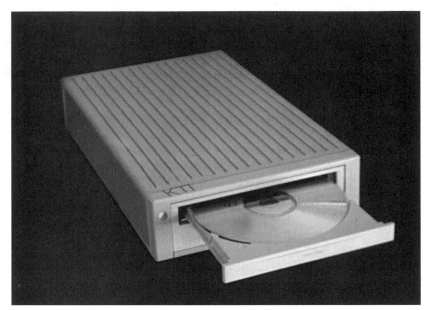

Figure 13-2: Even camcorder images can look good after they are processed in Photoshop.

Scanners

Most scanners these days come with both Mac and Windows software, and work equally well with both platforms. The Windows version may be provided with a proprietary SCSI card that works only with that scanner (and not with other SCSI peripherals you have), but drivers are also provided for use with a SCSI adapter already in your computer.

A scanner will be your first choice for capturing images for your Web page if you already have a lot of photographs or slides to use as a graphics source, or have the time to produce such pictures using conventional cameras, have them processed, and then scanned. Most scanners used for images these days fall into one of three categories: flatbed, hand-held, and slide scanners.

With only a couple exceptions, these devices all work by capturing an image a line at a time using a moving light source/sensor bar with 2,550 to 5,100 tiny CCDs arrayed across its width. The familiar flatbed scanner looks and works a lot like a digital photocopier, and is able to grab images from anything you can lay down on its glass platen. Hand-held scanners, which look like overgrown mice, are best for original images measuring about four inches or less wide (although, their software can "stitch" multiple passes together into a single image). Since flatbed scanners have dipped down to the $300 price level, hand-held models at $150-$400 have become less common.

If you're not in a hurry to get your images into Photoshop, you'll be happiest with a flatbed scanner. Some great models are available for $399 to $1,000. At the high end of the price range, you can get the latest HP ScanJet, which in its current incarnation offers 600 dpi, an 8.5 × 14-inch scanning bed, and the capability to capture 30-bit, billion-colors images. Check out HP's Web page at `http://www.hp.com` for more information about its scanner line.

While you think you might not need such high resolution and color depth for your Web pages, think again. A 600 dpi scanner lets you capture tiny images — say, engravings such as postage stamps — without losing important details. A stamp measuring .75 × .75 inches would produce an image just 450 × 450 pixels in size — not entirely outside the realm of Web graphics.

Nor will a billion colors go to waste in a Web image you've boiled down to 256 hues. Scanners like the HP ScanJet use their extra color depth to pull details out of inky shadows while retaining information in the lighter portions. You'll appreciate the ability to grab those images, and then decide on your own what to keep and what to throw away.

Umax is another leading vendor with affordable models dipping down to the $399 price range. Many Umax scanners are especially practical for LAN-linked users. They are furnished with drivers that allow the scanner to be controlled by any workstation on a network.

Other industry pacesetters include Microtek, which boasts a broad line of scanners that include everything from $399 entry-level models to pro-quality high-end scanners. And Canon (`http://www.usa.canon.com`) specializes in tiny 24-bit color models that won't hog your desktop.

While many flatbed color scanners can be fitted with a transparency attachment for around $700, you'll get better results from a dedicated slide scanner like the Nikon CoolScan scanner line. The Nikon and similar models do a better job of meeting the tough resolution requirements of the tiny 1 × 1.5-inch slide originals, since their high-resolution sensors (up to 2,700 dpi) are optimized for grabbing the broad range of tones you'll find in color transparencies.

You can find out more about digital scanners and cameras at my Web site, http://www.dbusch.com/Scanners/.

Another Option

Can't justify $500 or more for a digital camera or desktop scanner? If you have a CD-ROM drive (which costs about the same as a hand scanner and has a lot more uses), Kodak's Photo CD format can be your gateway to a wealth of high-quality images. You'll sacrifice only the fast turnaround that the other options offer. Just snap the images you want to include in your Web page with your existing snapshot camera, then ask for a Photo CD disc when you take the roll of film in for processing.

For about $20 more, your photofinisher can provide a CD-ROM-like disc with your images stored in five compressed Image Pacs, each at a different resolution ranging from 128 × 192-pixel thumbnails to more useful 512 × 768 "base" images to whopping 2,048 × 3,072 (18MB) Base X 16 versions. You can buy clip art and stock photos in Photo CD format as well. If you can wait a few days to get your pictures back in digital format, Photo CD saves you the expense of buying a scanner or digital camera, and provides a handy way to store digital images permanently without burdening your hard drive. Kodak's Web site (http://www.kodak.com) includes a form that you can fill out to find the closest vendor of Photo CD services in your area.

Moving On

Electronic cameras, scanners, and video capture devices can keep you supplied with plenty of digital images for your Web graphics. But what if you need a picture that you can't take yourself? Unless you live near a wild animal park, if you need a photo of an elephant thundering across the plain, you'll need some other sources for artwork. In the next chapter, I'll show you some good places to find low-cost or free images.

Finding Images

Not all people who work with Photoshop are photographers, even if they do tend to know quite a bit about photography, graphic arts, and imaging in general. If you're one who manipulates pictures more than originates them, your Web page work will have you constantly in search of new images to use. While, as you've seen in previous chapters, it's possible to create many stunning effects from scratch with Photoshop, when you need a picture of an elephant driving a car, somewhere along the line you'll have to locate a photo of an elephant, one showing a car, or, preferably, one that includes both.

This chapter offers tips for obtaining original images beyond those included on the CD-ROM packaged with this book. You'll learn how to scour the Web for photos, and I'll provide some links to a few especially suitable sites.

Clip Art

Although the term *clip art* has come to embrace any kind of image, in its original sense clip art is just that: printed images that you could clip out and paste into layouts for use in advertisements, brochures, newsletters, or whatever. Clip art illustrations are generic drawings, usually prepared by professional artists. Traditionally, clip art has been published in hardcopy form for use by graphics professionals. Clip books are printed on glossy paper on only one side of the page, so the images can be cut out and pasted directly onto a finished mechanical. Frequently, each illustration is supplied in several sizes, so additional reduction or enlargement steps are not usually required. Clip art is most frequently black-and-white line art, but more advanced renderings may also be included in some collections.

The artwork is offered more or less royalty-free. You are entitled to use it just about any way you wish without crediting the company. A key exception is that you can't include the artwork in a clip art collection of your own and sell it. Companies such as Dover Publications in Mineola, New York, and Dynamic Graphics in Peoria, Illinois, still do an excellent business producing original artwork of this type for business and advertising applications.

Most clip art of this type is line art that you can scan and open within Photoshop as bitmapped images. In such cases, the higher the resolution you use when scanning, the better the image will look and (perhaps) the better you'll be able to scale it up or down to fit your particular application. A typical example of line clip art is shown in Figure 14-1.

Figure 14-1: Typical line clip art like this is available from many different sources.

It's more common today for computer users to purchase this kind of clip art on CD-ROMs. These discs can easily hold 20,000 to 30,000 different images, which are usually cataloged in an accompanying guidebook. If you have an illustration package like Adobe Illustrator, Macromind FreeHand, or Corel Draw for the Macintosh, your software probably came with a good selection of line clip art. CorelDraw, for example, includes 25,000 clip art images and 1,000 photographs.

Other discs are available from companies such as Nova Development, which offers *Web Explosion 20,000*, a disc with 8,000 buttons, bullets and banners; 10,000 color clip art images and photos; and a 150-page printed catalog of the images. All of the images are already in GIF and JPEG formats. The company also offers *Art Explosion 40,000*, with twice as many images in EPS format (which can be imported into Photoshop), and 1,200 TrueType fonts.

ClickArt's incredible *Image Pak 65,000* ups the ante with 60,000 EPS and TIFF images; 5,000 photographs in JPEG format; and a huge 1,000-page full-color, fully indexed Visual Catalog. (It's software, folks!) Not enough images? Zedcor's *DeskGallery Megabundle* includes a mind-boggling 100,000 images in symbol, plant, animal, advertising, and lifestyles/occupations categories, all shown in a 1,100-page catalog.

There are a lot of applications for line art of this kind in Web design, since clean black-and-white artwork looks good and downloads quickly, and the color images and photos on these clip art discs also can be adapted in Photoshop for Web use.

Stock Photography

Advertising agencies and publishers have long drawn on stock photography houses for the images they need, and you can do the same for your Web pages. Stock photo collections are storehouses of images provided by professional photographers for "rent" and single use in publications or presentations. The fees vary depending on the use and size of the potential audience, as well as the content of the picture and the reputation of the photographer. If you just need a photo of an elephant, you can find one easily and pay only a small fee. If you decide you simply must have Dorothea Lange's famous photo of the migrant mother, prepare to cough up some cash. An example of the kind of stock photography you can expect to find is shown in Figure 14-2.

Web sites, even commercial ones, are unlikely to need expensive stock images. Fortunately, the CD-ROM comes to the rescue again. You'll find hundreds of discs of images that can be used on a virtually royalty-free basis for many applications. There will always be a restriction against recycling the images in a clip art collection of your own, but in most cases, once you've paid the fee for the photograph, you're free to use it as you wish.

Figure 14-2: Stock photography can be found to illustrate virtually any concept.

Corel, for example, offers an extensive collection of images in its Corel Stock Photo Libraries. There are three different libraries, each with 20,000 royalty-free images on 200 (yup, 200) CD-ROMs, and a mind-numbing price of about $900 per library. You can also buy individual discs for $20 to $40 if you're interested in a specific type of image. PhotoDisc and Image Gallery also have extensive lines of photographic stock discs.

While you're collecting clip art and photographic CD-ROMs, don't neglect some specialized offerings from Auto F/X. Their *TypoGraphic Edges, Photo/Graphic Edges,* and *Page/Edges* CD-ROMs are multivolume collections of very cool special-edge effects and textures you can use in Photoshop.

Other Sources for Images

There are many other sources of good Web-adaptable images that you can investigate, both offline and online. This section has some suggestions you'll want to explore.

Material with expired copyrights

A good source of copyright-free clip art is books published more than 75 years ago. Anything printed before 1922 can frequently be scanned and reused with few restrictions. I regularly haunt used bookstores looking for books with steel engravings, woodcuts, and other illustrations that can be used as charming illustrations in Web pages.

 What are the restrictions? You can't, for example, use the registered logo of a company — even if you happen to find it in a very old book — or a picture of the cartoon character, Popeye. The particular image might not be protected under copyright, but the logo or character is.

On the one hand, very old clip art probably looks dated. Illustrations of Victorian gentlemen and ladies playing croquet would look out of place in any sort of high-tech-oriented Web page — unless you want to cultivate an old-time image. Yet, these images would be quite suitable for, say, a page specializing in home-style recipes or anything dealing with nostalgia. The key is to use antique clip art in an appropriate manner and not to mix it with a more contemporary look in the same publication, chapter, or article. Figure 14-3 shows a page featuring an old image I collected on one of my forays.

Figure 14-3: Old books can be a source of good clip art for Web pages.

The best old books to look through are dictionaries and encyclopedias. They have many small illustrations, and you can look alphabetically for the topic you want to illustrate. Textbooks that cover the subject in which you are interested also make good sources. Don't overlook old college year-books for school- and sports-oriented drawings with a period look. I've found these for as little as 10 cents. Most of the other old books I use cost no more than two or three dollars. These editions are often damaged and of no use, even as reading copies, so you don't have to feel guilty about dis-mantling them.

Public domain work

Strictly speaking, works on which the copyright has expired pass into the public domain. However, some illustrations are created specifically for unrestricted use and are never copyrighted at all. Government publications are one example — you can often use artwork from publications prepared at public expense without any restrictions.

You can use illustrations from government publications in your own work if you wish. The Superintendent of Documents in Washington, DC, can pro-vide you with a list of available publications. Many are free, while others cost a few dollars.

The government also has many sources of photographs and other non-line art that you can obtain at low cost and use in your publications. The resources are too extensive to list here. Try the individual agencies that supervise your areas of interest. For example, the U.S. Forestry Service has an extensive library of aerial photographs. Satellite and space pho-tographs can be obtained from several agencies. Figure 14-4 is an example of government artwork.

Copyrighted works

Sometimes, you may be able to scan and use copyrighted material legally simply by asking the permission of the copyright holder, who may ask you to include a credit line. Rights to materials published in magazines may belong to the publication, the artist, or the photographer. Start with the magazine, unless the artwork has a credit line you can easily track down. Only line art can be usefully scanned from publications. If you want to reuse a photograph, you'll have to get the original to scan.

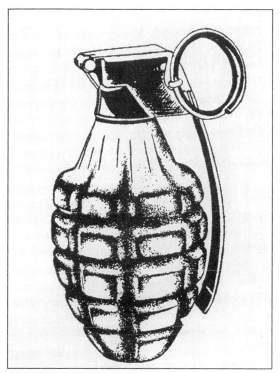

Figure 14-4: This image was created by the U.S. Government — but you're free to use it on your Web page.

Reference libraries

I've put the reference departments of public libraries, universities, and businesses as a separate category because they are often overlooked as sources for clip art. You'll find a great deal more than books in these libraries. They also hold brochures, photographs, drawings, and other materials.

Don't confine yourself to the obvious areas. Each university department may have a library of its own. The School of Architecture may have more drawings of buildings than the university's central library. Some of them may be student work that you can use with permission at no cost.

Businesses typically have libraries of their own, often specializing in a particular industry. If I wanted some pictures of babies or similar material that I couldn't find elsewhere, I'd probably check with Gerber before giving up.

Copyright questions

Keep copyright considerations in mind when you grab clip art for your own use — particularly if you're running a commercial Web site for a corporation with deep pockets. The issues involved are complex. For example, even if you create an image yourself, that's no guarantee you can use it. You can't draw your own rendition of Mickey Mouse and expect to use it with impunity, even if you are clever and make a few changes — like giving the rodent ten-fingered gloves.

Images can cause legal problems for you in other ways. If you take a photograph yourself, you still may not be allowed to use it if the people pictured are recognizable. A special document called a *photo release form* should be signed by each person in the picture, giving you permission to use his or her image in your publication. Most photo stores have pads of these releases you can use. Note that a photo release offers some protection, but is never absolutely ironclad. If you do a lot of scanning of such images, you might want to consult with an attorney who knows the field and who can also draw up a more binding release for you.

Locating Images Online

The Web itself is a treasure-trove of royalty-free clip art, including photographs, fractal backgrounds, line art, logos, and tons of other stuff available for downloading. Some can be used at no cost, while others entail a reasonable fee.

Clip Art and Image Paradise
`http://www.cybercomm.net/~pagemake/cliplist.html`
Links to more than 300, incredibly useful clip art servers, ftp sites, Web pages with free samples, government agencies with propaganda art to peddle, and other locations. There are 20 major category headings, such as Aircraft, Animals, Flags, Fractals, Icons, Landscapes, People, Space, and Transparent Images, each with a dozen or more links. This site is a treasure-trove — and it's free.

Casey's Page Mill, Ltd.
`http://www.caseyspm.com:80/`
Information about obtaining high-resolution, royalty-free photos on Photo CD.

Over The Rainbow
`http://cameo.softwarelabs.com/gini/index.htm`
A free service provided by Software Labs, a good source of graphics, clip art, HTML files, and shareware, in addition to images. Icon

librarian Anthony Thyssen has collected quite a few useful icons intended primarily for Windows users, but many have been converted to GIF format for HTML use.

Fractal Nirvana Club
http://www.algonet.se/~dip/kpt_b.htm
If you want to know what can be done with KPT Fractal Explorer, check out this site.

Metatools
http://www.metatools.com/metauniv/clipindex.html
A clip art library of amazing Web graphics that you can freely use in your own pages.

Dave's site
http://www.dbusch.com
If you're serious about photography, you'll want to check out many of the photography and scanning links you can find online, including my own site!

HyperZine
http://www.hyperzine.com
Includes photography and scanning links.

The National Press Photographers Association
http://sunsite.unc.edu/nppa
Candid assessments of equipment, film, and other products, and links to digital galleries.

The Digital Camera Club
http://www.digicam.org
You might want to explore the first online digital camera club at this site.

The New York Institute of Photography
http://www.nyip.com
Another good jumping-off place for photography.

PhotoDirect
http://www.photodirect.com/text/index.html
A site for digital portfolios.

Of course, you can always conduct your own searches for Web image sources using search engines like Yahoo! or AltaVista (http://www.yahoo.com and http://www.altavista.com, respectively). Yahoo! is an organized collection of sites with well-designed categories. AltaVista, on the other hand, is a massive repository of site information, gleaned by indexing virtually every word on every page of millions of Web sites. You can enter simple or complex searches with all kinds of AND/OR qualifiers, and turn up hundreds of hits. Type in "photo AND elephant" and you're likely to turn up thousands of possibilities, as I did recently.

Moving On →

Collecting images for Web pages can be a lot of work, but it's fun, too. You'll find that some of the eclectic graphics you turn up during your quests may, in fact, give you ideas for new page layouts or themes. Another way to spark your creativity is to use one of the many add-on products available to enhance Photoshop's capabilities. I'll look at several products in this category in the next chapter.

Beyond
Photoshop

In your quest for the ultimate Web page, don't be afraid to go beyond Photoshop to embrace some cool third-party plug-ins that work right within your image editor. The add-ons we'll look at in this chapter give you a powerful arsenal of special effects for that distinct look that makes your page stand out from the crowd.

KPT Convolver

If fine-tuning basic filter effects is your forte, you'll want KPT Convolver, from those amazing folks at MetaTools. This often-overlooked product is an Adobe Photoshop-compatible filter that offers complete dominion over image-tweaking parameters like relief angle, intensity, or tint, for a variety of blurring, sharpening, embossing, and hue-bending effects. For example, Convolver lets you mix filters in fine increments to meld edge detection with relief effects in one-of-a-kind combinations. A typical KPT Convolver effect is shown in Figure 15-1.

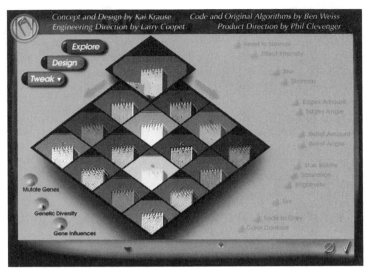

Figure 15-1: KPT Convolver offers effects like these.

Add the traditional Kai Krause interface-from-Mars, and you have a plug-in that's as powerful and temporarily disorienting as a direct hit from a Maui breaker. Once you get your bearings, you'll find that Convolver can replace most of the filters you're already using. You can use it to create textured backgrounds or tweak buttons and rules to the exact effect you want.

Convolver — a "fat" application for both Power Macs and 040/030 models with a floating point unit (FPU) — is also available in a Windows/Windows 95 version. The program has three modes. All operate so quickly that they lend themselves to wild experimentation. In Explore mode, a selection is previewed in 15 diamond-shaped slices, plus a larger window. Click the Mutate Genes button to generate 15 random versions. The Genetic Diversity button controls the amount of variation in the effects in five steps, while Genetic Influences produces a list of effects that will be combined in each new generation: Blur/Sharpen, Embossing, Edge Detection, Hue, Saturation, Brightness, Contrast, and Tint. You can choose and investigate any combination.

Tweak mode is a production tool that manipulates parameters individually using percentages; you can also specify edge or relief angle and amount or color contrast. The full preview area can be used to perform image correction and enhancement on a larger portion of your image, using combinations of conventional filter effects. Unlimited Undo allows backtracking to any desired point in the process.

Design mode assigns any filter parameter to two axes — the sample images displayed in the diamond preview area incorporate increasing amounts of the factors you've selected. Choose Edge Detection and Relief, for example, and you'll see an array of samples with combinations of both effects applied.

The 3D interface is quirky, but superior to the decade-old Macintosh/Windows conventions. Instead of using sliders to enter values, you click on a control and drag from side to side as the new values are displayed in a status bar. Controls that are not currently in use fade into the background, but pop back into view when you click them.

Convolver rewards intense use by progressively unveiling four new tools: a split-screen preview facility; a slick tint wheel that serves as a joystick-like color balancer; a set of nine memory dot scratch pads that can store effects combinations for instant recall; and an animation feature. A few minutes with this tool will convince you that the rewards are worth the journey.

Kai's Power Tools

This is the basic Photoshop plug-in set that everyone should have. The latest upgrade transforms this essential package into an integrated set of filter applications with the control and expanded real-time preview windows that serious image workers have been yearning for. A new Spheroid Designer, an incredible tool for creating 3D rounded buttons; revamped KPT Lens f/x, which provides KPT Convolver-like combinations of blur, noise, edge-finding, and smudging, and is also great for making buttons; and the texture-melding Interform plug-in, add wild new effects to the redesigned toolkit.

Previous versions of the MetaTools flagship product scattered dialog-less, single-step filters and several applications like Texture Explorer throughout your Photoshop Filter submenus. KPT 3.0 collects everything under a single listing, which also includes a Help entry. A typical KPT effect is shown in Figure 15-2.

Several groups of the old single-step filters — such as noise, edge, and pixel diffusing modules — are combined into a lens-like tool that can be moved around your image to preview effects as you "dial" them in. Even formerly unpredictable loose cannons like Vortex Tiling gain a dialog box that offers control over vortex angle, style, opacity, and composite effects. Some of KPT's more limited effects, such as Page Curl, take on a new life when given added controls and options.

Figure 15-2: A typical Kai's Power Tools effect is applied to a Web button.

Experimenters will love the new 4X larger previews (and an option to see a full-screen version before applying the effect), better controls, and a powerful, non-linear undo feature. KPT remembers your last 35 actions, which can be undone in any order.

The new effects will please those looking for new f/x worlds to conquer. Spheroid Designer creates three-dimensional spheres, complete with realistic ray-traced surfaces, using light sources, curvature, bump map textures, and transparency specified by the user. KPT Interform combines the look of any two Texture Explorer textures you select and combines them, either as a new texture, or in an animated QuickTime movie.

Also added are Planar Tiling, Twirl, and Video Feedback effects. Older tools like Gradient Designer and Texture Explorer have refinements such as hue, saturation, brightness, contrast, and blur tweaking. Try out the texture and fractal tools for creating eye-catching backgrounds for your Web pages.

KPT 3's installation routine doesn't overwrite or remove your earlier Version 2.1 filters, which can remain in your plug-in folder if you want. For example, those who have an extensive collection of Fractal or Texture Explorer presets will want to keep their older plug-ins, since the new engine can't use them.

This latest version of the serious image editor's most important add-on tool is a significant upgrade, with enough new features to satisfy the most jaded graphics professional. The quirky Kai Krause-designed interface — always a breeze to use, but a struggle to learn — has been made more friendly for new users without slowing down experienced workers.

KPT Bryce

Another entry from MetaTools, KPT Bryce doesn't plug into Photoshop. Instead, it's a single-function, stand-alone tool for designing realistic renditions of earthly or surreal other-worldly terrain. It is the 3D modeling equivalent of a paint-by-numbers set. Even if you have no artistic skill and think a wireframe is an eyeglass style, you can create breathtaking landscapes overnight. Drop one of these scenes into your Web page for an instant sci-fi moodsetter.

That's meant literally, too: a bare bones mountain scene measuring a mere 520 x 354 pixels took 32 minutes to render on a Quadra 650, then another half hour was spent antialiasing the results. More ambitious terrain designers will want to set up the program to render whole batches of images before retiring, then get up early to see what Bryce has wrought while they slept.

A color Mac with math coprocessor and 6MB of RAM is the minimum hardware necessary to run Bryce, and, since a Power Macintosh native version isn't available yet, Bryce should run its fastest on a speedy 68040-based Mac.

You never expected 3D modeling — even though strictly limited to landscapes — to be this easy. Using a typically Kai Krause-quirky interface (vaguely reminiscent of the Kai's Power Tools Photoshop plug-in), KPT Bryce (code-named in development after Utah's Bryce Canyon — the name stuck) quickly leads you through all the steps needed to generate your own scene. Choose sky and terrain types from a library of pre-set textures or your own creations, and populate your world with the objects supplied or those you design. An included CD-ROM has hundreds from which to choose.

Though un-Mac-like, the tools are powerful and easy to use: just click a control in its palette and drag to produce immediate on-screen effects in the wireframe preview model. Make your adjustments, add some fog and atmosphere, choose an angle, then start the rendering process. Bryce starts by painting a preview window with an extremely coarse rendition, then gradually brings the image into sharper focus as it calculates texture, lighting, and shading over the course of many minutes.

Paint-by-numbers never produced results that were as good as those you'd expect from a professional. KPT Bryce can give you something that's *better* than the output of pro 3D modelers: it can incorporate your own vision and creativity.

Terrazzo

Xaos Tools' Terrazzo is an image-enhancing filter and pattern factory, disguised as an Adobe Photoshop plug-in filter. It can quickly generate a never-ending array of kaleidoscopic patterns from portions of an image, while allowing the digital artist to control opacity, transitions, saturation, and dozens of other parameters. These patterns lend themselves to Web page backgrounds if you fade them out in Photoshop so that they're not quite so overpowering.

If you want to generate "tileable" patterns, spice up your images with wondrous textures, create imaginative textile designs, or just play with abstract geometry, you should add Terrazzo to your plug-in library. A typical Terrazzo effect is shown in Figure 15-3.

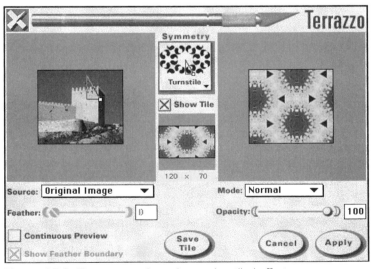

Figure 15-3: Terrazzo produces interesting tiled effects.

You can apply Terrazzo's transformations to an entire image or just a selection of an image. In either case, the filter's dialog box allows you to choose a portion of the original image — or another file, if you wish — to be reflected and twisted based on one of 17 different kaleidoscope-like symmetrical patterns. Warping an existing image is a slick way to generate patterns that are automatically color-coordinated.

Your tiles are built by reflecting, rotating, and repeating the portion of the image you select. Choose from Pinwheel, Whirlpool, Sunflower, or another arrangement, and then play with Terrazzos' controls in real time to preview thousands of effects in minutes. Xaos warns that this "continuous preview" can slow down some color Macs, but on anything faster than a Quadra 650, the display will be updated instantaneously.

The boundaries between portions of the pattern can be feathered to produce a smooth transition, and you may adjust opacity so that the underlying image shows through to varying degrees.

A Mode menu — which operates similar to the Mode menu in Photoshop — lets you control how the pattern is applied to a selection. The overlay can modify the image through Lighten, Darken, Hue, Saturation, Color, Luminosity, and other parameters.

Terrazzo can save patterns as PICT files that can be tiled seamlessly, for use as desktop wallpaper, or backgrounds in presentations or other images. The program is accompanied by a full-color manual that leads you through the process of creating stunning patterns and textures, with a generous gallery of examples.

The Black Box

The original version of Alien Skin's Black Box Photoshop-compatible image filters held more surprises than a moonlight drive and foggy windows. Now, navigating with four all-new special effects and six holdovers is more precise, thanks to the addition of a preview window and user-defined settings to the latest edition. Applying motion blurs, swirls, or bevel, cutout, and glass effects to selections — including those within Photoshop layers — has never been easier. A typical effect from this plug-in is shown in Figure 15-4.

Figure 15-4: The Black Box offers a selection of great filter effects.

Adobe now includes some Actions macros that duplicate some of The Black Box's effects (for example, drop shadows), but the rest of the effects are cool, and have many applications on Web pages. The add-on's spiffed-up 3D interface includes a preview that pans around the image, a Settings list of presets (with names like Scooped Out, Ugly Ridges, or Very Smooth). Save your own settings by clicking a camera icon.

All filters can be applied to Photoshop layers, so effects can be merged with various levels of transparency using the Opacity sliders. Although you can Undo all filters, several — such as the Drop Shadow, Outer Bevel, and Glow — "lose" the current selection if it isn't saved first.

New filters include Inner Bevel, Carve, Cutout, and Motion Trail. The first two are variations on the Outer Bevel and Glass filters from the original package. All create an adjustable-width bevel that appears to be sunk into the surface of the image (Inner Bevel), raised above it (Outer Bevel), roughly carved into the selection (Carve), or coated with a shiny raised layer (Glass).

The new Cutout filter turns the selection into a hole in the image with a feathered shadow, much as the original Drop Shadow filter adds a soft silhouette behind a selection. Both allow you to specify the opacity, shadow color, amount of blur, and x/y offsets for the shadow.

Motion Trail smears the selection in one direction, as if the object were photographed while moving rapidly. The blur direction is selectable from a rotating wheel, and sliders control the length and opacity of the smear effect. HSB Noise adds random texture to RGB images using subtle variations of hue, saturation, and brightness.

Swirl remains the coolest filter in The Black Box, creating unique, outrageously swirly effects unlike those provided by any other filter. Different transformations result from experimenting with the average spacing for the randomly-spaced whirlpools, the length of the smears, and the amount of twist.

While some of Black Box's effects, such as Drop Shadow and Glow (which adds a neon backlight to your selection), can be achieved using Photoshop commands, and even programmed yourself using Actions, these filters encourage experimenting with two or three variations in about the time it would take you to select, feather, and add Gaussian Blur to a manually-created drop shadow.

Though accelerated for Power Macintoshes, The Black Box remains slow on 680X0 Macs. On a Quadra 650 with 24MB of RAM (16MB of it set aside for Photoshop using the Get Info setting), it took 10 to 15 seconds to preview most effects, and up to a minute to apply them to moderate-sized selections. The Windows version of this plug-in set is also relatively slow. While many of this packages' effects may seem to be just variations on a theme, they're all useful and worth the modest price.

Andromeda Filters

Two series of filters are available from Andromeda Software: the Series 1 Photography filters and Series 2 3D filters. The Series 1 filters include the cMulti and sMulti filters to create kaleidoscopic effects; Designs Pattern bends and warps a 102-pattern library; Designs Mezzo converts continuous tone images to a mezzo-line screen effect; Rainbow, Prism, and Diffract are used for spectral effects; Halo is used for controlled highlight diffusion; Reflection, for clear pool reflections; Star, for adding glints and sparks to night lights or glossy surfaces; Velocity, for unique motion trails.

The Series 2 filters let you wrap an image onto a shaded 3D surface. You may shift, scale, rotate, or tile the image. The variable viewing angle and distance provides many perspectives. You can work with a resizable predefined sphere, cylinder, plane, or box in any color or render the image transparent. The filters feature a movable light source, and high-quality, anti-aliased 3D images.

Paint Alchemy

Here's another entry from Xaos Tools. Paint Alchemy ranks as one of the most flexible and interesting image processing add-ons, particularly if you're looking for more artistic brush type effects than those built into Photoshop.

Paint Alchemy is a user-configurable, brush-stroke filter that is furnished with 36 predesigned brushes (50 more are available for $20) and 75 preset styles such as Pointillist, Screen Door, Ripple, or Sponge Print. In addition, any grayscale PICT file can be imported as a brush.

Parameters such as Color, Size, Angle, and Transparency are available from handy "file folder" tabbed dialogs and sets of slider controls. Brush strokes can be varied according to the hue, saturation, or brightness of the pixels being painted over. You can paint a scenic image's blue skies with one type of brush and amber waves of grain with another, if you like.

Moving On

Given Photoshop's popularity, you can count on third-party vendors introducing a constant array of plug-ins and add-ons that you can use to enhance your Web page graphics. Don't forget the dozens of shareware filters available online.

Now that I've taken you beyond Photoshop, I'll go beyond basic HTML in the final chapter of this book to examine what changes in how pages are prepared and used you can expect in the future, and how they may affect you.

Beyond HMTL

If you're serious about creating cool Web pages with Photoshop, this book should just be your starting point. Even after you've mastered creating graphics and placing them in Web pages, you'll want to explore all the non-image-related tags and features of HTML, and probably become proficient with a WYSIWYG Web page authoring program such as PageMill. There are also alternate types of multimedia technologies, from virtual reality 3D worlds to streaming video, along with dozens of site administration tasks to learn.

In this final chapter of the book, I give you a preview of what may lie ahead for you, today and in the future. I also look at why Web pages aren't just for the Web anymore, and at some of the alternate technologies that may take your Photoshop graphics to broader audiences than you ever dreamed.

In This Chapter

New Uses for HTML

Other Applications for Web Pages

What to Expect in the Future

Emerging Uses for HTML

When you think of HTML you probably think of Web pages, and with good reason. Today, most beginning HTML authors get started creating pages for distribution on the World Wide Web. However, the applications for HTML are still in their infancy. It's probably safe to say that in the future Web applications will make up only a fraction of the uses for HTML.

Some 18 or so years ago, many business owners purchased Apple II computers just so they could run an early spreadsheet program called VisiCalc. Recently, I've seen dozens of my photographer friends buy Macs or PCs solely to get access to Photoshop. Yet, every new user of a personal computer discovers that they can do so much more than run spreadsheet or image editing programs. HTML, too, has a lot more potential than just Internet applications. In this section, I look at some of them.

Corporate intranet information systems

Not all Web sites are publicly available over the Internet. Indeed, the largest application for Web-style pages in the future may well be for corporate intranets, which use HTML pages to distribute information internally to employees over an organization's network. Netscape estimates that 90 percent of all Fortune 1,000 companies already have an intranet up and running.

An intranet is set up and operated much like an Internet Web site. It consists of a server; TCP/IP protocols that are used for communication between the server and individual users, or clients; and the same graphics-rich HTML pages you learned to create in this book. The key differences (not all of which have an impact on how you create graphics) include the following:

➡ Intranets are much, much faster to access than an Internet site, since internal networks operate hundreds of times more quickly than a 28.8Kbps modem or even an ISDN connection. That makes the information more accessible, and means that you, a Web page designer, can use larger, more detailed Photoshop graphics without bogging down your users. If you've been trying to keep individual images smaller than about 20K, you'll find that richer-looking 50K images are now feasible over an intranet.

➡ Intranets are typically available only to the workers at a particular organization, and the goals of these Web pages are slightly different. Intranets are designed to provide a company with a better and more efficient way to communicate, rather than capture the attention of reluctant viewers. So, your Photoshop graphics will need to be more down-to-earth, rather than flashy. Buttons, images, and other components you create must help lead employees to the information they need, instead of distract them from their jobs.

➡ Intranets potentially offer a more standardized environment for your graphics. If you know, for example, that everyone in the company who will be viewing your pages has a video display with at least 800 × 600 or 832 × 624 resolution, you can create larger, more vivid images and know that they can be viewed as you intended. A company that standardizes on browsers, hardware, or other variables can make the Web designer's life a lot easier.

➡ If you're working within a corporate environment, even if you're the internal Webmaster, you'll often need to work with other authors and information providers while maintaining the company intranet. Why? One of the strengths of intranets is that HTML pages are easy enough to format and create that vital information can be collected, maintained, and posted by those who actually have the responsibility for that data. Instead of waiting in a queue while the information systems staff gets enough time to prepare a Web page, project leaders, middle managers, and others can all provide updates on their own. If they like, pages can be updated weekly, daily, or hourly. In contrast to working on a World Wide Web-oriented site, you may find yourself creating pages and graphics in concert with — or even in competition with — others.

➡ Because they are internal, intranets can easily include more sensitive and proprietary information than what is usually found in World Wide Web sites.

For some types of communication, intranets threaten to partially supplant humongous groupware environments such as Lotus Notes — although, oddly enough, the latest release of Notes itself includes a built-in quasi-Web browser and support for connections to URLs. Lotus also announced Domino II, a Web server that merges Internet protocols with Notes-like functions.

Working with graphics for an intranet has a hidden advantage, too. An internal Web site provides a corporation with the opportunity to gain experience and to get all of the bugs out of the system — out of the eye of public scrutiny — before the organization rolls out onto public Internet Web pages. Figure 16-1 shows how a typical company intranet might look.

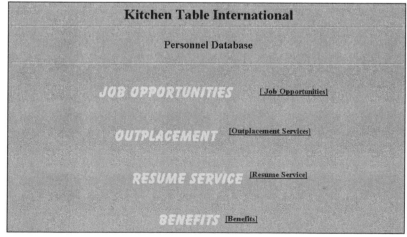

Figure 16-1: Intranets offer the opportunity to disseminate information efficiently to employees.

Other Applications for Your Web Graphics

HTML makes creating attractive, interactive pages so easy, and lends itself to other cool applications for your Photoshop graphics. These applications are described in the sections that follow.

Catalogs

A catalog that can be viewed with any Web browser is a flexible, easily modified sales tool. You can actually create the catalog using another Adobe application (PageMaker 6.5 or Framemaker 5.1.1), drag images you've created in Photoshop directly into the new HTML pages, and add links to move customers quickly from one product to another, entice them with photographs, or lead them to an order page. Small catalogs with efficiently-sized JPEG images can easily fit on a floppy disk and be mailed out with a brochure. Larger catalogs can be copied to a CD-ROM. As a bonus, you can place the exact same material on your Web page for online access. A typical catalog-type application is shown in Figure 16-2.

Figure 16-2: Catalog pages can be attractively formatted with HTML.

Desktop presentations

If you'd rather not master a complex desktop presentation package, such as Adobe Persuasion, you can easily create sophisticated desktop slide shows using Photoshop, then format the productions in PageMill, PageMaker, or another HTML authoring tool. The presentation can proceed in linear fashion like most such productions if you like. Just place Forward and Back buttons on the pages to link to preceding and subsequent pages. However, there's no reason why you can't include links to other branches of the presentation, allowing the presenter to jump around if he or she senses that the audience would be better served by viewing different sections, or seeing the material in a different order. This technique makes it possible to create one presentation that can be given to employees, customers, stockholders, new recruits, and other audiences, and customized on-the-fly.

Photo galleries

You've got tons of great images you've manipulated in Photoshop. Why not create an image gallery for a portfolio or clip art CD-ROM? Thumbnails can be displayed on some pages, with full-size images available for viewing with a click on a link. A whole disk full of images can be sorted, previewed, and presented with a well-organized set of pages. This is a good way for photographers to distribute portfolios. Images that have been compressed using the JPEG file format may amount to 20 to 30K of disk space each, so it's possible to include a fair number of pictures, even on a floppy disk. Figure 16-3 shows a photo gallery formatted as an HTML page.

Software distribution

Place your software on a CD-ROM, use Photoshop to create or modify screen shots that you can couple with descriptions of the software. Then, build into your pages a link that viewers can use to "download" the software to their hard disks. For security reasons, HTML doesn't allow you to execute installer programs directly, but is perfectly capable of opening a standard File Save window that the user can activate to transfer software from your CD-ROM to his or her computer's hard drive.

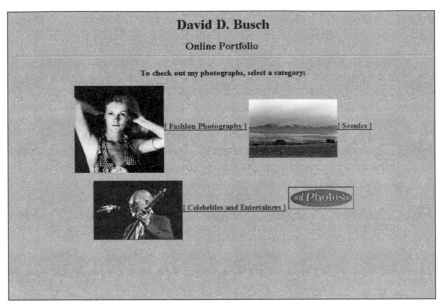

Figure 16-3: HTML pages can effectively present photographers' portfolios.

Employee "business card" databases

Here's a perfect intranet application: Some fast-growing companies may add employees at a 50 to 100 percent clip for the business' first few years. It makes sense to produce pages with a head shot or picture of a new employee at work on an HTML page, packed with background information, a job description, and how he or she fits into the organization. Other workers can access the page immediately to match a name with a face and job, and then refer to it in the future as they renew dealings with an individual.

Memos and reports

Here's another intranet goodie: Even routine memos can become more memorable when they're delivered with attached graphics you create in Photoshop. Who says a memo or other document can't be done as an HTML page, especially if a special occasion — such as a product introduction — warrants it?

Training

Multimedia authoring software is complex to learn, and time-consuming to use. Simple kinds of training can be done as HTML pages that can be distributed on a CD-ROM or over a company intranet. Your Photoshop images can lead students through new tasks on a step-by-step basis. If necessary, employees can download the pages and graphics to their own computers, use a browser as needed, and then erase the pages and/or graphics when finished.

Employee newsletters

Why fill up your corporate newsletter with bowling scores when you can display images of the actual bowlers? Seriously, not only can a company newsletter be spiced up with Photoshop images, but it can be opened to submissions from anyone with a digital camera, camcorder, or scanner. Or, you can accept snapshots and digitize them yourself, then update the company newsletter as often as required.

Farther Down the Road

Within the next few years, the need for Web-style pages will expand dramatically because of some new technologies that are on the horizon, but not quite ready for prime time. This section describes some of them.

Better display and faster access

We have spent a lot of time in this book learning how to create Photoshop images that are compatible with the lowest common denominators of Web access: slow modems and small, coarse display screens. In the future, both these limitations should vanish. As older computers are replaced, full-color computers with 832×624 screens capable of displaying thousands of colors will become a virtual standard.

Working with larger, full-color JPEG images will become practical from a display standpoint. Progressive (interlaced) and transparent JPEG images will eliminate much of the need for those old 256-color GIFs before long.

Faster access will make larger image files and bandwidth hogs like image maps more practical. The key question is how we'll get faster Internet connections. The current crop of 33.3Kbps modems are just about the speediest possible with analog phone lines. Indeed, most users of this device find they rarely are able to connect at speeds much faster than 24 to 26Kbps, anyway. There are a few 56Kbps modems on the market, but they only work that fast when they are communicating with a special digital modem on the other end. Some users have satellite modems that *download* at high rates from signals beamed from orbiting platforms — but still require conventional (slow) modem connections over phone lines to send commands and upload.

ISDN (Integrated Services Digital Network or, popularly, It Still Does Nothing) service offers 56 to 128Kbps connections, but your home or office must be relatively close to the telephone company's switching office (typically five to six miles). Moreover, ISDN is still relatively expensive, and most ISPs don't support it, anyway.

Cable modems are great if you live in a city that offers that service. Keep in mind that cable modems give you super-high speeds only between your home and office computer and the cable company's server. The rest of the Internet can be accessed quickly, too, but you'll still suffer the same wait for a response. Downloading pages and graphics very, very quickly is less attractive if you have to wait 30 seconds for the remote server to start delivering. Will we all be using juiced-up T1 direct lines? Not at $1,000 or more per month.

So, what's the key to faster access to the Internet in the future? I can't even hazard a guess at this point, but I am confident of one thing: the popularity and potential of the Internet is strong enough that some combination of the technologies I just mentioned, or something entirely new, will definitely be perfected in order to tap all the demand for Internet access. When everyone has quick connections to the Net, designers like yourself will benefit from greater freedom to use Photoshop to create the dazzling graphics you've always wanted to show to the world.

Beyond HTML 3.2

When extensions to HTML were largely the whim of large software developers like Netscape and Microsoft, the Web was a mess. We had pages that could only be viewed with a particular release of Netscape Navigator, and others that looked best on Microsoft Internet Explorer. Web designers often used HTML features for the sole reason that, like climbing Mt. Everest, they were there. That led to a proliferation of blinking, scrolling, marquee-laden pages with dozens of useless frames or other artifacts that were difficult for Internet neophytes to navigate, and even confusing to Internet veterans.

When you consider that, even today, most Internet visitors are neophytes, you'll see why piling dozens of extensions onto HTML haphazardly wasn't a good idea. Fortunately, the language has been taken under the wing of the International Standards Organization (ISO)'s World Wide Web Consortium (W3C), an organization that seeks to guide standards related to the World Wide Web and that works in concert with the Internet Engineering Task Force. Funded by contributions from a diversity of member organizations, we can expect the W3C to lead us to a more organized, structured approach to expanding the HTML specification in the future. Look for extensions that support newer graphics formats, like PNG, and perhaps even Web graphics with layers, animation, and other features — something like the animated GIF features already available.

Beyond HTML, expect programming and scripting languages such as Java and JavaScript; application program interfaces (APIs) such as Microsoft's ActiveX; and applets, plug-ins, and controls, like Apple's QuickTime; to expand the capabilities of graphics on the Net.

Java is a C++-type language developed by Sun Microsystems that turns the Web from an information delivery system to an interactive environment, by enabling developers to create small applets that can download and run automatically on any platform (Mac, Windows, Unix, and so on). It has a browser with an interpreter capable of interpreting Java code. Incoming Java applets are recognized as MIME (Multipurpose Internet Mail Extensions) type files that require the Java interpreter, already included in Netscape and Microsoft Internet Explorer. If the browser doesn't support Java, the Web page can display a still image or text message instead.

Java applets can display a series of Photoshop-generated images as a slide show, or perform other online magic. Java frees developers from the vagaries of developing applications in Perl for Common Gateway Interface (CGI)-compatible servers. Java takes the workload from the server and puts it on the client workstation, which can be a significant benefit with graphics-intensive applications. It can easily be used to create animated sequences, scrolling text, slides shows, and other content.

Of course, Java applications won't run until the entire applet is transferred, either directly from a Web page, or when embedded in an e-mail or news-group message. The delay isn't usually a problem over a fast connection.

Moving On

It's time to move on now, creating cool Web pages with Photoshop 4 and the techniques you've learned in this book. As I said at the beginning of this chapter, the material I presented should just be the beginning. Tackle some other books on HTML crafting, if you like, but the real key is to just create as many pages as you can, trying out new ideas you see elsewhere on the Internet, and melding them with your own imagination.

Glossary

Appendix A

This glossary contains words used in *Creating Cool Photoshop 4 Web Graphics* that you might not understand, and other terms you might encounter either when working with Photoshop, or when creating or traversing Web pages. Although I tried to define most words you might not understand the first time they were used in this book, you'll find this guide a handy place to look up terms without hunting through the index.

Additive colors: The primary colors of light — red, green, and blue — which, when combined, produce white light. Your monitor or TV is probably the most common source for RGB images you see on a regular basis, and most Photoshop images are manipulated in this mode.

Adjustment layer: A new kind of layer added to Photoshop 4.0 used to preview changes to one or more other layers without actually applying those changes until you are ready.

Alpha channel: An optional, grayscale layer of an image created to store selections and other modifications, and saved with the image if it is stored in TIFF or Photoshop's proprietary PSD format. See also *Channel.*

Ambient lighting: The overall directionless lighting that fills an area.

Anamorphic: An image that has been enlarged or reduced more in one direction than another. The image looks squashed or stretched in a given dimension.

Antialiasing: A process that can be used to remove jaggies or stair-stepping in an image. Antialiasing smoothes out diagonal lines by placing dots of an in-between tone in appropriate places.

Animation: Computer graphics used to prepare moving sequences of images. On the World Wide Web, you'll find animations in the form of animated GIFs and QuickTime movies, among other formats.

Aspect ratio: The relative proportion of the length and width of an image.

Attribute: Characteristics of a page, character, or object, such as line width, fill, underlining, boldface, or font.

Authoring tool or **authoring system:** Software that generates code from the user's input, such as HTML.

Background: In Photoshop, the background is the bottom layer of an image. In Web pages, the background is the color or image that appears behind the page's text or image content.

Backlighting: A lighting effect produced when the main light source is located behind the subject. If no frontlighting, fill, or ambient lighting is used in conjunction with backlighting, the effect is a silhouette. You can simulate backlighting with filters.

Bit: A binary digit — either a 1 or a 0. Image files typically use multiple bits to represent information about each pixel of an image. A 1-bit image can store only black or white information about a pixel. A 2-bit image can include 16-bit ("thousands of colors" or 65,535 hues) and 24-bit color ("millions of colors" or 16.8 million hues).

Bit map: A representation of an image in row and column format in which each individual pixel is represented by a number. A single bit, up to as many as 32, can be used to represent a larger amount of gray or color information about the pixel. You'll often hear service bureaus and others talking about a bit map as a bilevel, black-and-white image.

Blend: To create a more realistic transition between image areas, as with Photoshop's Smudge tool. Image editing software will often allow you to merge overlapping sections of images to blend the boundary between them.

Blur: To soften part of an image, making it less distinct.

Brightness: The balance of light and dark shades in an image. See also *Luminance*.

Browser: An Internet application, such as Netscape or Microsoft Internet Explorer, that lets users access World Wide Web servers and view HTML pages and other content.

Buffer: An area of computer memory set aside by a computer or an application like Photoshop to store information meant for some sort of Input/Output, such as printing or writing to disk.

Burn: In photography, to expose part of a print for a longer period, making it darker than it would be with a straight exposure. Photoshop's equivalent is the Burn mode of the Toning tool.

Byte: Eight bits, which can represent any number from 0000000 to 11111111 binary (0 to 255 decimal).

Cache: A fast memory buffer used to store information read from disk or from slower RAM that allows the operating system to access the information more quickly.

Calibration: A process used to correct for the variation in output from a device like a printer or monitor when compared to the original image data you get from the scanner.

Cast: A tinge of color in an image, particularly an undesired color.

CCD: Charge-Coupled Device. A type of solid state sensor used in scanners and video capture devices. Compared to older imaging devices, including video tubes, CCDs are more sensitive and less prone to memory problems that can cause blurring of images.

CERN: Centre European Researche Nucleare. The Center for High-Energy Physics in Geneva, Switzerland; the birthplace of the World Wide Web, which is now overseen by the World Wide Web Consortium (W3C).

CGI: The Common Gateway Interface. A way in which Web clients such as a browser can pass input to Web servers and on to specific programs written to the CGI specification.

Channel: One of the layers that make up an image. An RGB image has three channels: one each for the red, green, and blue information. A CMYK image has four channels: cyan, magenta, yellow, and black. A grayscale image contains just one channel. Additional masking channels, or *alpha channels*, can be added to any of these.

Chroma: Color or hue.

Clickable image: A graphic in an HTML document that can be clicked to retrieve associated URLs and content.

Client pull: A method through which a Web browser instructs a server to send it a particular set of data.

Clip art: Artwork that is purchased or otherwise available for scanning or other uses in desktop publishing with few restrictions.

Clipboard: A memory buffer that can hold images and text so that they can be freely interchanged within and between Macintosh applications. Photoshop uses its own internal clipboard, but can export and import to and from the Mac's Clipboard.

Clone: In image editing, to copy pixels from one part of an image to another, as with Photoshop's Rubber Stamp tool.

Color correction: Changing the color balance of an image to produce a desired effect, usually a more accurate representation of the colors in an image.

Color depth: The number of bits of information used to represent color values in an image; the higher the number of bits, the greater the number of colors (and shades) that can be represented.

Color wheel: A circle representing the spectrum of visible colors.

Complementary color: Generally, the opposite hue of a color on a color wheel, which is called the direct complement. For example, green is the direct complement of magenta. There are also two other types of complements: the split complement (a color 30 degrees away from the direct complementary color) and the triadic (a color 120 degrees in either direction from the selected color).

Compression: Packing a file or image in a more efficient form to improve storage efficiency.

Constrain: To limit in some way, as to limit the movement of a selection by holding down the Shift key as you begin to move it with the mouse.

Continuous tone: Images that contain tones from black to white with an infinite range of variations in between.

Contrast: The range between the lightest and darkest tones in an image.

Convolve: To twist, roll, or twine together. As applied to imaging, the term is used to describe the way filters use the values of surrounding pixels to calculate new values when generating a special effect, as with MetaTools' KPT Convolver.

Crop: To trim an image or page by adjusting the side or boundaries.

CYMK color model: A model that defines all possible colors in percentages of cyan, magenta, yellow, and black.

Darken: A feature found in Photoshop that allows gray values in selected areas to be changed, one value at a time, from the current value to a darker one. This is equivalent to the burning procedure used in conventional darkrooms.

Default: A preset option or value that is used unless you specify otherwise.

Defringe: To remove the outer-edged pixels of a selection, usually to merge the selection with the underlying image more smoothly.

Desaturate: To reduce the purity or vividness of a color. Desaturated colors appear washed out and diluted.

Diffusion: The random distribution of gray tones in an area of an image, often used to produce a mezzotint effect.

Digitize: To convert information, usually analog information, such as that found in continuous tone images (or music), to a numeric format that can be accepted by a computer.

Dithering: A method of simulating gray tones by grouping the dots shown on your CRT display or produced by your printer into large clusters of varying size. The mind merges these clusters and the surrounding white background into different tones of gray.

DNS: Domain Name Service. An Internet service that maps symbolic names (like www.dbusch.com) to actual IP addresses.

Dodge: In photography, to block part of an image as it is exposed to lighten its tones.

Dot: A unit used to represent a portion of an image. A dot can correspond to one of the pixels used to capture or show an image on the screen, or groups of pixels can be collected to produce larger printer dots of varying sizes to represent gray.

Dots per inch: The resolution of an image, expressed in the number of pixels or printer dots in an inch. Abbreviated dpi. Scanner resolution is also commonly expressed in dpi but, technically, scanners use an optical technique that makes *samples per inch* a more accurate term.

Download: To receive a file from another device. For example, soft fonts are downloaded from your computer to your printer.

Downsampling: To reduce the number of colors or bit depth, or otherwise lower the amount of data details in a graphics file.

Dynamic RAM: Type of memory that must be electrically refreshed many times each second to avoid loss of the contents. All computers use dynamic RAM to store programs, data, video information, and the operating system.

Emboss: To change an image or selection so it appears to be raised above the surface, for a 3D effect.

Export: To transfer text or images from a document to another format.

Eye Dropper: An image editing tool that is used to pick up color from one part of an image so that the color can be used to paint or draw with elsewhere.

Feather: To fade the edges of a selection to produce a less-noticeable transition.

File: A collection of information, usually data or a program, that has been given a name and allocated sectors by the operating system.

File format: A set way in which a particular application stores information on a disk. This standardization makes it possible for different applications to load each others' files, since they know what to expect from a predictable file format. PICT and TIFF are examples of image file formats found on the Mac.

Filter: In image processing, a device used to process an image — to blur, sharpen, or otherwise change it. Programs like Adobe Photoshop have advanced filters that will spherize, change perspective, and add patterns to selected portions of the image.

Fill: To cover a selected area with a tone or pattern. Fills can be solid, transparent, or have a gradient transition from one color or tone to another.

Flat: A low-contrast image. Also, the assembled and registered negatives or positives used to expose a printing plate.

Floating selection: A selection that has been pasted into an image from another image or layer is said to be floating. It's above and not part of the underlying image; that is, you can move it around without affecting the image beneath. Once it has been defloated, the selection becomes part of the underlying pixels, and cannot be moved or cut without leaving a hole.

Font: A group of letters, numbers, and symbols in one size and typeface. Garamond and Helvetica are typefaces; 11-point Helvetica Bold is a font.

Fractal: A kind of image in which each component is made up of ever smaller versions of the component. Sets of fractal images can be calculated using formulas developed by mathematicians such as Mandelbrot and Julia, and used as textures in images with tools like KPT Fractal Explorer. More recently, fractal calculations have been used to highly compress image files: when the image is decompressed, fractal components are used to simulate portions that were discarded during the archiving process.

Frame grabber: A device that captures a single field of a video scanner or camera.

Frequency: The number of lines per inch in a halftone screen.

FTP: File Transfer Protocol. An Internet protocol used to provide network file transfer between any two network nodes for which a user has file access rights (especially a remote host and your local host or desktop machine).

Gamma: A numerical way of representing the contrast of an image, shown as the slope of a line depicting tones from white to black.

Gamma correction: A method for changing the brightness, contrast, or color balance of an image by assigning new values to the gray or color tones of an image. Gamma correction can be either linear or nonlinear. Linear correction applies the same amount of change to all the tones. Nonlinear correction varies the changes tone by tone, or in highlight, mid-tone, and shadow areas separately to produce a more accurate or improved appearance.

Gamut: A range of color values. Colors present in an image that cannot be represented by a particular process, such as offset printing or CRT display, are said to be out of gamut.

Gaussian blur: A method of diffusing an image by using a bell-shaped curve to calculate which pixels will be blurred, rather than uniformly blurring all pixels in the selected area.

Gigabyte: A billion bytes of information; a thousand megabytes. Only ten 8.5 x 11-inch full color images scanned at 600 dpi would be needed to fill up a gigabyte of disk space.

Grayscale: The spectrum of different gray values an image can have.

Guides: New to Photoshop 4.0, a set of user-defined grid lines used to help position objects in an image.

Handles: Small squares that appear in the corners (and often at the sides) of a square that are used to define an area to be scanned, or an object in an image editing program. The user can grab the handles with the mouse cursor and resize the area or object.

Helper application: An application that is invoked by a Web browser but runs in a separate window on your desktop to display or play back information that the browser cannot directly handle.

Highlight: The brightest values in a continuous tone image.

Histogram: A bar-like graph that shows the distribution of gray tones in an image.

Host: A computer that provides services to users, usually through a unique name and network address.

HSB color model: A model that defines all possible colors by specifying a particular hue and then adding or subtracting percentages of black or white.

HTML: Hypertext Markup Language. The computer code that tells a Web browser what to place on a page and where to place it. By convention, a file containing HTML code ends with an *.html* or *.htm* file extension. HTML is derived from SGML, or Standard General Markup Language.

HTTP: Hypertext Transfer Protocol. The TCP/IP-based communications protocol developed for the World Wide Web. HTTP defines how a browser and host servers communicate.

Hypermedia: Any of the methods of computer-based information delivery — including text, graphics, video, animation, and sound — that can be interlinked and treated as a single collection of information.

Hypertext: A method of organizing text, graphics, and other data for computer use that lets individual data elements point to one another; a nonlinear method of organizing information, especially text.

Hue: A pure color. In nature, there is a continuous range of hues.

Image acquisition: Capturing a digitized version of a hard copy or real-world image, as with a scanner or video camera.

Input: Incoming information. Input may be supplied to the computer by the user or to a program by either the user or a data file.

Instruction cache: A type of high speed memory used to store the commands that the microprocessor used most recently. A cache "hit" can eliminate the need to access slower RAM or the hard disk, thus increasing the effective speed of the system.

Interlacing: A way of displaying a video image in two fields: odd-numbered lines first, even-numbered lines second, thereby having to update or refresh only half of the image on the screen at a time.

Image map: An HTML object identified by the <ISMAP> tag, an image map is a graphical image that has an associated map file that lets users select links by clicking certain portions of the image. Also called a clickable image or clickable map.

Internet: The worldwide, TCP/IP-based, networked computing community with millions of users that links together government, business, research, industry, education, and individuals. The World Wide Web is one portion of the Internet.

Intranet: An internal, TCP/IP-based network within an organization that is based around the same services as the Internet, which may or may not be accessible to or through the Internet.

IP: Internet Protocol is the primary network protocol for the TCP/IP protocol suite.

ISP: Internet Service Provider. Any entity that provides Internet access to a consumer, usually for a fee. Most commonly, ISP is used to refer to an independent, third-party access business. However, ISP is often also used to refer to online services, such as CompuServe and America Online, through which a user can access the Internet.

Interactive: Allowing user input during run time.

Interpolation: A technique used when resizing or changing the resolution of an image to calculate the value of pixels that must be created to produce the new size or resolution desired. Interpolation uses the tone and color of the pixels surrounding each new pixel to estimate the correct parameters.

Invert: To change an image into its negative. Black becomes white, white becomes black, dark gray becomes light gray, and so on. Colors are also changed to the complementary color: green becomes magenta, blue turns to yellow, and red is changed to cyan.

I/O: Input/Output. Used to describe the process in which information flows to and from the microprocessor or computer through peripherals such as scanners, disk drives, modems, CRT screens, and printers.

Jaggies: Staircasing of lines that are not perfectly horizontal or vertical. Jaggies are produced when the pixels used to portray a slanted line aren't small enough to be invisible, because of the high contrast of the line and its surrounding pixels, for example, at the edges of letters.

JPEG compression: Reducing the size of an image through algorithms specified by the Joint Photographic Experts Group. The image is divided into blocks, and all the pixels within the block are compared. Depending on the quality level chosen by the user, some of the pixel information is discarded as the file is compressed. For example, if all of the pixels in a block are very close in value, they may be represented by a single number, rather than the individual values.

K: Kilobyte. In computer terminology, 1 K is equal to 1,024, so that 16K represents 16,384; 64K equals 65,536; 512K corresponds to 524,288; and so on.

Layers: Separate, transparent overlays of a drawing or image, which can be edited or manipulated separately, yet combined to provide a single drawing or image.

Layer mask: A kind of grayscale mask applied only to one layer of a Photoshop image.

Leading: The amount of vertical spacing between lines of text from baseline to baseline.

Lens flare: In photography, an effect produced by the reflection of light internally among elements of an optical lens. Bright light sources within or just outside the field of view causes lens flare. It can be reduced by the use of coatings on the lens elements or with the use of lens hoods, but photographers (and now digital image workers) have learned to use it as a creative element.

Lighten: An image editing function that is the equivalent to the photographic darkroom technique of dodging. Gray tones in a specific area of an image are gradually changed to lighter values.

Line art: Usually, images that consist only of black and white lines.

Linking: The ability to join several Photoshop layers together.

Luminance: The brightness or intensity of an image. Determined by the amount of gray in a hue, luminance reflects the lightness or darkness of a color. See also *Saturation.*

LZW compression: A method of compacting TIFF files using the Lempel-Zev Welch compression algorithm. It produces an average compression ratio of 2:1, but larger savings are produced with line art and continuous tone images with large areas of similar tonal values.

Magic Wand: A tool that selects contiguous pixels that have the same brightness value, or that of a range you select.

Mapping: Assigning colors or grays in an image.

Marquee: The selection tool used to mark rectangular areas.

Mask: To cover part of an image so that it won't be affected by other operations.

Midtones: Parts of an image with tones of an intermediate value, usually in the 25 to 75 percent range.

Navigator palette: The new Photoshop 4.0 palette that can be used to move the cursor and viewed area of an image quickly, using a miniature preview.

NCSA: National Center for Supercomputing Applications. The arm of the University of Illinois that originally developed Mosaic, the first World Wide Web browser generally accessible to the public and justifiably credited with today's tremendous popularity of the Web.

Negative: A representation of an image in which the tones are reversed. That is, blacks are shown as white, and vice versa.

Neutral color: In RGB mode, a color in which red, green, and blue are present in equal amounts, producing a gray.

Noise: Random pixels added to an image to increase apparent graininess.

NTSC: National Television Standard Code. The standard for video in the United States.

Opacity: The opposite of transparency; the degree to which a layer obscures the view of the layer beneath. High opacity means low transparency.

Point: A unit of typographic measurement. There are approximately 72 points in one inch.

Palette: A set of tones or colors available to produce an image, or a row of icons representing tools that can be used.

Parallel: To move data several bits at a time, rather than one at a time. Usually, parallel operation involves sending all eight bits of a byte along eight separate data paths at one time.

Parameter: A qualifier that defines more precisely what a program is to do.

Peripheral: Any hardware part of a computer system other than the microprocessor itself and its directly accessible memory. We usually think of peripherals as printers, modems, and so on.

Photo CD: A special type of CD-ROM developed by the Eastman Kodak Company that can store high-quality photographic images in a special space-saving format, along with music and other data. Photo CDs can be accessed by CD-ROM XA-compatible drives, using Kodak-supplied software, or through compatible programs such as Photoshop.

PICT: A graphic image and file format used by the Macintosh and its Clipboard. PICT2 is an enhanced version, which can be used in both 8-bit and 24-bit formats.

Pixel: A picture element of a screen image; one dot of the collection that makes up an image.

Plug-in: A module that can be accessed from within a program like Photoshop to provide special functions. Many plug-ins are image processing filters that offer special effects.

Point: Approximately $1/72$ of an inch outside the Macintosh world, exactly $1/72$ of an inch within it. Points are used by printers to measure things like type and other vertically oriented objects.

Portable Network Graphics: A new RGB file format supported by Photoshop 4.0. It offers progressive, interleaved display, like GIF and progressive JPEG, for the gradual display of images on Web pages, but it is lossless (unlike JPEG, which can discard some image information).

Portrait: The orientation of a page in which the longest dimension is vertical; also called tall orientation.

Posterization: A photographic effect produced by reducing the number of gray tones in an image to a level at which the tones are shown as bands, as on a poster.

Raster image: An image defined as a set of pixels or dots in row and column format.

Rasterize: The process of turning an outline-oriented image, such as a PostScript file or an Adobe Illustrator drawing into a bit-mapped image.

Ray tracing: A method of producing realistic highlights, shadows, and reflections in 3D by projecting the path of an imaginary beam of light from a particular location back to the viewpoint of the observer.

Rendering: To produce a realistic 3D image from a drawing or other data.

Resampling: The process of changing the resolution of an image, adding pixels through interpolation, or removing pixels to reduce resolution.

Rescaling: The operation of changing the dimensions of an image by reducing the height and width in proportion to its overall dimensions.

Response time: The amount of time between the transmission of a request for service and the arrival of the corresponding response.

Resolution: The number of pixels or dots per inch in an image, whether it is displayed on the screen or printed.

Retouch: To edit an image, usually to remove flaws or to create a new effect.

RGB color correction: A color correction system based on adjusting the levels of red, green, and blue in an image.

RGB color model: A way of defining all possible colors as percentages of red, green, and blue.

Rubber Stamp: A tool that copies or clones part of an image to another area.

Saturation: The purity of a color. An attribute that describes the degree to which a pure color is diluted with white or gray. A color with low color saturation appears washed out; a highly saturated color is pure and vivid.

Scale: To change the size of a piece of artwork.

Scanner: A device that captures a photographic image and converts it to a bit-mapped image the computer can handle.

SCSI: Small Computer Systems Interface. An intelligent interface, used for most scanners in the Macintosh world and for other devices, including hard disk drives.

Secondary color: A color produced by mixing two primary colors. For example, mixing red and green primary colors of light produces the secondary color, magenta. Mixing the yellow and cyan primary colors produces the secondary color, blue.

Selection: The act of marking various portions of an image or document so that you can work on them apart from the rest of the image or document. As a noun, a selection is the area that has been marked, usually surrounded by a marquee or an outline that is sometimes colorfully called "marching ants."

Serial: Passing information 1 bit at a time in sequential order.

Server: A network computer that responds to requests from a client computer.

Shade: A color with black added to it.

Shadows: The darkest part of an image, generally with values ranging from 75 to 100 percent.

Sharpening: Increasing the apparent sharpness of an image by boosting the contrast between adjacent tones or colors.

Smoothing: To blur the boundaries between tones of an image, often to reduce a rough or jagged appearance.

Smudge: A tool that smears part of an image, mixing surrounding tones together.

Snap: A feature that causes lines or objects to be attracted to a visible or invisible grid or special guidelines in an image or drawing.

Solarization: In photography, an effect produced by exposing film to light partially through the developing process. Some of the tones are reversed, generating an interesting effect. In digital photography, the same effect is produced by combining some positive areas of the image with some negative areas.

Subtractive colors: The primary colors of pigments. When two subtractive colors are added, the result is a darker color, which further subtracts from the light reflected by the substrate surface.

TCP/IP: Transmission Control Protocol/Internet Protocol. The set of rules through which computers on the Internet (such as yours and a host system that you're calling) communicate.

Text file: Usually an ASCII file, often created by selecting Save Text Only from within an application.

Thumbnail: A miniature copy of a page or image, which gives you some idea of what the original will look like without having to open the original file or view the full-size image.

TIFF: Tagged Image File Format. A standard graphics file format that can be used to store grayscale and color images.

Tint: A color with white added to it. In graphic arts, tint often refers to the percentage of one color added to another.

Tolerance: The range of color or tonal values that will be selected, with a tool like the Magic Wand, or filled with paint, when using a tool like the Paint Bucket.

Type code: A four-letter code that tells the Macintosh what kind of document a file is. It is used with the creator code, which represents the particular application that created the file. Some applications can create several different types of documents.

Unfragmented: A hard disk that has most of its files stored in consecutive sectors, rather than spread out over the disk. Such an arrangement allows more efficient reading of data, and requires less time to move the read/write head to gather the information.

Unsharp masking: The process of increasing the contrast between adjacent pixels in an image, which raises the apparent sharpness of the image.

URL: Uniform Resource Locator. The complete address of a file or some other destination on the Internet.

Utility: A program that performs some useful system or maintenance function, as opposed to an applications program.

Vector image: An image defined as a series of straight line vectors. The beginning and ending points of each line are stored and later adjusted as the image is sized.

Virtual memory: The hard disk space used when there is not enough RAM to carry out an operation. Photoshop and your Mac each have their own virtual memory systems. If you use Photoshop a great deal, you'll want to turn off the Mac's version and let Photoshop work exclusively with its optimized version.

W3C: World Wide Web Consortium. An organization that seeks to guide standards related to the World Wide Web and that works in concert with the Internet Engineering Task Force. It is funded by contributions from a diversity of member organizations.

Web site: A term used both to mean a particular Web page or, more precisely, all documents that together comprise the destination. A typical Web page contains several files, including the main HTML file and associated graphic, sound, animation, and other files that it specifies. That HTML file usually also contains hypertext links to other HTML documents at the same overall Web site.

Webmaster: The individual responsible for managing a specific Web site.

Wire frame: A rendering technique that presents only the edges of a 3D object, as if it were modeled from pieces of wire. This is much faster than modeling the entire object.

Zoom: To enlarge part of an image so that it fills the screen, making it easier to work with that particular portion.

About the CD-ROM

Appendix B

Creating Cool Photoshop 4 Web Graphics Directory

In the *Creating Cool Photoshop 4 Web Graphics* directory you'll find all of the files used in this book, subdivided by chapters, appendixes, and color insert. Each chapter contains the following two folders:

➡ Figures

➡ Working Files

The Figures folder contains the figures used throughout the book. The Working Files folder contains the artwork in the various stages of each project, plus HTML pages.

Extras

In the Extras folder, you'll find a Clip Art folder that contains photos and art files from the author for you to experiment with, as well as the following items:

EarthLink Total Access Software, Including Netscape Navigator

Total Access from EarthLink Network provides a top-quality, easy-to-use Internet connection with an Internet Dialer and Netscape Navigator 2.0. Macintosh installation: Double-click on the Total Access Installer in the EarthLink folder. Windows 95 installation: Launch SETUP.EXE from the EARTHLINK: WIN95 folder/directory. Windows 3.1 installation: Launch SETUP.EXE from the EARTHLINK: WIN31 folder/directory.

3D Web Workshop Demo Suite (Mac only)

This rich offering includes Macintosh demos of Specular's powerful LogoMotion, TextureScape and WebHands applications. Macintosh installation: Double-click on the application icons in their respective 3D WEB WORKSHOP folders.

WebTools 1.4 Tryout

Macintosh installation: click on the Start icon or access individual folders from the Finder. Windows installation: Run DEMOSTRT. (*Note to Windows users:* If WebTools displays a dialog box requesting file location for any of the clip media samples, make sure the file format field is set correctly and indicate a path to the appropriate folder on the CD-ROM.)

Backgrounds from Texture Farm

Superb photographic-quality background images in Kodak Photo CD format. Access from Adobe Photoshop or other Photo CD-savvy graphics application and adjust resolution.

DeBabelizer Lite LE (Macintosh only)

This "lite" version of the award-winning Macintosh graphics translator will read and write BMP, GIF, PICT and TIFF (Mac & IBM) files. To run, click on the Demo Version icon.

DeBabelizer Toolbox demo (Macintosh only)

A full demo of the premiere Macintosh graphics translator, which reads and writes 64 graphics formats. To install, double-click on the installer icon. Check the Readme files on the CD-ROM for updated, detailed contents information.

DeBabelizer Web Scripts (Macintosh only)

Several pre-made scripts that you can import into your DeBabelizer Toolbox program and execute. Once you've imported the scripts into DeBabelizer, all you need to do is to customize them to utilize your own batch of images, and to set up the Input and Output folders, which are located in the WebScripts folder. Included: WebSaveToTNail, WebSaveToGIF, WebSaveToJPEG, WebSaveToAll.

B

D

(continued)

(continued)

(continued)

(continued)

Credits

Senior Vice President and Group Publisher
Brenda McLaughlin

Director of Publishing
Walt Bruce

Acquisitions Manager
John Osborn

Acquisitions Editor
Michael Roney

Marketing Manager
Melisa M. Duffy

Managing Editor
Andy Cummings

Development Editor
Barbra Guerra

Copy Editor
Katharine Dvorak

Technical Editor
Eric Thomas

Editorial Assistant
Tim Borek

Production Director
Andrew Walker

Supervisor of Page Layout
Craig A. Harrison

Project Coordinator
Ben Schroeter

Layout and Graphics
Vincent F. Burns
Tom Debolski
Jude Levinson
Andreas F. Schueller
Mark Schumann

Quality Control Specialist
Mick Arellano

Proofreader
Mary C. Oby

Indexer
Ty Koontz

Production Administration
Tony Augsburger
Todd Klemme
Jason Marcus
Christopher Pimentel
Leslie Popplewell
Theresa Sanchez-Baker
Melissa Stauffer

Book Design
Theresa Sanchez-Baker

Cover Design
Craig Hanson

About the Author

David D. Busch

Since 1980, David D. Busch has demystified computer technology for busy professionals through more than four dozen books and thousands of magazine articles in such publications as *Macworld* and *HomePC*. The first two-time winner of best book honors from the Computer Press Association, Busch earned his first award in 1986 for an exposé of Kitchen Table International, the world's leading fictitious supplier of hardware, software, firmware, and limpware. More recently, he's been creating Web pages online at `http://www.dbusch.com`, and covering Photoshop developments in books such as *Macworld Photoshop 4 Instant Expert* for IDG Books Worldwide.

IDG BOOKS WORLDWIDE, INC.
END-USER LICENSE AGREEMENT

4. **Restrictions on Use of Individual Programs.** You must follow the individual requirements and restrictions detailed for each individual program in Appendix B, "About the CD-ROM." These limitations are contained in the individual license agreements recorded on the disk(s)/CD-ROM. These restrictions may include a requirement that after using the program for the period of time specified in its text, the user must pay a registration fee or discontinue use. By opening the Software packet(s), you will be agreeing to abide by the licenses and restrictions for these individual programs. None of the material on this disk(s) or listed in this Book may ever be distributed, in original or modified form, for commercial purposes.

5. **Limited Warranty.**

(a) IDGB warrants that the Software and disk(s)/CD-ROM are free from defects in materials and workmanship under normal use for a period of sixty (60) days from the date of purchase of this Book. If IDGB receives notification within the warranty period of defects in materials or workmanship, IDGB will replace the defective disk(s)/CD-ROM.

(b) **IDGB AND THE AUTHOR OF THE BOOK DISCLAIM ALL OTHER WARRANTIES, EXPRESS OR IMPLIED, INCLUDING WITHOUT LIMITATION IMPLIED WARRANTIES OF MERCHANTABILITY AND FITNESS FOR A PARTICULAR PURPOSE, WITH RESPECT TO THE SOFTWARE, THE PROGRAMS, THE SOURCE CODE CONTAINED THEREIN, AND/OR THE TECHNIQUES DESCRIBED IN THIS BOOK. IDGB DOES NOT WARRANT THAT THE FUNCTIONS CONTAINED IN THE SOFTWARE WILL MEET YOUR REQUIREMENTS OR THAT THE OPERATION OF THE SOFTWARE WILL BE ERROR FREE.**

(c) This limited warranty gives you specific legal rights, and you may have other rights which vary from jurisdiction to jurisdiction.

6. **Remedies.**

(a) IDGB's entire liability and your exclusive remedy for defects in materials and workmanship shall be limited to replacement of the Software, which may be returned to IDGB with a copy of your receipt at the following address: Disk Fulfillment Department, Attn: Creating Cool Photoshop 4 Web Graphics, IDG Books Worldwide, Inc., 7260 Shadeland Station, Ste. 100, Indianapolis, IN 46256, or call 1-800-762-2974. Please allow 3-4 weeks for delivery. This Limited Warranty is void if failure of the Software has resulted from accident, abuse, or misapplication. Any replacement Software will be warranted for the remainder of the original warranty period or thirty (30) days, whichever is longer.

(b) In no event shall IDGB or the author be liable for any damages whatsoever (including without limitation damages for loss of business profits, business interruption, loss of business information, or any other pecuniary loss) arising from the use of or inability to use the Book or the Software, even if IDGB has been advised of the possibility of such damages.

(c) Because some jurisdictions do not allow the exclusion or limitation of liability for consequential or incidental damages, the above limitation or exclusion may not apply to you.

7. **U.S. Government Restricted Rights.** Use, duplication, or disclosure of the Software by the U.S. Government is subject to restrictions stated in paragraph (c) (1) (ii) of the Rights in Technical Data and Computer Software clause of DFARS 252.227-7013, and in subparagraphs (a) through (d) of the Commercial Computer— Restricted Rights clause at FAR 52.227-19, and in similar clauses in the NASA FAR supplement, when applicable.

8. **General.** This Agreement constitutes the entire understanding of the parties and revokes and supersedes all prior agreements, oral or written, between them and may not be modified or amended except in a writing signed by both parties hereto which specifically refers to this Agreement. This Agreement shall take precedence over any other documents that may be in conflict herewith. If any one or more provisions contained in this Agreement are held by any court or tribunal to be invalid, illegal, or otherwise unenforceable, each and every other provision shall remain in full force and effect.

Specular 3D Web Workshop™

The Ultimate Companion to Adobe PageMill™

Blast Your Web Pages Into The Next Dimension!

Specular 3D Web Workshop™ makes your Web page stand out above the rest. In an ever-growing sea of Web pages, 3D Web Workshop's stunning graphic elements, 3D animations and beautiful background textures give your page the edge. Whether you're a beginning Web enthusiast or an experienced Web Master, 3D Web Workshop gives you a high-impact Web page that draws in Web surfers and keeps them coming back.

Packed With Hundreds Of Ready-To-Use Web Graphics!

Specular WebHands™ are a collection of high-quality graphic elements, professionally designed for the Web. Choose from hundreds of sophisticated 3D buttons, bullets, rules, background textures and animations—each optimized for the Web. WebHands are grouped into different design styles—including metallic, glass, chrome, retro, engraved, industrial and Renaissance—so it's easy to make your Web page fit your style!

Easy-To-Use Design Tools Won't Limit Your Imagination!

Not only are WebHands ready-to-use, they're also easily customizable. Change text, color, size and shape to suit your style perfectly. Then simply drag your new WebHands directly onto your Web page. You can also design your own graphics completely from scratch! With Specular 3D Web Workshop, you have an infinite variety of possibilities for high-impact Web pages.

Commonly Asked Questions About 3D Web Workshop

What is 3D Web Workshop?

3D Web Workshop is a complete set of award-winning, easy-to-use graphics tools optimized for creating high-impact Web pages. 3D Web Workshop includes:

- Specular TextureScape™
- Specular LogoMotion™
- Adobe PageMill™ (optional)
- Vividus Web Workshop™
- Over 1500 Customizable WebHands™
- Essential Web utilities including: GifBuilder™ & Specular ImageRoller™

Do I need to know HTML?

Not at all. 3D Web Workshop works seamlessly with any WYSIWYG Web page layout program (such as Adobe PageMill) so you can create amazing Web pages with no HTML programming!

Do I need design or 3D experience?

No. 3D Web Workshop's tools are easy to learn and use. Even a novice designer can quickly create fantastic-looking Web pages.

Can I design my own Web graphics?

Of course! All WebHands are completely editable and can be easily incorporated into any HTML document. You can also create your own 3D graphics, textures and animations from scratch—perfect for seasoned Web designers.

Is 3D Web Workshop only for designing Web pages?

Absolutely not! Multimedia, print and video designers will find the award-winning design and animation power of LogoMotion and TextureScape invaluable for all their projects.

Specular
The 3D Graphics Company
http://www.specular.com
7 Pomeroy Lane • Amherst, MA 01002